ADVANCED PRAISE FOR
OUTFITTING THE OFFSHORE CRUISING SAILBOAT

In *Outfitting the Offshore Cruising Sailboat* author and cruising sailor Peter Berman presents a compelling case for finding an affordable, used sailboat—and then paints a realistic picture of the work and expense that getting it blue-water ready will entail. Starting with rig and engine and concluding with tips on seaworthy accommodations and boat-buying advice, Berman walks a potential buyer through some of the many tradeoffs involved in finding just the right boat. His best advice? Focus on the essentials and then go sailing.

—Mark Pillsbury, editor in chief, *Cruising World*

The tagline for Peter Berman's new book, titled *Outfitting the Offshore Cruising Sailboat*, tells why it's an important new reference for good old boaters: *Refitting Used Sailboats for Blue-Water Voyaging*. Peter's basic premise is that *new* offshore cruising sailboats are prohibitively expensive and somewhat uncommon, while the market in *used* cruising sailboats is rich and vast and flourishing. There's something there for everyone.

His 45-year experience as a cruiser in nearly a dozen different designs (CCA through modern racing designs) is enlightening. While Peter has formed strong opinions about many features, he does not recommend one design type over another. He knows, perhaps better than most, that every sailboat is a compromise and that priorities and budgets will vary from sailor to sailor.

What he offers is a series of observations and a logical review of onboard systems that will help any prospective offshore cruiser consider the pros and cons of each system, feature, and sailboat type. In the end, the reader of *Outfitting the Offshore Cruising Sailboat* will be able to determine which features are personally important and which have a lower priority.

I chuckled occasionally at Peter's dry wit and found that I didn't agree with every word of his sage advice. I'm just one sailor, after all, with one set of values and preferences. I was surprised, for example, to note that Peter overlooked the value of freshwater sailboats, as they apparently do not figure in the experience of this East Coast (and beyond) sailor.

Peter starts his discussion of good used boats by ranking the most expensive systems: the rig, the engine, and the ground tackle. As these are the most expensive items to replace, he gives each system a thorough and thoughtful critique based on his experiences as a cruiser. There are many nuggets here for every would-be cruiser. In particular, he includes good tips about good and bad construction features in the rig, bearing in mind intended use for coastal vs. offshore work. This section clearly spells out features to look for if you will be cruising offshore.

Over all, Peter offers great advice about buying a good old cruising sailboat and how to refit it for several more decades of offshore cruising adventures. Like the rest of us, Peter has conflicts about the best possible cruising sailboat. After saying that larger is always better, that system redundancy is critically important, and that you should replace practically everything before going offshore, Peter admits that his first cruiser was probably his favorite. A primitively equipped wooden Dickerson, this boat cost only $16,000, had fewer systems to maintain, and was his most affordable cruiser. After telling readers they should probably invest the purchase price of the boat in the refit and to replace all the important and expensive systems, he reminds us that the first priority is to "just go." Time is the enemy, he says, so don't spend your life in "endless outfitting."

In the end, as in all things, it's up to the reader to make his own choices based on his own list of priorities. But Peter offers great advice that may help each reader rank his own list of priorities and consider some systems and construction methods that he may not have thought about.

If you're still searching for your offshore sailboat and juggling the hundreds of variables, Peter Berman — a guy who's been there and done that — has some very useful advice for you.

Read this book. Then go get the boat, get to work on the refit, and get going . . . now while you can.

—Karen Larson, editor, *Good Old Boat Magazine*

Our thoughts are that it is VERY in depth and very well put together.

If a person is serious about putting together a used boat for extended offshore cruising this is a MUST read. The depth that this book covers would shame most and I use the word MOST surveyors.

The best use for this book would probably be for the person who already has this type of boat that would use it as a guide to improve/repair.

Peter has done a great job and from the sound of it he has faced most everything in the book head on.

—Clarke Coit & Bronson Lamb, St. Johns Boat Co., Jacksonville Fl.

Whether it's the world voyager, occasional coastwise passage maker or the first time sailboat owner, Peter Berman's new book *Outfitting the Offshore Cruising Sailboat* better be packed in your ditty bag. Establishing which is the best ground tackle, how to rebuild your electrical panel or the importance of professional radar training, Peter's insight from practical experience and industry research is clearly presented and easy to read. Even with my background, I found myself making notes in the columns of the book and learning something new in each chapter. He writes with experiential authority and research, yet not so "academic" that you get bored and frustrated trying to understand the book's contents, laid out for its wide range of readers.

Peter's chapter on "Buying the Boat" contains numerous pearls of advice for doing just that. I'd rather call them "Pearls of Economic Wisdom." Follow these pearls and they will pay you back ten-fold.

—Capt. Bob Glover III

I consider Peter's book it to be a complete guide to buying, outfitting and maintaining an offshore blue-water cruising sailboat. Everything in the book is also applicable to those sailors cruising near shore. Peter's years of offshore cruising have given him the wisdom and experience to pass along to future cruisers. He delves into all the critical and non-critical areas every owner needs to consider when readying a sailboat for offshore adventures. I will recommend this book to my clients who plan to cruise both offshore and near shore.

—Jack Zacks CPYB, FYBA Sparkman & Stephens

Outfitting the Offshore Cruising Sailboat

Refitting Used Sailboats
for Blue-Water Voyaging

Peter I. Berman

Cover design by Rob Johnson, www.toprotype.com
Editing and interior design by Linda Morehouse, www.WeBuildBooks.com
Editing also by Matt Morehouse

All photos credited to Samuel L. Berman

Printed in the United States of America

ISBN 9780939837991

Published by Paradise Cay Publications, Inc.
P. O. Box 29, Arcata, CA 95518-0029
800-736-4509
707-822-9163 Fax
paracay@humboldt1.com
www.paracay.com

To Samuel L. Berman

Whose superior seamanship, unfailing courage,
and good cheer over two decades
always ensured happy endings to our adventures.

ACKNOWLEDGMENTS

Among the many blue-water veterans who contributed to this book, a very special appreciation goes to Bob Zarchen, who read the entire manuscript, provided numerous thoughtful suggestions for its improvement, and corrected more than a few errors. Bob, a Yale-trained engineer, arranged the purchase of our current boat, *Celebration*, some six years ago and encouraged the writing of this volume. Bob was formerly president of the Florida Yacht Brokers Association and is currently treasurer. He's in the Ft. Lauderdale office of Sparkman & Stephens, and to my mind is the consummate professional yacht broker. And a dear friend.

Thanks are due to Captain Pawel Menz, circumnavigator Gary Wood, and George Rommel, all blue-water veterans who read parts of the manuscript and made thoughtful suggestions.

Thanks are also due Ms. Heather Whyte of Glasgow, Scotland, an artist who crewed aboard *Celebration* in the Bahamas and greatly assisted in the preparation of the manuscript.

I am greatly indebted to my editor, Linda Morehouse, who skillfully narrowed a longish manuscript. She was a delight to work with and a consummate professional. Thanks also to Captain Terri Tierney, a distinguished blue-water sailor and dolphin naturalist, who carefully read the entire manuscript with keen insight.

Finally, special thanks to my son Samuel, who has ably joined me in tens of thousands of miles of blue-water voyaging these past two decades. A superb seaman with a cheerful disposition ever willing to explore new horizons, he truly has salt water in his veins.

CONTENTS

PREFACE

This book discusses the gear that any well-found offshore cruiser requires for safe and comfortable offshore voyaging; it also discusses the necessary refits involved with older fiberglass production sailboats. Hopefully it will encourage adventurous souls to undertake blue water voyaging—one of life's most rewarding joys—even if they have modest budgets.

Our book discusses what to look for in selecting an older boat for refit. It provides some guidance in the major required refits and focuses on the really essential offshore cruising gear—the must-haves. Surprisingly, once the older boat has been properly refitted, the costs of the necessary offshore cruising gear as well as the list of equipment are quite similar for both new and older cruising boats.

This book largely reflects the author's 40+ years of experience more than 100,000 miles with nearly a dozen offshore cruisers: a traditional wooden ketch, centerboard CCA design ketches, high-tech state-of-the-art ocean racers, cutters, center cockpit Caribbean "charter type" ketches, and, more recently, a large performance-oriented center cockpit cutter displacing nearly 40 tons.

Outfitting an Offshore Cruiser also reflects discussions with hundreds of blue-water voyagers and inspections of literally hundreds of cruising boats over many years. Proper cruising gear is always a good topic for discussion wherever cruisers gather. Indeed, a trademark of the blue-water cruising fraternity is sharing knowledge and lending a helping hand.

INTRODUCTION

Offshore blue-water sailing is one of life's great pleasures. All too often, offshore cruising is delayed until retirement or thereabouts, with the would-be cruiser focused on finding the "right" affordable boat. But that can be a never-ending search, for there is no "perfect" boat—just look at the profusion of boats in any of the world's major cruising anchorages: no two are the same.

To be sure, some boats are better designed for blue-water cruising than others, but in our view all cruising boats are forever works in progress. Our fundamental premise is that successful blue-water cruising is not about obtaining the perfect boat, but rather about choosing a structurally sound boat from a known designer/builder and then properly outfitting and refitting her.

Fiberglass has proven to be an unusually durable material. Consequently, when they are properly refitted with suitable rigs and engines and equipped with the necessary cruising gear, most well-maintained fiberglass production cruising boats built by well-known yards since the early 1970s are capable of extended blue-water passages.

Few cruisers can afford to go offshore in shiny new boats, so as a practical matter, most blue-water cruisers begin by purchasing an older fiberglass boat that's been used for coastal sailing. They then undertake a serious refit. This is economically feasible because many times an older, structurally sound boat can be fully refitted for less than one-half the cost of a newer one of the same length. And many of the CCA designs of the 1970s make splendid offshore cruisers.

The 30-70 rule helps explain why sailboats markedly depreciate to the point where most of us can afford to go sailing: The builder creates 30 percent of the boat while purchasing the other 70 percent from various suppliers, some good, others not so good. So over time, virtually all the purchased 70 percent needs to be replaced anyway.

An important corollary of the 30-70 Rule is that the boat is bought twice during the first 5 years of ownership. In other words, the costs of refitting an older boat—replacing the essential components and then acquiring the necessary gear for blue-water voyaging—will likely equal the acquisition cost of the boat. Many, if not most, cruisers learn this the hard way and are forced to delay cruising. So the prudent cruiser will put together a 5-year budget including acquisition, and then use only half the funds to buy the boat.

That may sound like harsh medicine, but it's one that many experienced cruisers can relate to. Bigger is not better when cruising. Successful cruising really depends on refitting the key components—the rig and the engine—updating other systems, and then purchasing the essential cruising gear.

Although fiberglass hulls, if well maintained, may last virtually forever, the two principal components—the rig and the engine—need periodic major attention once the boat has logged more than 10 years in southern climates or more than 20 years in northern, seasonal-use climates.

Ordinarily the rig—mast, components, hardware, lines/sheets/blocks, and sails—is the most costly component of the boat. With the exception of the mast, the rig's components are, basically, consumables. Moreover, the prime directive of any offshore cruiser is that the rig must be sufficiently robust to really be bulletproof—able to stand up to serious weather for extended periods when necessary.

The second major refit of an older boat concerns its engine. Despite their name "diesel," the practical realities are that the diesels installed in cruising sailboats are light-duty diesels and only distantly related to the everlasting behemoths that power overland trucks. Just about all diesels in cruising sailboats are shoehorned deep down in the bilge where they typically receive minimal and indifferent care. After all, it's a sailboat. Yet most cruisers will spend about one-half their under-way time under power, often with the assist of sails. That's especially true in the Pacific.

While light-duty marine diesels with good care can last 20 or more years and log 5,000 or so hours, the odds are that an older fiberglass production sailboat will be ready for an engine replacement/rebuild. Quite often the labor costs for removal, rebuilding, and replacement are equal to the cost of installing a new engine, so economics usually argue not only for a new engine but also a new transmission, the Achilles Heel of engines. To be sure, it is usually cheaper to rebuild the engine than secure a new one, but the warranty is likely to be short and not helpful in remote areas where obtaining parts is always a real hassle. Engine problems have probably derailed and shortened more offshore cruises than any other factor.

All in all, the money spent in thoroughly surveying the engine might be better spent to replace/rebuild. And when replacing engines it's important to install one well known to mechanics everywhere, with easily available parts, with a good track record for durability.

While every cruiser's boat is fitted out differently, there is a great commonality in the essential cruising gear carried. Interestingly, whether the boat is small and modest or large and elegant, the list of essential cruising gear is pretty much the same. Of course, it's important to have a well-found and structurally capable boat, and here one needs input from a capable surveyor.

But the unusual variety of different boats easily observed in any of the major cruising grounds suggests that it's not the boat but the time and energies used to properly refit the rig and engine, along with obtaining the essential cruising gear, that is really the key ingredient towards successful blue-water cruising.

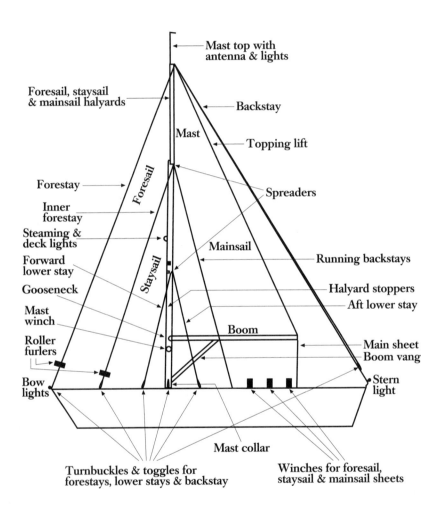

FIG. I.I

THE RIG AND ITS COMPONENTS

1

THE RIG

The unique feature of cruising sailboats is their complex rigs designed to capture the propelling forces of the wind. While cruising sailboats can get by without an engine, the rig is really the critical gear. Like engines, the rig is a consumable item needing both attention and periodic replacement. *Rigs are the most complex cruising gear on the boat and the most expensive to replace.*

Rigs of boats designed for coastal cruising usually need some upgrades for offshore duty; in fact, most boats older than 10 years usually require a substantial refit, including the installation of new standing rigging (shrouds, headstay, backstay), running rigging (halyards, sheets), sails, and a variety of rig-related gear.

The rig (see Fig. 1.1, opposite) includes the mast itself; the spreaders; the stays, shrouds, and various components that hold the mast in place and control the boom; the sails; halyards to hoist the sails, sheets to control the sails, and various deck gear to facilitate handling the sheets, including winches, travelers, cars, cleats, jammers, vangs, preventers, and various blocks. Additionally, there are some navigation lights and antennas attached to the mast. Typically more than a dozen such stainless steel components are attached to the aluminum mast, which invites some interesting corrosion issues.

Cruising boats often have additional components that greatly facilitate sail handling. These include roller furling devices attached to the forestays to handle the fore sails. Sometimes the mainsail is also controlled by furling gear. Jib and mainsail furlers can be controlled manually, by electric motors, or by hydraulic motors, operated from the cockpit. Larger boats often have electric winches to control the sheets and, sometimes, the furling gear.

Using furling gear allows even quite sizeable boats to be sailed with small crews, since sail control can be easily managed from the cockpit. In contrast to earlier days when half a dozen crew were often necessary on a 50-footer, with modern furling gear and electric winches, boats of this size can be effectively handled with crews as small as two or three.

Outfitting the Offshore Cruising Sailboat

The downside is the initial cost of furling gear and power winches, which can easily equal the cost of a quite nice mid-size cruiser with basic equipment. Moreover, furling gear and power winches require maintenance and eventual replacement.

It's not often realized, but the cost of outfitting and maintaining the rig increases disproportionally to the size of the boat. For example, a 30-foot cruiser may weigh about 5 tons, have a rig weighing about 200 to 300 pounds, and do quite nicely without furlers. But a boat twice as long, 60 feet, will have a rig weighing upwards of 2 tons complete with several jib furlers and power winches. The cost for all this gear can easily exceed six figures, along with the six-figure cost of pulling and refitting the rig. Indeed, maintenance costs in general for large boats have prompted more than one owner to put his boat in charter service to help earn her keep.

While rigs of many coastal cruisers can last a decade or more without much attention, rigs of offshore cruisers are *consumable* items that require periodic inspection and replacement. Even though the mast can last for several decades, just about every part of the rig requires periodic replacement over the useful economic life of the boat. For offshore boats, replacing rig components begins at 5 years, becomes quite extensive at 10 years, and at 20 years it's time for a major refit. By the time a cruiser is 20 years old or so, the cost of replacing both the engine and the rig components (excluding the mast) can become large relative to the value of the boat.

Unlike engines, which can often be readily inspected by a skilled engine surveyor, a thorough inspection of complex sailboat rigs usually requires mast removal and disassembly of the individual components. The nemesis of aluminum masts is corrosion arising from the many attached stainless steel fittings. The nemesis of the standing rigging is the condition of the terminals. While there is often visible corrosion on the surface of the mast around the stainless steel attachments, there can be deep-seated corrosion not visible from the surface. That deep-seated corrosion can be sufficient to cause failure at sea.

Rigs are also subject to component failure due to repeated stress loadings and associated metal fatigue. Clearly a rig that's been used for coastal sailing for 20 years will have a very different history of stress loadings than a rig for a similarly sized boat that's been actively ocean sailed. Storm conditions at sea can place severe stress on the rig that is of special concern. *Casual inspection is unlikely to reveal the real condition of the rig.* The upshot is that a prospective purchaser looking at a boat that's 10 to 20 years old will prudently set aside some considerable funds for a major rig refit—at the very least, new standing and running rigging. Other items requiring special inspection are turnbuckles and chain plates.

Fig. 1.2a High-Tech Masts
These high-tech 7/8ths double and triple spreader masts belong on the racing circuit, not offshore sailing.

It can't be emphasized enough that losing a rig offshore in heavy weather is a very serious event, especially for a larger boat where the sheer size and weight of the rig can be quite destructive. Even if the damaged rig can be safely deep-sixed, most sailboats have quite limited fuel supplies, so prospects for continuing by engine alone are limited. When all or part of a rig comes down offshore in heavy weather, there's almost always damage to the boat and her crew. For example, the rig of a 50-footer can easily weigh a ton and for a 60-footer the rig can approach two tons. The rig is the one major component of the boat whose failure can really imperil the safety of the boat and her crew.

Sailboat rigs are usually designed with at least a 3-fold factor of safety. But the factor of safety is different between coastal cruisers and offshore cruisers. *The basic rule for offshore cruisers is to upgrade the rigging gear so that it just doesn't break.* We expect the rig to remain intact even if a rogue wave upends the boat and puts the mast momentarily into the water, or worse, causes the boat to turn turtle rolling over 360 degrees. Prudent offshore cruisers improve their safety margins by installing larger size rigging than required, frequently inspecting and paying attention to their rigs, and seeking out potential weak links. When docked after a long ocean passage, the prudent cruiser will inspect the entire rig from a bosun's chair.

Another feature of sailboat rigs is that they usually have very limited re-dundancy, so they are dependent on a variety of critical components. Experienced offshore cruisers usually build redundancy into their rigs through the use of staysail jibs, running backstays, and spare halyards. When refitting the wire mast supports, offshore sailors often go up a size, especially for the lower shrouds and the forestays and backstays.

As a practical matter, when buying a 10- or 20-year-old boat that will be used for serious offshore cruising, it's usually both prudent and economical at the outset to unstep the rig and take it apart for a serious inspection. At the very least, the shrouds, terminal ends, halyards, and sheets will require replacement. Maybe the rigging turnbuckles and toggles and much of the sail handling gear will, as well. Most would-be purchasers fret about the engine and the sails. But it's the rig that really should command their attention. More than a few sailors have cruised extensively without a working engine. But none without a standing rig in good order.

MASTS

Aluminum masts and booms, along with Dacron sails and fiberglass hulls, are post-War inventions that have greatly expanded the availability of affordable cruising sailboats. In the halcyon days of wooden-built boats, masts and booms were crafted of spruce and received careful attention. Typically the varnished spars were stored indoors during the off season. Even in larger boats it was common to see crews sanding and varnishing masts several times yearly, at the same time inspecting the various components of the standing rigging.

With the advent of aluminum and its seemingly carefree requirements, masts seldom receive the attention they deserve. It's not uncommon to see aluminum masts remain standing for years, even a decade or longer, without being removed for inspection and repair. Sometimes the only impetus to un-step the mast is for cosmetic purposes when the original anodized or painted surface becomes unsightly. Relatively few coastal sailboat owners unstep the mast to examine the components.

Often the full extent of the mast corrosion is not realized until the mast fittings have been removed and the mast has been completely disassembled preparatory for painting. Indeed, it's not uncommon to find that the costs of repairing hitherto unknown corrosion and fully prepping the mast to avoid future corrosion actually equal the costs of painting itself.

Without periodic disassembly it's difficult or impossible to determine the extent of corrosion to the mast and its components. Corrosion around fittings can be serious and lead to rig failure. Even with large sailing vessels where some serious engineering went into rig design and construction, it's common for the rig to be disassembled and carefully inspected periodically in order to maintain the vessel's compliance certification.

As long as the mast is kept straight in column, all the forces upon it will be transferred by compression to the keel. As the mast is loaded with the forces of the sails, these forces are transferred to the shrouds and chainplates, which compress the mast into the keel. The failure of any mast fitting connecting the shrouds or fittings can lead to mast failure. While it's uncommon for straight-run shrouds themselves to fail, they can suffer serious corrosion as they pass over the ends of the spreaders, especially if the spreader ends are covered with leather or plastic sail protectors. These protectors, which retain moisture, hide what is happening inside. Disassembly is necessary for proper maintenance.

Fig. 1.2b Aluminum masts are quite flexible without adequate support. This swept-back double spreader rig omits the conventional forward lower shroud but is strictly for the inshore racing fraternity.

HOW WELL WAS SHE BUILT IN THE FIRST PLACE?

Standards for securing metal fittings to aluminum masts vary greatly among builders. Conscientious builders always use aluminum fittings wherever possible, to minimize corrosion. Most builders, however, use stainless steel fittings attached to the aluminum mast. The best builders use machine screws, tapping threads into the mast together with sealant and, often, using protective isolation gaskets to separate the stainless fittings from aluminum. Some builders go to the trouble of drilling holes in nuts, allowing the use of cotter pins to prevent the nuts on the machine bolts from loosening. Other builders, working to a price point, use self-tapping stainless screws wherever possible.

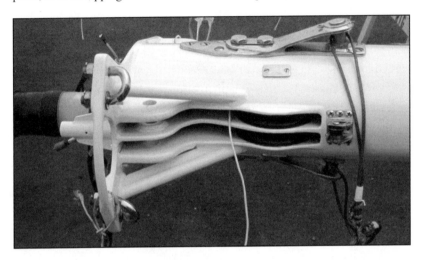

Fig. 1.3a Sturdy mast top with protected double crane. Notice double thru-bolts for spreader assembly and mainsail halyard protector and provision for additional halyards.

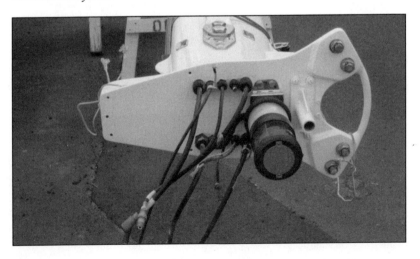

Fig. 1.3b Seen from above, an anchor light with a tri-color light and a forest of antennas and connections for sailing instruments. Better to have fewer electrics on top and more spare halyards.

Fig. 1.4 The modest forestay attachment above is only attached with screws. For offshore work a robust attachment is required; this should be thru-bolted to the mast. Note that the exit plate for the staysail halyard is also screwed to the mast rather than thru-bolted. The exit plate does have a preventer keeping the halyard properly aligned.

Fig. 1.5a Carbon fiber makes for elegant masts but they are usually restricted to the racing community owing to frightful costs and difficulty of repair and attachment. See also Fig. 1.5b following page.

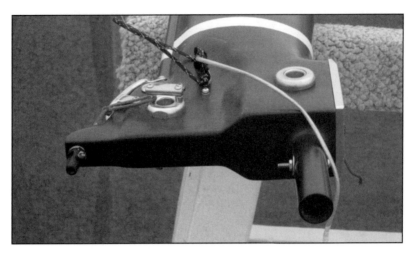

Fig. 1.5b Carbon fiber masts are attractive but very expensive.

It's not often appreciated that the cost of the metal aluminum extrusion used in cruising boats is a relatively minor cost of the entire rig. It's the components and required hand-assembly of those components that's costly. A walking inspection around the boat at deck level is not apt to reveal the care and effort put into building the rig. But if you look at how the winches attach to the mast, you'll have a good indicator. Most builders fabricate stainless steel plates and then fasten winches to those plates. Some builders use wooden mounting blocks to separate the stainless or bronze winches from the aluminum mast. On high-end assemblies, aluminum base plates are welded to the mast, and sometimes large aluminum castings are used as base plates.

Even to the casual observer there are noticeable differences between masts built by production spar builders and those built by specialty yards. For example, spars custom-built by Hinckley have long had a reputation for high standards. And for sheer attention to engineering detail and heavy-duty construction, the Hood custom in-mast furling spars are hard to beat. They are veritable aluminum oak trees.

How the mast was originally put together is hardly academic when it comes to disassembling the mast to remove fittings and/or fix corrosion. A mast put together by a budget-minded production builder can impose some serious disassembly costs a decade or two down the road. It's not uncommon for stainless steel machine screws and even machine bolts to break when being removed from aluminum masts. Sometimes it's a quick fix to grind the surface flush and replace the fitting close by with a new set of holes while the old holes are painted over. Caveat emptor.

BEWARE CORROSION

Two places on aluminum masts simply invite corrosion. The first is around the mast where it enters the deck. Typically the mast is held in place with wooden or rubber wedges over which a rubber or Dacron cloth is fitted. The end result is that this area remains wet, and over the years the mast suffers serious corrosion.

Fig. 1.6 Masts held together with rivets do not inspire confidence. They are usually put together to save money, and are not suitable for offshore use. Rivets and salt water invite corrosion.

The best way to prevent corrosion in this area is to fit a fabricated metal *mast collar* to the deck, leaving about 1 inch of space between the collar and the mast. Usually the base of the mast collar extends about 2 inches outward, while the collar itself is about 2 inches high. The 2-inches-wide by 1-inch-deep space between the mast collar is then filled with high-grade rubber caulking.

This system lasts practically forever, provides some flexibility, and is easily removed. Mast collars are usually made from welded 3/16" aluminum plate and cost about $500 to $1,000 to fabricate for medium-sized cruisers. They're expensive, but they protect the mast at a vulnerable spot and keep the water from running down the mast into the boat. High-end boats often have spiffy stainless steel mast collars.

Fig. 1.7 Close-Up View of Mast Boom Vang Attachment Plate and Mast Plate
The highly loaded boom vang attachment is thru-bolted to the mast. Note that
the mast plate makes a watertight seal because it is made in two pieces and is
filled with flexible rubber so the mast can work against the mast partners while
preventing any water from running down the mast into the interior of the boat.

The second place aluminum masts invite corrosion is the mast step that sits atop the keel in the bilge. This area is perpetually wet, since water invariably enters the mast and then collects inside the bottom of the mast. Quite often builders forget to drill several weep holes around the mast step to allow water to easily escape. Here, too, builder standards vary. Some install heavy-duty aluminum castings that last forever despite the inevitable corrosion. Others use thin welded aluminum plate, or, worse, a mast step made of painted steel.

It's always a good idea to inspect the mast plate immediately after the mast has been removed. The corruption and accumulated debris can be quite awesome. Sometimes the inside of the mast at its base is heavily corroded and needs repair. And sometimes the fiberglass and plywood supports used to hold the mast plate need repair or reinforcement. Some high-end builders fabricate large metal weldments supporting the mast step that are truly works of art.

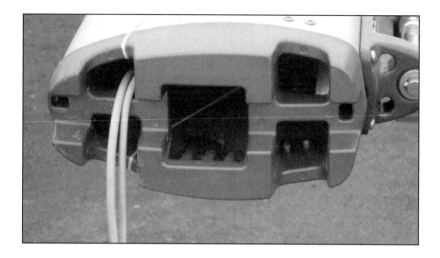

Fig. 1.8 Mast Step
Cast aluminum mast male step attached to the mast with just rivets for a
mast stepped on deck—generally not a good idea for offshore cruisers since the
failure of any single shroud is likely to send the entire rig overboard. Note the
cast fitting to the right for the boom vang swivel attached with sheet metal
screws—not a good arrangement either.

Another place to look for corrosion is the masthead. Over the years, various instruments, anchor lights, navigation lights, and antennae are installed, removed, and replaced, so there tend to be lots of holes and unused screw fittings. Sometimes a brass or bronze anchor light will be installed directly on top of the aluminum mast, with impressive corrosion consequences. Since replacing mast top equipment is typically outsourced, it's not surprising that over the years the mast top invites corrosion.

PROBLEM AREAS

Mast sheaves at the top of the mast that handle the genoa and mainsail halyards can be a source of trouble if not inspected once in a while. Usually large aluminum sheaves are fixed to stainless steel bolts or pins as axles with thin aluminum plates (the box) fixed to prevent the halyards from jumping out of the sheaves. Over time the sheaves can wear from corrosion, especially if flexible stainless steel wire is used for halyards. When the halyard gets jammed between the sheave and its box plate, there's just no way of taking down the

11

sail short of heroic measures. This actually happened to us once early in our cruising career when we tried to take down a mainsail while on a reach. We spent the next 24 hours sailing squares until the wind died sufficiently so we could approach a dock and send a crew up to the mast top.

Another problem area can be external halyard genoa or spinnaker blocks installed in a crane at the top of the mast. Over time, the plastic sheaves and block bodies corrode from the ultraviolet rays and can actually break under load. Similarly, continuous movement can wear the shackle pins attaching the blocks. We always use halyard blocks with all aluminum sheaves, metal bodies, and beefy stainless steel shackles, while the blocks themselves are rated at twice the working load of the halyards. That's overkill, to be sure, but an extra 6 or 12 ounces at the mast top for truly robust halyard blocks is good insurance over the long haul. Also, we're extra careful in seizing the shackle pins so the blocks remain well attached to the mast crane.

WATCH THOSE SPREADERS

Spreaders need special attention. On most aluminum masts the spreaders are hollowed-out thin aluminum weldments that are affixed to the mast by means of flexible hinge attachments allowing the spreaders to flex up and down at their attachment points. Sometimes on older boats one finds spreaders made of spruce. That's OK if they were made correctly to begin with and kept varnished, but not OK if they're painted and allowed to hide rot.

Fig. 1.9 Lightweight spreader attachment assembly to mast that is thru-bolted to the mast and then fitted with sheet metal screws. Note that the spreader ends can only move sideways, not up and down as required in a proper attachment. Note that provision is made only for one shroud attachment. Given their importance there is no reason to skimp on spreader attachment fittings.

A really good mast builder will fabricate beefy spreaders with heavy-duty cover plates that secure the shrouds to the spreader ends by means of Allen machine screws that are tapped into solid metal at the spreader ends. The idea is to lock the windward spreader ends into the stainless steel shroud. To be sure, the shroud itself will expand and contract under load, but the spreader itself flexes where it's attached by a hinge device to the mast. These arrangements are always used on large boats where the rig receives very serious attention.

Many builders take a shortcut and simply cut a groove in the windward spreader end and then use stainless steel wire to hold the shroud into the groove so it doesn't come loose. Then to keep things tidy, the spreader end is taped up with rigging tape. The spreader is no longer fixed in position relative to the mast at approximately right angles. Over time the spreader will fall below horizontal or creep upwards above horizontal. Under these arrangements, when the shroud is under load the windward spreader can now move up and down and is no longer fixed in position relative to the mast. That degrades the purpose of having a spreader in the first place.

Fig. 1.10 A lightweight aluminum spreader attachment assembly fastened with rivets unsuited for offshore sailing. Note the spreaders can only move in one plane rather than vertically as required.

Walk down any dock and look up: you'll always find spreaders fixed so they bisect the angle made with the shroud. That looks nice, but once a real load is placed on the shroud, the shroud stretches under load and the windward spreader end will tend to move even higher, effectively reducing the length of the spreader as a supporting strut. If things get really messy, the spreader end will keep rising so that the shroud is no longer in tension. When that happens, the mast will no longer remain in column and things can get sticky real fast.

Correctly set spreaders should be set parallel to the water, not sweeping up to heaven, with the shroud firmly secured to the outboard spreader end. Until we had *Celebration*'s rig pulled out at Thunderbolt Shipyard in Savannah, Georgia, I, too, was a firm believer that spreader ends need to bisect the angle and reach upwards to heaven. After all, everyone did it this way. But the head rigger insisted that they should be parallel to the water. After consulting an old engineering statistics textbook I used eons ago, I, too, saw the light. Nonetheless, the practice of installing spreader ends pointing upwards is so well ingrained it will be followed for posterity. It does look odd to see one's spreaders flat while everyone else's point skywards.

HOW'S SHE SET?

Sometimes the hull flexes sufficiently so that when sailing to windward the leeward shrouds really flex and the mast is thrown out of column. The usual fix is to install a half-inch or larger *stainless steel tension rod* just forward of the mast. The rod is tied to both the deck and the keel and tensioned, usually with a turnbuckle. This method works wonders. Such rods were often used in wooden boats and aren't seen very often in modern fiberglass boats. Sometimes this fix is needed in older fiberglass boats where the builders did not attach the plywood bulkheads near the mast to the underside of the decks. We once sailed across the Pacific in an early production fiberglass boat where the bulkheads noticeably flexed. The mast tension rod worked wonders.

Whereas racing boats can oft be identified with masts bent backwards near the top to allow adjustment of the draft of the mainsail, cruising boats do well enough with masts kept in column. This is especially important for masts that have in-mast furling systems. If the mast is bent backwards at the top, the furling system will not work properly, or at least as well as it should.

Nowadays just about every aluminum mast is a double spreader rig. For ocean cruising purposes there's no special advantage in double spreader rigs

14

over the old-fashioned single spreader rigs—just more components to fail. Ocean cruisers avoid sailing close to windward, so having the chainplates set a few inches inboard doesn't yield any real advantage, but it does complicate construction of the hull. Over open water there's almost always bound to be seas and significant swells from hundreds or thousands of miles distant. Once the breeze picks up to 15 or 20 knots, there's bound to be 3- to 4-foot seas. Sailing close-hauled to windward in those conditions for any length of time isn't pleasant, no matter how expertly designed, built, and sailed your boat.

The upshot is that while a modern double spreader rig set inboard from the toerails may look more functional and perhaps even more impressive or seaworthy for cruising boat purposes, the real onions lie in a well built and well maintained rig. To be sure, a lighter rig will improve motion and perhaps even performance, but the difference in weight isn't likely to have a significantly noticeable effect, especially when the boat is loaded with cruising gear. Of course, with deep pockets and carbon fiber masts, some interesting arrangements can be devised, but that's beyond the range of most cruiser folks.

KEEP IT SIMPLE, SAILOR

Other things being equal, the more complex the rig, the more parts to fail. One often sees double spreader rigs with the shroud to the lower spreader terminating at that lower spreader. Then another shroud runs from outboard the lower spreader all the way to the mast top. That system requires just 3 chain plates: two for the lowers and one for the intermediate and upper middle shroud. Much better is an arrangement with 4 separate shrouds, where separate shrouds are used for the lower spreaders, another shroud for the lower spreader, and a fourth shroud that runs over both spreaders before ending at the mast top. In this case one chainplate is extra large, handling the shrouds for each of the spreaders.

WIRE SHROUD TERMINAL ENDS

The weak links in any rig are usually the terminals that are fitted to each end of the wire shrouds. Most production sailboats use swage fittings to attach terminals (usually marine eyes and sometimes forks) to the wire shrouds; great hydraulic pressure is used to squeeze the stainless steel marine eyes or forks into the wire. Swage fittings are fairly inexpensive and can be attached fairly easily to the wire, provided the proper swaging equipment is available.

In northern waters where boats are used seasonally, swage fittings can often last 15 or 20 years. But in tropical waters, swage terminal ends are often replaced after just 5 or 10 years. Usually it's the terminal ends at deck level that fail first—they're usually sprayed frequently with sea water.

Fig. 1.11 Stay-Lok Fittings

The usual recommendation for cruisers in tropical waters is to switch to the more expensive mechanical or Sta-Lok terminals machined from solid stainless steel. Properly installed, they will last just about forever, can be easily disassembled, and can be installed by most crews with appropriate hand tools. Sta-Loks are especially handy when replacing just one failed swage fitting, by virtue of using Sta-Loks with *extender rods*. However, when replacing all the shrouds, the usual practice is to replace the wire as well. Otherwise, if the original wire is retained, then extender rod Sta-Loks must be used all around and they are expensive, especially in the larger wire diameters.

The 20-year rule for replacing swage fittings for boats isn't a hard and fast one. We once brought a 45-foot centerboard CCA design ketch from San Francisco through the Canal up to New England with its original 20-year-old rigging and sails. But the boat had a traditional low-aspect sail plan, was a ketch rig, and we didn't press her too hard. We kept her running off the wind, where she had a good turn of speed. Before she was put up for sale she did have new rigging all around.

When refitting a cruising boat, or when purchasing one that's 10 years or older and for which replacing the shrouds is in order, it's good economy to use Sta-Lok fittings rather than the less expensive swagings. Most boats one sees when out cruising typically have Sta-Lok refits. Even for newer boats with swage terminals, it's a good idea to carry a supply of Sta-Loks with some extender rods. Then when a swage fitting fails the wire shroud can continue to be used if a Sta-Lok with an extender rod is available. New boat or used boat, it's always a good idea to have an extra-long spare shroud wire on board, along with a dozen or more heavy-duty stainless steel wire clamps and several dozen heavy-duty shackles of various sizes to take care of a rigging emergency.

Common practice calls for surveyors to briefly inspect the mast fittings and terminal ends with a ride to the mast top. Often surveyors will use a magnifying glass to look for surface stress cracks. But some years ago when purchasing our current boat we learned a thing or two about inspecting swage fittings. The surveyor's real weapon is not just a magnifying glass: *It's a small triangular machinist's file*. The trick, we learned, is to look for faint surface signs of rust. And then to go "exploring" with the file for signs of *internal corrosion*.

After finding some very, very faint signs of surface rust on several lower swage fittings, the surveyor began patiently exploring with his small machinist's file. It was painful to watch. Rust became more noticeable at just 1/16" under the surface, and by the time the file had worked to 1/8" below the surface there were signs of rust apparent to the naked eye. The surveyor explained that the swage fitting fails from within, so it's what's inside that counts. That lesson cost us several thousand dollars. For 3 decades previous we had always believed the conventional wisdom that surface cracks are the guide. Some 6 months later, after a long ocean passage, we bit the bullet and replaced the entire rig with new wire, Sta-Loks all around, and turnbuckles and toggles as well.

Other than perhaps replacing the engine there is no other major refit outlay that provides more lasting peace of mind than replacing the complete set of wire shroud terminal ends. When the boat is working hard and the squalls pop up out of the blue, it is comforting to know that the rig is going to stay on the boat. Losing a rig offshore is a terrifying experience and the potential damage to boat and crew is frequently quite awesome. There is simply no other cruising experience more terrifying than losing a rig offshore in heavy conditions. It's the ultimate blue-water learning experience.

Losing an aluminum mast is also bloody inconvenient, especially if the rig is lost quite some distance away from a major boating repair center. Then it's easy to lose a major chunk of time and cruising budget when replacing the rig. Losing a rig offshore is always a game-changing experience no one ever quite forgets. So look upwards for impending trouble, and take an occasional inspection tour in the bosun's chair.

TURNBUCKLES AND TOGGLES

Whether or not to replace turnbuckles and toggles when the wire rigging is replaced is sometimes a difficult call. Much depends on whether the original turnbuckles were made of machined stainless steel or forged bronze, whether they were made by a known and reputable firm, and the condition of the thread—and the depth of one's remaining pockets. Given the cost of replacing the wire and purchasing Sta-Lok fittings, the additional expense of purchasing new toggles and turnbuckles is substantial, but not hugely so. Over the years, when changing rigging, we've stuck with tried and true forged bronze turnbuckles and paid the piper. Bronze turnbuckles are the century-old standard largely because they were forged, and marine-grade bronze has an impressive ability to resist salt water. Moreover, the rigging screws are open, so the threads of the turnbuckle are easily visible.

In contrast, stainless steel turnbuckles are typically machined and can be made by any competent machine shop. There are various grades of stainless. Some stainless turnbuckles use internal threads. That looks nice and makes a shorter turnbuckle. But it's hard to inspect the threads.

To the best of my knowledge it is very rare for a properly sized forged bronze traditional turnbuckle made by a reputable builder to fail, and the threads seem to remain tight forever. But the reputation for stainless steel turnbuckles is more problematic, especially for galling of the threads when under load. On several occasions we've had to replace stainless steel turnbuckles when the threads were obviously galling to the point where the turnbuckle itself was loose fitting when relaxed from load. On the other hand, stainless turnbuckles when polished up look spiffy. In contrast, the chrome plate on bronze turnbuckles eventually wears off.

Fig. 1.12 Rigging Details
Note the 3 chain plates with 4 shrouds and the use of Stay-Lok terminal ends,
open bronze rigging screws (turnbuckles) and stainless toggles. Each of the
3 chain plates carries a shroud to the lower spreader attachment where the
forces on the mast are the greatest. The middle chain plate also carries a
shroud to the top of the mast over both spreaders. It is usually one wire size
smaller than the shrouds to the lower spreader. When properly sized with
robust mast fittings this 3 chain plate 4 shroud arrangement has proven very
durable in offshore sailing with two spreader mast arrangements. Note the
spare mainsail halyard tied to the aft shroud and the robust running back stay
arrangements for supporting the forestay when required.

Sometimes a builder will omit toggles on the stays. So it's good practice to make sure that toggles are used. Toggles at both ends of the stays allow them to easily flex. Here, too, our preference is for forged bronze fittings from a recognized manufacturer.

Common practice is to replace cotter pins when reassembling rigging parts. Our practice is to always use new cotter pins of the largest diameter that will fit. There's no virtue in using extra-long pins. Bending the outboard pins 30 degrees is all that's needed to avoid cold-welding the material. Reapplying rigging tape every 6 months or so is good practice, as is polishing the metal fittings.

Outfitting the Offshore Cruising Sailboat

JIB FURLERS

Roller furling devices for genoas, jibs, and staysails are one of sailing's most user-friendly innovations. In halcyon days jibs and genoas were hanked on the forestay, and it took some serious heroics and physical ability to raise and lower such sails on a pitching foredeck. Even for a 40-foot boat it was a two-man job in the ocean, complete with safety harnesses, foul weather gear, and boots. Moreover, in those "golden days," crews carried an inventory of jibs stored in the forepeak, where it was an ongoing effort to prevent the spread of mildew on the sails and in the boat. Wet sails stowed below dry slowly.

Early iterations of roller furling had the sail furl around a luff wire sewn into the sail. This arrangement had only limited success. The sail was still hoisted on a halyard and sagged to leeward when any real force was placed on it. The real advance came with aluminum extrusions set in place around the forestay with the luff edge of the sail held to the extrusion by means of a sturdy luff tape built into the leading edge of the sail. Early extrusions, pioneered by Hood, were elliptical, with opposing outboard pieces dovetailing into a central core extrusion that held the forestay——an elegant if expensive construction, since they could easily be taken apart for inspection and had no mechanical fastenings between lengths of adjoining extrusions.

Presently the standard cruising arrangement calls for round aluminum extrusions fastened to one another mechanically with either machine screws or rivets, with sturdy bearings at either end. It's a fairly simply matter to furl the sail, either partially or all the way. However, when there's some force on the sail from a good breeze it can take some serious muscle power to completely furl the luffing sail. And for genoas in larger boats, say 50 to 60 feet, it's handy to have an electric winch available.

Roller furling has so many advantages that it's pretty much standard equipment on mid-size and larger cruisers and on many smaller ones as well. The sail is always at the ready, furled up on the forestay. It's relatively easy to furl it after use. It can even be used partially furled in a pinch, although using a partially furled sail in heavy weather is hard on the sail and the furling line. Many offshore cruisers have twin roller furlers, one forward for the genoa (usually a 110 percent sail) and one several feet aft for the staysail. If the staysail is cut flat and made bulletproof, it can serve as a storm jib even partially furled. When motor sailing, a flat cut staysail sheeted really hard to the center is also handy for reducing the rolling.

As with every piece of mechanical assist on sailboats, there are some caveats when using furlers. First, the furled-up edges of the sail, which are exposed to the sun's ultraviolet rays, need protection, so a sacrificial cloth about 12 to 18 inches wide is sewn into the foot and leach of the sail. Typically Sunbrella or Dacron is used. Over time that sacrificial cloth will require replacement and/or restitching every year or two, especially in the tropics. A really good sailmaker will use UV-resistant heavy-duty sail thread and double-stitch the cover ends. Even better is extra stitching in an X format running back and forth along the heavy sacrificial cover.

Second, while it is convenient to partially furl the genoa when the winds pick up, doing so strains the sail and eventually distorts its intended shape. Hence, serious cruisers nearly always install a much smaller staysail. A partially furled sail also puts quite a load on the furling gear and line. Retrieving a sizeable roller furling jib that's blowing wildly on a pitching deck in heavy seas is a very demanding and dangerous task.

Third, over time the bearings at either end of the extrusions need attention and perhaps replacement. The better-made and more expensive units designed for offshore use feature sealed bearing arrangements with steel, rather than plastic, ball bearings.

Fourth, furlers are heavy, so the tendency among coastal sailors is to use the lightest one. Cruising sailors are advised to go up one step from the manufacturer's recommendation.

Fifth, after 10 or 15 years furlers are good candidates for refits and replacement of the forestays. Furlers can wear out from hard use, the extrusions can be bent when the mast is removed for winter storage, and the roller units at each end can have damaged bearings.

Sixth, the furling line, typically ⅜" or so, requires periodic replacing. Typically it runs through half a dozen blocks on its way to the cockpit, sometimes taking a hard load when the sail is partially furled. More than one mast has come down when an inept crew continues grinding away at the furling line with an electric winch—or when the furling line breaks in heavy weather and the genoa flogs its way to destruction.

Seventh, halyards don't last forever, so every six months or so it's important to take down the furled jibs and check out the halyards that are tensioned over the mast sheaves. When installing new halyards, add another 10 to 12 feet to allow periodic shortening of the halyard at the mast head, to account for wear and tear.

MAINSAIL FURLERS

With the development of jib furlers it was only natural that furlers would be used for the mainsail. Early innovations were installing jib furlers externally behind the mast to furl the mainsail. These installations required fabricating mast hardware to firmly hold the top and bottom of the furler just behind the mast itself. This "poor man's mainsail furler" continues to be used by many mid-size center cockpit cruisers. With an electric winch the mainsail can easily be furled.

Certainly these furlers are not as elegant as dedicated in-mast furlers, since the furling rod inevitably sags to windward and there is a gap between the mainsail's luff and the mast. While these are limitations compared to the dedicated in-mast systems, most offshore sailing is done off the wind. So for modest budgets, fitting a behind-the-mast mainsail furler is recommended over the in-mast or in-boom mainsail furlers.

Hood Yacht Systems was an early leader in developing a series of sophisticated in-mast furling system—Stoway masts—with internal electric and hydraulic motors for custom masts, with accompanying booms, up to about 120 feet or so. These incorporate some nifty engineering and many have been in service for decades. These systems support the entire luff of the mainsail no matter how much the sail is furled. With powerful electric or hydraulic motors, the mainsail can be furled when under reasonable load even when running before the wind, if absolutely necessary.

In-mast mainsail furling systems are ideally suited for larger center cockpit boats and older sailors reluctant to raise and lower sail outside the cockpit. Together with roller furling jibs, the entire sail inventory can usually be easily handled from the security of the cockpit; moreover, this method doesn't require any storage space for sails, since they are always ready to unfurl. Once boats are in the 50- to 60-foot range, in-mast furling systems are quite attractive assists, since a genoa or mainsail for these size boats can easily reach 100 pounds or more. So hoisting and furling such behemoths by conventional means (sail tracks) can be a chore even for beefy crew.

Mainsails used in in-mast furling systems are typically cut quite flat, with a hollowed-out leech, so some sail area is lost compared to conventional sails. The in-mast furling system is designed to allow any portion of the sail to be unfurled to balance the forces on the mainsail. The open extrusion in the back of the mast provides continuous support for any portion of the sail that's been unfurled. Quite often the mainsail will be furled about one-third when the wind pipes up and furled as much as one-half in heavy weather.

It's hard to overstate the advantages of being able to quickly adjust, with an electric switch from the comfortable cockpit, the available mainsail area projected against the wind. In contrast, roller furler jibs are usually all-in or all-out affairs. With a roller furler jib, the sail needs to be always luffed before furling, since when furling there is no mast extrusion to guide the sail and keep it from fouling the reefing line. A particularly nice feature of in-mast furling is that you can extend the sail out halfway to assist when motor sailing. Usually only about 6 inches or so of protective material is required on the leech to protect against UV rays.

Of course, in-mast powered furling systems have their maintenance issues. Greasing the mast top bearing for the extrusion is an annual task for the Hood systems. The electric motors and the gearboxes can require expensive repair and/or replacement. And when the internal extrusion fails, it usually takes a professional rigging crew to undo the damage, although usually the extrusion can be removed without unstepping the mast.

Even with their powerful electric furling systems, it is possible for the partially furled mainsail to literally get stuck in the aft groove of the mainmast. For example, this can happen if the crew is not attentive to keep the boom both level and stable when furling so the sail is doubled up as it is furled. It can also happen if the boom's gooseneck fails, as with an unintended jibe of the main boom in heavy weather. The only recourse then is to manually unfurl the sail with a socket wrench designed for this purpose—which is easier said than done, since the power ratio is 1:1, not 60:1 as with the electric motor.

For smaller and mid-size boats, *manually operated* in-mast furling systems have been developed. These have the obvious advantage of avoiding the complications of an electric or hydraulic motor inside the mast. Quite often a dedicated electric cockpit winch is used to assist in the furling. On occasion one sees quite a large sailboat with a custom manual furling system using electric sheet winches in the cockpit to do the heavy lifting.

A more recent furling development has been in-boom furling systems.

These have the advantage of keeping the weight of the furled sail and furling mechanism low, facilitating easier removal when problems arise and allowing full size mainsails with horizontal battens. However, they do require external aft extrusions fastened to the aft edge of the mast, adding weight and expense. In-boom furling systems usually require furling to be done when the sail is headed into the wind.

FULL LENGTH BATTENED MAINSAILS

A widely used improvement over conventional mainsail arrangements employs full length battens together with special cars riding in an extrusion aft of the mast. These systems can be retrofitted to existing mainsails at considerable expense and the systems themselves involve some expensive components. Typically the mast is removed to allow the retrofit of a special track. When hoisted, the fully battened mainsail is usually more efficient than the conventional mainsail and has more roach area.

Since the battens are more or less permanently mounted to the sail (at least for the season), the sail cover along the boom is modified to provide vertical covers on either side of the boom; these covers range from a foot at the aft end of the boom to about 3 feet at the forward end. With the installation of several connected jacklines between the mast and boom, the sail will nicely fall into the sail cover sleeve—at least in theory.

Our experience with a new, fully battened mainsail system in a 50-foot center cockpit boat was problematical. Once hoisted, the sail worked quite nicely, with greatly reduced luffing. The fully battened mainsail was splendid downwind. But the aft battens in the sail's over-extended roach tended to get caught up in the backstay during light breezes. The additional weight of the full-length battens with their associated hardware was considerable, so raising the sail by a conventional two-speed mast winch became an unpleasant chore. Moreover, despite some very aggressive experimentation over several years, it was just not possible to fully collapse the sail within the two vertical sail covers on the boom. So a long wooden boat pole was used to literally pound the sail more compactly between the vertical sail covers. Only then could the zipper be used to fully enclose the sail covers. All in all, the benefits of a fully battened mainsail were not, in our view, sufficient to overcome the difficulties in furling the sail within the two vertical sail covers and adjusting the various jacklines.

For the beginning cruiser, the conventional mainsail, with sail slides attached to the old-fashioned sail track screwed or bolted into the aft portion of the mainmast, is a pretty good and durable system without fancy hardware. It works fine with aft cockpit boats that have sufficient cabin top space to easily furl the sail. But it's bloody difficult to use in a center cockpit sailboat. Since the available supply of used sailboats is mostly aft cockpit boats, the beginning cruiser will likely select an aft cockpit boat with a conventional mainsail system.

Under current technology, a manually operated in-mast furling system with an assist from an electric cockpit winch looks attractive. The older technology of retrofitting a jib furler right behind the mainmast should not be dismissed out of hand. Pound for pound, dollar for dollar, that system has probably produced more joy than any other mainsail furling system. But it doesn't look very elegant. For those with deeper pockets, in-mast furling systems are attractive, especially if they are manually operated.

SAILS

A new suit of sails ranks pretty high on the must-have list of most purchasers of new boats. After all, sails are the engine, and new sails always outperform more experienced sails. Yet most newly acquired boats will have a still-serviceable sail inventory, and it shouldn't take a local sailmaker more than an hour or so to inspect the sails.

Usually the costs of restitching and any necessary repairs to the inherited sail wardrobe are fairly modest, relative to a new inventory. Most sailmakers can readily determine the cloth weight and the expertise that was involved in the construction and design of sails, and can give you an estimate of their remaining life. Modern Dacron cruising sails are quite durable. Typically their major repairs involve restitching, replacing the sacrificial cover cloths for the furling sails, and repairing the corners of the sails.

With the advent of computer assisted sail design and production in Southeast Asia, most sailmakers can estimate the cost of new sails with just a few clicks. Local sailmakers whose hand-stitched works of art lasted for a generation are pretty much gone now. Within a few weeks of the order, new sails are flown in and their quality, judging from some recent purchases, seems quite suitable—at least for cruising sails. Unlike other cruising gear, prices of cruising sails haven't changed much over the past several years as production shifted overseas.

Outfitting the Offshore Cruising Sailboat

When ordering new cruising sails, ask for tradewind quality; this sends the message to the sailmaker that the sails are intended for offshore use. Triple stitching with heavy-duty UV-resistant thread is the way to go, plus reinforced leeches and corners. Specialization works well here. Sailmakers whose bread and butter is racing sails are not apt to design bulletproof offshore cruising sails that take hard abuse.

The basic cruising inventory includes a mainsail, 110 percent or 130 percent genoa, a staysail, and perhaps a cruising spinnaker or lightweight genoa. Nice to have for those "special situations" is a storm jib. Few cruising boats carry large sail inventories and when they do, they're mostly toting around older sails with limited usefulness. Gone are the days when cruisers carried large sail wardrobes in the forepeak with large crews to adjust the sail plan. If the budget permits, it's helpful to carry a spare 100 percent "get home" sturdy genoa. It need not be new. If the roller furler fails, the spare genoa can be hoisted on a halyard. Most offshore sailing is done off the wind anyway.

Depending on the crew's experience and agility, cruising spinnakers can be great fun in light airs. But taking one down when the breeze pipes up can be character-building. A special device—a spinnaker sleeve (sock) or sally—greatly assists in keeping the sail out of the water when hoisting or retrieving.

Not often seen anymore is a riding sail, typically a flat sail made of heavy-duty cloth with no more than 30 or 40 square feet. Hoisted on backstay just above the boom, a riding sail keeps the bow pointed into the breeze when anchored and reduces the oscillation of the bows. In a strong breeze it can make a big difference.

SAILING HARDWARE

Modern cruising sailboats, unlike their forebears, come with a large and varied assortment of sailing gear: winches, line stoppers, cleats, mainsheet travelers and cars, outhaul track and cars, genoa track and cars, staysail sheet and cars, boomvangs, preventers, various blocks, and a bewildering variety of lines for controlling and hoisting sails. Some of this gear—for example, the various tracks—lasts forever if properly sized and installed to begin with. Similarly, well-made winches are very durable if periodically lubricated.

Most sailing gear deteriorates with age, neglect, and/or if it is undersized to begin with. Failure of critical sailing gear can jeopardize the rig and even cause serious injury. *Our advice, based on long experience, is to always regard sailing gear that comes with a used sailboat with varying degrees of suspicion.* Early on it's prudent to replace critical gear such as genoa cars, mainsheet traveler and outhaul cars, and various blocks and shackles with the next largest size from a well-known manufacturer. Chances are that much if not all of the sailing gear is original to the boat and was selected by the builder for coastal or limited cruising loads. In production boats, decisions on hardware are often influenced by budget considerations.

Over time, metals corrode and their characteristics are degraded by repeated shock loads. Under any reasonable costs/benefits analysis relative to the cost of the boat and its rig, replacing the critical sailing gear warrants high place on the to-do list. Skeptics might argue that gear that's done its duty still has plenty of life. True enough, but the point is that remaining hardware life just can't be judged by appearances. Moreover, under previous owners the boat may have had a hard life. *Prudence suggests a high degree of confidence that the hardware can survive intact when subject to high shock loads during serious weather for extended periods.* Moreover, the cumulative stresses on hardware over a long time can weaken even seemingly robust fittings to the failure point. A rig that does well at 30 knots but can't take 50 or 60 knots isn't very reassuring.

Mainsheet and outhaul travelers and genoa blocks need special attention. Often they're sized by the builder or hardware manufacturer based on the catalog working load specifications. The problem is that those specifications are usually for static loads. Over time, metal fatigue sets in and the hardware can and does fail when heavily stressed. *Over the years, we've had a number of incidents in which seemingly robust cars and blocks from well-regarded manufacturers failed, once where a crew narrowly missed serious or even fatal injury.*

Occasional gear failures and even mast failures are sometimes tolerated by the racing fraternity seeking cutting edge performance. But they have no place on a well-found cruising boat headed out for weeks or months of blue water. The consequences of rig failure are so challenging and threatening to life and limb that it's prudent to take sensible precautions by installing sail handling gear that can take unexpected loads with aplomb.

Of course, bad seamanship can destroy the best-laid precautions. For example, unexpectedly jibing the mainsail in heavy weather or putting the mast top temporarily in the water or keeping the genoa up too long so that the decks are continuously submerged can overload even a well-found craft.

Outfitting the Offshore Cruising Sailboat

One of the best guides to high quality sailboat gear is whether the hardware can be taken apart for inspection and lubrication. Favor aluminum and stainless components over plastic, since plastic is usually employed to save weight. *On a cruising boat, robust construction always trumps weight savings.* At the very least, your crew and the next owner will be impressed with an owner who favors larger than customary safety margins.

To be sure, replacing critical sail handling gear may seem like overly cautious advice. Mainsheet traveler cars are expensive. The upside is that replacing sailboat hardware should not have to be done again. When looking at apparently robust sailboat fittings, size can be misleading. We have the remains of a very robustly constructed stainless steel mainsheet traveler with ⅜" bales from a well-known manufacturer that literally exploded when subjected to an unexpected jibe. Add to that instance the remains of a cast aluminum gooseneck some ½" to ¾" thick, cracked turnbuckles, broken shackles, and so on.

Cruising sailboats have dozens of shackles and they need special attention. Often the shackles that came with the original gear have been replaced with others from unknown makers. Every sailboat owner borrows shackles from one piece of gear for use in another at some time. We have a box of shackles that have failed their duty and some of them are quite sizeable. Our experience has been that no matter how many different spare shackles we carry, we sometimes come up short and borrow from another piece of gear until we can find the next chandlery.

All shackles are not made equal even when they're made of stainless steel: some are forged, some are cast, and the material composition can be quite different. Our experience is that there is only one dependable method of obtaining high quality stainless steel shackles. Buy them from a well-known manufacturer that tests its product. Both Wichard and Schaeffer meet these requirements. Most shackles for sale at boat supply houses these days seem to be made in the Far East from either unknown or obscure manufacturers. Our advice is to run the other way and use the largest known-brand stainless steel shackles that fit the gear. And keep a supply kitty of half a dozen or more of various size shackles just in case.

Blocks also need attention. In halcyon days blocks were built robustly and lasted almost forever, especially when made of bronze. At the behest of the racing fraternity major innovations have been made in block design and manufacture. Some lightweight marvels have truly impressive load ratings with plastic ball bearings. Our advice is to rely on old-fashioned technologies whenever possible, looking for aluminum sheaves and stainless steel bodies with hefty straps. A good rule of thumb is to use blocks with safe working load (SWL) figures twice the expected load in the most strenuous expected condition—a full-blown gale. That gives a 4-to-1 safety margin, since the failure load is typically twice the SWL.

Blocks on top of the mast need special attention. Here it's good advice to use ones with twice or three times the expected maximum working load. Mast top blocks should always be substantially stronger than the halyard. Sometimes they go for years and years without inspection.

Winches are by far the most expensive sail hardware items. These are typically used on the mast for tensioning halyards, on the deck for the same purpose, and in the cockpit for tensioning various sheets. Before the advent of dependable "line stoppers," it was not uncommon to see a virtual forest of winches in high-end sailboats, both at the mast and in the cockpit. However, with the judicious use of line stoppers, one winch on either side of the mast should be sufficient, using enough cleats so they can carry the load along with the line stoppers.

Fig. 1.13a These winches are bolted to aluminum plates which are then riveted to the mast—not a good idea. Machine bolts should be used so the mast bases can be inspected for corrosion. Just two winches and the use of line stoppers would improve matters here. Even better would be winches with self tailers. Several aluminum folding steps are fitted. These fail too often in our experience. Better to climb using the winches themselves.

Fig. 1.13b Another example of poor winch attachment to masts. Here one winch base is simply riveted to the mast while the other two are attached with just sheet screws. Both methods invite trouble and preclude easily disassembly to check for corrosion. Just two properly mounted winches with line stoppers would make for a better arrangement, as would winches with self tailers.

In the cockpit the usual installations call for one winch per sheet or 5 winches, one each for the staysail and genoa sheets and one for the mainsheet, plus line stoppers for mainsheet traveler control cars and perhaps one for the boom vang. Genoa winches are usually used when flying the spinnaker. A nice arrangement is to have one winch handle holder installed near each winch to avoid passing heavy winch handles around the cockpit. Modern plastic winch handles have largely replaced the heavy duty ones made of chromed bronze or stainless steel. But for heavy loads such as hoisting the crew to the mast top, stick with metal ones.

Boat builders almost always install winches that are too small, at least for crew with modest physical capabilities. It's rare to find a boat where the winches are too large for the least able crew. Replacing or adding larger cockpit winches ranks high on the to-do list. Unfortunately, new winches are expensive and used winches are not often the bargains they appear to be unless replacement parts are available. Several reliable winch manufacturers, such as Barient, are long gone, and parts are available only from offshore specialist suppliers on the Web. A reasonably sized new winch might well cost as much as a new sail.

Formerly reserved only for high-end yachts, electric winches are increasingly found on cruising boats. They are expensive, especially considering that they employ just a starter motor and a gearbox. Then there's the considerable installation cost, including heavy cables to the distribution box, remote switches, solenoids, and so forth. Most electric winches allow the winch to be used manually by disengaging the clutch. However, this may be scant comfort if the loads are large enough so that electric winches are required in the first place.

Used actively, electric winches place a significant load on the battery bank. Their motors draw upwards of 100 amps or so as they slowly grind away. Active sail trimming with an electric winch over a 24-hour period can easily run down even a fairly large battery bank. Sometimes the genset has to be kicked in just to provide the juice to keep up with sail trimming using electric winches. Newcomers to electric winches often delight in grinding away seemingly forever with their new toys.

If the budget doesn't permit a battery of electric winches, there may still be a role for a single electric winch installed just behind the helmsman. Then, providing the sheets for controlling the jibs and mainsail are long enough, the single electric winch can be used when necessary anywhere in the cockpit. Electric winches are handy for furling in genoas, hoisting a crew to the mast top, docking against an unfavorable cross wind, hoisting dinghies and motors aboard, and reeling in a large dinghy when towed behind. With suitable gear an electric winch can even substitute for a failed windlass. Electric winches have even been used to hoist sails for senior citizen sailors. The uses of electric cockpit winches are almost endless.

Once the boat length reaches 50 to 60 feet or more, electric winches are pretty much required for boats with small crews, especially when large genoas are used. Indeed, the cost of large electric winches required to operate large boats with small crews is by itself a good argument to consider more modest vessels in the first place.

An important innovation has been self-tailing devices on top of the winch. One can often guess the age of the boat by whether it has self-tailers installed. They became fairly common in the mid-1980s. Self tailers do just what their name implies. Just one crew is needed to operate the winch without having another crew keep tension on the other end of the line. Various efforts have been made to retrofit earlier capstan style winches with self-tailers, but these remain a work in progress. Even when using self-tailers, there's still a role for securing sheets with a cleat.

BOOM VANGS AND PREVENTERS

Boom vangs control the boom so it stays more or less level with the deck when the forces working on the sail are pushing upwards. Otherwise the boom will tend to rise and fall with each passing wave and wind gust. A secondary role for boom vangs is supporting the boom when the sails are stowed. Some boats use a block and tackle arrangement to restrain the boom from lifting upwards. That keeps the boom from rising but it doesn't support the boom.

Fig. 1.14 Boom Vang
A good example of a heavy-duty solid boom vang installation. Note the welded attachment on the boom, the large gooseneck mast fitting thru-bolted, the vang's mast base fitting also thru-bolted to the mast, and the large turning blocks allowing the vang to be properly tensioned with line leading to the cockpit. Note the running backstays for the staysail and spare mainsail halyards. Note the aluminum winch base through bolted to the mast and the use of just one winch serving 3 halyards with line jammers. Also, note the mast deck plate fitting making for a completely watertight arrangement.

Much better are solid boom vangs that have two interconnecting aluminum tubes with a heavy-duty spring inside. These are much more costly than block and tackle arrangements, but they restrain as well as support the boom.

Solid boom vangs rather than block and tackle boom vangs are essential on boats with booms weighing several hundred pounds.

Fig. 1.15a Gooseneck and Boom Vang

Fig. 1.15b Gooseneck and Boom Vang

Fig. 1.15a, top, represents the undersized gooseneck fitting for an 80-foot mast attached with just machine screws. Fig. 1.15b, bottom, represents the boom vang attachment. The rough quality of the welds doesn't inspire confidence. Note the hollows in the fittings as they attach to the mast, suggesting low quality metalcraft. Just because stainless steel was used doesn't mean the fittings were adequately crafted.

Outfitting the Offshore Cruising Sailboat

Our experience has been to ignore the manufacturer's claims and install the largest solid boom that will fit as essential cruising gear. Even when solid boom vangs are used to hold the boom in a horizontal position, they should always be used with topping lifts or lines from the boom end to the mast top as a secondary support. The topping lift should be properly sized so that it will support the boom under all expected extreme conditions and, if necessary, so that it can be used as a crane to lift a heavy dinghy or to remove/install a genset or engine. A nice arrangement is to fit the topping lift to a block at the boom end and thence to the mast and to the cockpit so the line can be kept from flailing at the mainsail in heavy seas. That arrangement makes for a quieter sail by preventing the topping lift from banging into the sail. To reduce sail chafe, it's also helpful to use a beefy vinyl-covered wire as the topping lift, rather than an unsightly large diameter line.

A preventer is a line from the end of the boom to the deck or genoa track forward of the mast that keeps the boom in place when running before the wind. Such lines are especially helpful in rough conditions where an unintended jibe can damage the mast. Typically preventers are kept in storage until conditions warrant, at which time they are installed on both sides of the deck. The usual arrangement calls for a heavy-duty block forward of the mast on a track near the toe rail to bring the line back to the cockpit.

The problem with preventers is that when it becomes necessary to deploy thep, it takes a brave heart with chest harness and safety straps to set them up. We've learned from long experience to always set up preventers when leaving port.

LINES AND SHEETS

Halyards, sheets, and dock lines are disposable items that degrade under continued UV exposure. When refitting a new boat it's a good idea to buy several 600-foot reels of braided polyester line (Dacron) in just two sizes. The heavier line is for the sheets and dock lines; the next smallest size is for halyards. Standard braided polyester (Dacron) line with covers seems to give several years service. Unlike 3-stranded line, braided polyester line is difficult to splice.

Generally we make do with a bowline tied around neat fittings made by Wichard that incorporate a soft rubberlike thimble attached to either a snap shackle or standard shackle. The thimble prevents the line's assuming too narrow a radius under heavy load and the consequent need to splice the line.

34

Halyards typically wear at the mast head where they run over the mast top sheaves, so periodic inspection is recommended. Some cruisers keep their halyards as short as possible on the twin grounds of saving money and avoiding the messy look around the mast. We do the reverse and always install halyards 10 to 12 feet longer than required. That allows the fully extended line of an unused halyard to reach down the water to hoist dinghies or even an overboard crew when necessary. And with an overlong halyard it's an easy matter to shorten the worn-away halyard end attached to the sail at the mast top.

For a simple rig just two halyards are needed—one for the main sail and one for the genoa, plus one for the boom topping lift, which may or may not be adjustable. Adding a staysail makes for three halyards and with a spinnaker or two we're up to 5 halyards. However, for serious cruising we'd want a spare genoa halyard and two halyards at the mast top facing aft. These two can be used as a spare mainsail halyard, dinghy lift halyard, and especially as a lift for an overboard crew.

Hoisting an overboard crew in heavy weather requires halyards long enough so one end can be dropped into the water while the other end leads to a mast or cockpit winch. Having spare halyards on either side of the aft portion of mast is ideally suited for retrieving an overboard crew, since the boat will usually be moving forward. Only these halyards can be kept out of the way of the side shrouds or rigging holding up the mast, as is the case with the usual spinnaker halyards set on cranes forward of the mast.

Even if the boat doesn't carry spinnakers, it's helpful to have spinnaker and spare mainsail halyards installed. Sooner or later the boat will run aground in skinny water. Using a halyard to lean the boat over with a motorized dinghy is the time-honored way of breaking the suction holding the keel in place. Sometimes two motorized dinghies are used. One hauls on the halyard, the other hauls on the hull itself.

It's helpful to have a reel of ⅜" and ⅛" braided Dacron line available for various projects. Line seems to find its own uses: dinghy painters, fender lines, furling sails, securing the life raft, and keeping gas cans in place on the deck. We like to keep several lengths of spare halyards stored below decks and a variety of different diameters stuffed in a pail in the lazarette. No boat ever has too much line aboard. Even when halyards are replaced they are generally strong enough to serve other purposes.

Outfitting the Offshore Cruising Sailboat

SPLIT RIGS

So far we've only talked about single mast rigs, properly called sloops, or cutters when fitted with a staysail. With modern sail handling gear— *e.g.* roller furlers, aluminum masts, and winches—single mast rigs dominate the field. However, many years ago wooden masts and cotton sails split rigs were popular. Ketch rigs with the main mast moved forward to accommodate a smaller aft mizzenmast ahead of the rudder post are especially versatile offshore. Yawl rigs with tiny mizzens were creations of the racing fraternity.

Many oldtimers and circumnavigators of the old school claim the ideal offshore rig is a double headsail ketch rig. The modern incarnation includes roller furlers for the jibs and the mainsail. With four sails, the combinations are virtually endless. The best feature of a ketch is that when the wind pipes up, the main is furled and rig is balanced *jib and jigger*, i.e. staysail and mizzen. Since the staysail and mizzen are small, this balanced sail combination allows the boat to go to weather even in heavy stuff, *e.g.* 30 to 35 knots, without heeling too much. Nothing beats a ketch on a reach or a run with the wind on a quarter. In moderate winds all four sails can be set. But the ketch gives way to a single mast rig when close hauled, for then the mizzen has little use.

Ketch rigs are more expensive to build and maintain than single mast rigs. Moreover, the mizzenmast in the cockpit ahead of the helmsman is cumbersome and blocks forward vision. Plus there are more sheets and halyards to take care of. With a mizzenmast the backstay must be split into a Y, and that complicates fitting a single-side-band antenna, which requires an insulated stay of 30 feet or longer. Refitting a ketch rig costs about 50 percent more than for a similarly sized sloop or cutter. The mizzenmast is a neat place for radar antennae, horns, GPS antennae, flag halyards, and so forth. Plus, ketches look salty.

Alas, in order to keep mast height within reasonable bounds, the ketch rig is nowadays built only for truly large yachts, and that's a pity, for the enduring quality of the ketch rig is its unmatched ability to easily alter the sail plan to suit, as well as the variety of combinations that can be set without fancy sail-handling gear. For example, when sailing at night with the conventional cutter or sloop rig, the tall mainsail is always at risk of catching the power of an unexpected squall. Indeed, many cruisers reef the mainsail just for that reason. But with a ketch rig using staysail and mizzen, the comfort level is much higher under such conditions. All in all, jib and jigger is the true "old man's rig." As the years go by, ketch rigs in moderate-sized cruising boats will become a relic from a bygone era.

Having sailed tens and tens of thousands of miles in three ketches, an aft cockpit 36- and 45-footer and one 50-foot center cockpit, I found that their sea-keeping and handling properties are unparalleled. Typically we always set the jib and jigger (mizzen), secure in knowing that we could handle 40 to 50 knots in stride from any direction. We never had a knockdown until we moved to more modern tall rigs and fancy gear in our cutter rigged boats.

MAST ELECTRICS

Most masts for cruising boats built in the last 20 years or so have a thin-walled plastic tube about 2 inches in diameter that's riveted to the forward face of the mast for the purpose of carrying electric cables. Some larger boats have two tubes in parallel. Even if one is not installed, it's a worthwhile refit that requires the mast to be upstepped and also requires access to a small rivet gun. Over time the rivets tend to pull through the thin plastic tubing walls. So a common refit item is removing the original rivets and installing larger ones and more of them, especially near the mast top. Since the new rivets can damage the mast wires, it's helpful to replace rivets before replacing the wires.

Diamonds may be forever, but electric wires in sailboat masts are not. To keep weight down, minimum-sized electric cables are used. That invites problems when the insulation fractures or fails. So when the mast is unstepped, replacing the electric wires has high priority. Mast wires can also be refit when the mast is standing, providing one has patience to sit in the bosun's chair at mast top and has access to a long fish wire used by electricians. The job can be done but it's not recommended. More than a few boat builders cut costs by threading only single wires, using a single common ground wire through the mast conduits, to save both cost and weight. New wires should always have insulated jackets over the insulated wires.

The basic electric wires are for spreader lights, steaming light, deck light, and anchor or top light. The first three will exit near the spreaders. Installing a combination mast top navigation light (red/green) and anchor light will require a 3-connector cable. When refitting electric cables, it's important to arrange matters so that the weight of the cables is borne by a mast fitting, not the electric fixtures. Otherwise there is bound to be trouble. Forcing the wires to carry their own weight almost always means they'll stretch and sometimes fail. And if there is space within the electric mast tube, it's handy to put in a spare wire or two, or at the very least a spare messenger cord for future installations.

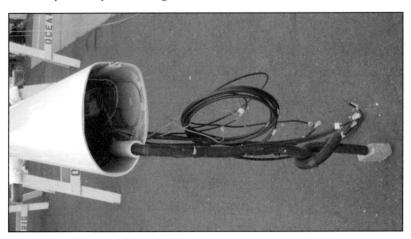

Fig. 1.16 Mast Wire Assembly
A nice example of mast wire assembly with a protective sleeve inside a mast wire tube together with a subsequent set of additional wires running loose within the mast. Much better would have been a larger original mast wire tube. Refitting the wires inside this mast will be challenging.

Fig. 1.17 Mast Electric Fixtures
Mast electric fixtures: steaming light with cage, deck flood light, and upper mast floodlight. Note the lightweight shroud attachment assembly. It's not fastened with a mast thru-bolt, making it unsuitable for offshore work.

The largest mast cable will be the co-axial conductor for the VHF antenna. Co-ax is fairly fragile, so replacement is a good idea when replacing mast wires in a refit. The Achilles heels of VHF installations are the end fittings of the co-ax and their attachment to the antenna base. Over time, the connections corrode and degrade the signal. Given the importance of a VHF antenna, if space permits inside the mast tube, it's a good idea to have a second antenna cable and antenna mounted. That provides redundancy with two independent VHF antennas and radios installed. Whenever possible, purchase freshly manufactured co-ax cable made to U.S. mil-spec standards—freshly made because given enough heat and time, all plastic insulation eventually turns solid. Even better is purchasing a sealed 100-foot reel of co-ax. It's also a good idea to leave several feet of spare cable appropriately coiled at the mast top and mast exit so new fittings can be installed.

When restepping the mast, it's a good idea to replace every electric fixture mounted on the mast plus the VHF antenna(s). Chances are they were installed using self-tapping stainless screws and they have degraded over time. Much better is using stainless machine screws with proper sealant so the fixtures can easily be replaced.

Spreader lights have been around a long time using just inexpensive sealed beams. Carrying spares is recommended. Our experience is that even new spares are sometimes defective, so testing right out of the box is in order. There's no better way to attract attention at night than putting on the spreader lights. Against a raised mainsail they can be seen a long way.

GROUNDING THE MAST

Lightning loves sailboat masts and can do quite impressive damage even when the boat is docked in a marina. Even high-end builders usually short-change lightning protection. Our recommendations for a proper mast grounding arrangement may well be overkill, but over the past four decades or so, our strategy has done the job for us, including some direct hits.

We connect #4 copper insulated cables from each of the eight chain plates directly to the mast step and then connect the mast step to a large, heavy-duty external grounding plate similar to one used as a ground poise for a single sideband installation. We use #4 rather than #8, the usual installed size. That gives us four times the current-carrying capacity. This approach provides multiple paths for the lightning to find the ground plate. Sometimes lightning hits the mast top directly. But in our experience there's more often a heavy discharge near the boat that's carried by the wire rigging to the ground plate. In any event, we want ample opportunities for lightning discharges to be carried to the ground plate through the rigging.

Most builders, if they use mast grounding wires, simply tie all three chain plates together and then bring one undersized wire to the mast base. That's not good enough. Sometimes one sees uninsulated wires used for grounding purposes. That surely invites trouble, since the huge amperages associated with lightning heat up the copper, and the heavy insulation normally found on #4 copper cables is designed in part to contain the momentary burst of current.

When connecting the insulated grounding wires to the chainplates and the mast plate, it's very important that the metal contacts be shined bright and coated with a preservative to reduce corrosion. There's no virtue in going through the time and expense of setting up a good grounding system if the connections corrode. Similarly, there's no virtue to grounding the chainplates to the mast base if the grounding wires are not carried to the external grounding plate. For boats fitted with external metal keels, the grounding wire can be carried from the mast plate to keel bolts.

To be sure, redoing the mast grounding system and removing interior cabinetry so the chainplates are accessible is both time-consuming and tedious. But this is one area where builders economize and surveyors often ignore. Only one of the boats we've owned ever had a proper mast grounding system prior to purchase. And we can count on one hand the numbers of boats with proper mast grounding systems from among the hundreds that we've inspected. There's a real safety aspect here that goes well beyond saving the electric and electronics gear from a lightning strike. Lightning has been known to punch holes in the boat's hull.

The Rig

Fig 2.1 Desirable Engine Installation Features

Engine start switch mounted near engine

Emergency engine stop switch

Oversize switchable diesel fuel filters

Dozen spare primary and secondary fuel filters and engine lube oil filters

Heavy-duty exhaust and intake fans connected to watertight deck ventilator boxes

Electric engine oil removal system

Separate sump fitted under the engine with pump

Double stainless steel hose clamps on all engine hoses

Double stainless steel exhaust hose clamps on exhaust system components

Automatic fire extinguisher system and separate large manual extinguisher

CO_2 monitor

High bilge water alarm

High temperature alarm

Water backflow trap on exhaust hose

Exhaust hose mounted well above knockdown water level

Visible window into engine room

Emergency fire hose pump

Easily accessible shaft log

Convenient access to all engine components

Easily accessible raw water intakes

Fire retardant engine compartment wall and ceiling insulation

200 ampere hour heavy-duty engine battery mounted above bilge

Easily accessible engine/battery house switches

Heavy-duty 1/0 or 2/0 welding cables used for battery cables

Heavy-duty high amp at alternator with large frame and sturdy mount

Good 12 volt and 110 volt lighting w/trouble light

Waste oil container

Large portable pump

Spare engine oil

Spare transmission fluid

2

THE ENGINE

The engine is the most important machinery on the cruising boat. Most voyagers spend 50 percent of their cruising time under power. Unfortunately marine diesels are typically shoe-horned into the bilges under the cockpit stairs or below the floorboards. So maintenance and repair can be challenging and frustrating. Difficulty of access means the engine tends to be looked at only when trouble arises.

Engines, like most machinery, are consumable items and eventually need rebuilding or replacement. For engines tucked deep in the bilges the top ends (valves, injectors, pressure pipes, distributor high pressure fuel injection pump) can sometimes be replaced economically. But a major engine rebuild requires lifting the engine to remove the oil pan to replace rods, bearings, pistons, oil pump and so forth. That's usually not possible with most sailboat engine installations. So when major engine failure occurs, the entire engine needs to come out.

Typically the costs of rebuild in the shop aren't much different than replacement with a complete new unit with a new warranty. It's not uncommon for the cost of labor to remove an existing engine and install a new one to equal the cost of a new engine. So a useful rule of thumb is to double the cost of the new engine when repowering. All the more reason to give the engine loving attention at all times.

It's understandable why engines are frequently "out of sight, out of mind." The features of cruising boats that really interest prospective buyers or dreamers are the sailing rig, deck layout, and interior accommodations. Engine installations do not sell cruising boats. The knowledgeable buyer of a used boat will examine the engine with meticulous care, keeping in mind the future cost of replacement.

Surprisingly, engine installations in upscale cruising sailboats may be no better arranged than production sailboats. Only on sailboats of the 50-foot range does it become feasible to install separate engine rooms—and then only with center cockpit designs where the engine room sits below the cockpit. Indeed, for the long term cruiser the advantages of a separate engine room are so great that a center cockpit design can often be more appealing than a traditional aft cockpit. Separate stand-up engine rooms facilitate both repair and maintenance—and also eventual engine replacement.

Fig. 2.2 Center Cockpit Engine Room
A center cockpit engine room installation permits handy access to the boat's machinery. Note the handy shelves for the desalinator pumps an also storing tools and fittings. Also, note the all-important Firebuoy automatic fire extinguishing system in the upper right corner.

MARINE DIESELS

Just about all inboard engines found in cruising sailboats nowadays are marine diesels ranging from 30 to about 100 horsepower. The engines really are "marinized" versions of land vehicle or equipment diesels. They're not designed from the ground up as true "marine diesels" for obvious reasons: the market is just too small. Moreover, they are not usually designed for continuous duty at high load.

To make a marine diesel out of a common production transportation or equipment service-type diesel usually requires installing some additional parts: water-cooled exhaust manifold, salt water pump and cooling system, wire reinforced exhaust hose, and simple forward/neutral transmission. Sometimes a water-cooled transmission oil cooler is added. Each of these modifications will eventually have to be replaced or rebuilt. Transmissions are usually the most expensive component that requires eventual replacement, followed by the exhaust manifold. Typically, engines outlast two or more transmissions.

With reasonable care, light-duty marine diesels may give 4,000 to 5,000 hours of service before requiring major rebuild. Typically they are replaced every 20 years or so. They usually rust out before they wear out or suffer the slings and arrows of inferior and infrequent maintenance. It's not uncommon to replace the starter motor during that period and perhaps have some work done on the fuel injectors and injector pump. The injector pump is the most expensive component of the engine to manufacture and repair.

Note that just because these engines are diesels doesn't mean that they are designed to provide continuous high-load service, nor are they more durable than gas engines of the same size, design, and intended use. Diesel is no magic bullet. It's how the diesel is designed, built, and used that determines its magic qualities. Longevity is often a function of whether the basic, naturally aspirated block is used or whether it is souped up with a turbocharger to increase horse-power by 50 to 100 percent. Relatively few marine diesels give long service, because they suffer from intermittent use and long periods of inactivity.

The small marine diesels used in sailboats are a far cry from the much larger and more robust heavy-duty workboat marine diesels that often give 10,000 to 20,000 hours before in-frame overhauls. GM (Detroit Diesel), Cat-erpillar, and Cummings come to mind. The big difference with the light-duty marine engines is that the commercial big marine diesels are much more ro-bust to begin with and almost always receive superior service and attention by knowledgeable mechanics in more user-friendly installations.

It's certainly rare to find an engineering log for a cruising sailboat of the size and variety we are considering here, even for crewed boats. That puts the burden of proof on a prospective purchaser to find out the true condition of the engine. The typical marine surveyor will not perform a diesel survey. During a brief sea trial the marine surveyor will note the maximum speed and engine RPM under load. That's a far cry from a detailed test of a commercial marine diesel by a competent diesel surveyor or diesel mechanic, where the better part of the day may be involved in testing and evaluating just the engines.

In contrast to commercial boats, the initial cost of installing a diesel in a sailboat during new build is fairly low relative to the cost of the boat. But the cost of removing and replacing the engine long after the boat is built can be quite large relative to the market value of the boat at that time. A complete rebuild that requires removing the engine from the boat—an expensive task.

Because of the labor involved in removing most sailboat diesels tucked away deep in the bilge under the cockpit stairs, a good rule of thumb is to double the cost of the replacement engine when considering repowering. Since most cruisers keep boats for at least 5 to 10 years, if there are any doubts about the engine it's good strategy to replace it upon or soon after purchase. Usually the costs of removal and an engine rebuild are similar to the cost of buying a new engine with a warranty, though sometimes the top end of the engine can be economically rebuilt.

When replacing an engine it's usually a good idea to go bigger. Boats usually acquire weight with advancing years, since more gear is added and their hulls absorb seawater. Not only are the larger engines generally more robust, but they also provide reserve power when it's necessary to plough through some nasty weather. It makes good sense to purchase a well-known brand that has a wide global distribution network so parts will be readily available, along with a plentiful supply of mechanics familiar with the engine. Since it takes a decade or two to gain experience about the reliability of a new engine, it's a good idea to stick to tried and true diesel designs by manufacturers with strong reputations.

While going bigger is recommended, there's a restriction in terms of the size of the propeller shaft. Changing to a larger propeller shaft and shaft log is a major expense. Similarly, a larger engine will require a different propeller. Changing engines allows refurbishing the engine compartment with improved or new insulation, exhaust fans, engine intake and exhaust hose replacements, and so forth. The costs add up quickly and your boat will be out of commission for an extended period. Best bet is to have engine replacements done by yards or crews that regularly do such installations.

An important decision when repowering is whether to go with a heavy, naturally aspirated diesel or a more modern, lightweight turbocharged unit. The difference in weight is quite considerable even though the difference is not reflected in the cost. For example, the venerable and widely used naturally aspirated 6-cylinder 135 horsepower Perkins 6-354 diesel with gear weighs almost a ton. But a modern Yanmar turbo diesel of the same power weighs only about 500 pounds. The reliable Perkins have been built on every continent with parts and knowledgeable mechanics widely available. While the lighter turbocharged Yanmars so far have good reliability records, their longer term reliability remains unknown.

Replacing the engine is likely to be the largest expense of refitting an older boat. For example, a 5- to 10-year-old boat will likely have an engine that has another 10 years of life without requiring major repair. But with a 20-year-old boat, a knowledgeable buyer will need to factor the cost of an early replacement, even though the engine currently runs just fine. Engine replacements often run between $20,000 and $30,000, including a new prop and perhaps some changes in the engine compartment.

In sum, the light-duty marine diesels commonly found in cruising sailboats are usually marinized versions of land-based vehicle or generator engines. They are consumable items and ordinarily very costly to replace because of the labor involved in removing the engine from deep in the bilge. A common rule of thumb is that repowering costs twice as much as replacing an engine. While it's possible to get 5,000 hours or so out of the engine, once the engine is 15 to 20 years old it's good practice to set aside an engine replacement fund. Typically the costs of an engine rebuild are not much different than installing a new engine with its warranty. Replacing an older engine (20 years plus) early on when purchasing a new boat is usually a good strategy. Unfortunately, the costs of replacing a diesel will be large relative to the market value of an older boat. That is one of the major factors behind boat depreciation.

ENGINE INSTALLATION IMPROVEMENTS

Several improvements to the usual sailboat engine installation will markedly increase the ease with which maintenance and repair can be carried out. These include better lighting, installation of an oil removal pump, increased exhaust fan capacity, a remote engine starter switch, larger switchable primary fuel filters, and an electric fuel pump. Together these improvements will likely cost between $1,000 to $2,000, depending on who does the installation.

Since engines are typically installed either tucked into the bilge below the stairs to the cockpit or below the floorboards, several fixed 12-volt and 110AC lights will prove invaluable, along with a flexible 12-volt or 110AC trouble light. Similarly, a remote starter switch will prove invaluable when you're called upon to bleed the fuel lines. However, installation of an electric fuel pump will eliminate this chore.

An oil removal pump, such as those made by Reverso, connects to the engine oil pan sump fitting and allows removing and replacing engine oil in just a few minutes. Such an installation is a worthy addition because it encourages more frequent oil changes.

Outfitting the Offshore Cruising Sailboat

Most sailboat engine installations have a single 3- or 4-inch light-duty exhaust fan connected to an outlet in the cockpit. Much better is to have two heavy-duty commercial-grade exhaust fans whose hoses exit into Dorade type ventilators on deck in a protected area. The ventilators protect both fresh and salt water from running down the exhaust hose into the blowers. With a larger engine it's often a good idea to install an intake blower as well. Even in the tropics, with a good blower installation it's usually possible to cool a hot engine space within 30 minutes or so.

Fig. 2.3a Engine Room Exhaust Ventilators
These large Dorade ventilators with heavy-duty 4-inch commercial-grade exhaust blowers keep the ambient engine room temperature below 100 degrees and will cool off the engine room in just an hour, even after a long run in the tropics. A really large engine exhaust system is essential in the tropics.

Moving up a size in primary fuel filter—say, from a Racor 500 to a Racor 1000 filter—provides an important margin of filtering capacity. Even better is a dual filter arrangement where the engine can run on either filter or both. Still better is installing a reliable electric fuel pump inline ahead of the primary fuel filter. With an electric fuel pump, filling up the fuel filter after a filter change takes but 30 seconds or so. The pump is especially useful when bleeding the fuel lines. Electric fuel pumps are helpful on older engines where the suction fuel lines are not completely airtight and the mechanical fuel pump needs some assistance.

If the budget permits, another helpful device is a fuel polisher. This continuously cycles the diesel fuel through a special filter, thus ensuring that the fuel is really clean before it reaches the primary fuel filter. Fuel polishers and electric fuel pumps are commonly installed on mid-size and larger powerboats.

Fig. 2.3b Generator and engine fuel filters with individual electric fuel pumps below (black cylinders) allow quick filter changes and can assist in priming the pressure diesel fuel circuit on a cold or balky diesel engine.

ENGINE SPARES

For long-distance cruisers, a good list of engine spares is an important insurance policy costing about a thousand dollars or so. When purchasing a boat, if you find a good set of engine spares it often suggests a mechanically knowledge-able prior owner. Some spares are likely to be needed over the expected service life of the engine: salt-water pumps, starter motors and solenoids, alternators, thermostats, injectors, belts, copper compression washers, pressure cap for the cooling system, water pump impellors, engine zincs, and so on. Other spares, such as high-pressure fuel lines and a set of gaskets, are likely to remain stored for the life of the engine. Even if one is all thumbs, it's a good idea to carry engine spares. There's almost always a nearby cruiser or local mechanic who can work wonders, providing the spares are available. If the budget is tight, at the very least consider a starter motor, raw water pump, and a spare alternator.

Fig. 2.4 Basic Engine Tool Kit

S.A.E. and metric deep socket sets: ½", ⅜"

S.A.E. and metric socket sets: ½", ⅜"

Torque wrench: ⅜" and ½"

S.A.E. and metric open end wrenches: ⅜" to 1"

Set of S.A.E. and metric allen wrenches to ⅜"

Set of punches to ⅜"

Set of pliers: channel, lineman's needle nose, regular, vice grip

Set of jeweler's pliers/screwdrivers

Set of ball peen hammers up to 1 pound

Pipe wrenches: 14" and 18"

Complete set of screwdrivers, regular and Phillips

S.A.E. and metric set of nut drivers

Set of metal files

Several hack saws and set of blades

Feeler gauge for setting valve clearances

Bearing puller for rebuilding pump bearings

Tool for tensioning alternator belts

Special set of pliers for removing rubber water pump impellors

Electric impact hammer: 12 or 110 volt

Rolls of electric, self-amalgamating and duct tape

Multimeter

Infrared temperature gun

Infrared RPM meter

Stuffing box wrench

Emery cloth

Bronze wool

Tube of Plyobond for making gaskets

Nut breaker set

Electric drills (battery and 110 volt) and set of carbide drill bits

Broken stud removal set

Breaker bar

Stainless steel coil of wire

Tube of waterproof grease

Spray can of penetrating oil

How you create your spares list depends upon where the cruising takes place, the age of and hours on the engine, intended hours usage of the engine, and difficulty in obtaining parts. The first task in creating a spares list is to purchase a rebuild manual and a parts manual, and identify several reliable suppliers.

Starter motors can be expensive, but carrying a rebuilt one should do fine. When changing a starter motor, it's a good idea to have the old one rebuilt with a new solenoid assembly. Starter motors on the larger diesels are plenty robust, but this is not always the case for lighter-duty engines. More than a few starter motors have given up the ghost when the bilges are partially flooded or a burst water hose showers the engine compartment. If a starter motor becomes submerged, it invariably requires replacement.

Spare salt- and fresh-water engine pumps are high on the spares list for two reasons. First, they are critical to the operation of the engine. Second, when they fail, speedy replacement is important so it's helpful to have a complete unit available rather than rebuilding the failed unit. (An impellor removal tool will help remove the neoprene impellor in the salt-water pump). Matters are less critical with the fresh-water pump, whose impellor is typically made of metal. A leaking pump will eventually destroy the pump bearings, and replacing the bearings typically requires a specialized tool and a bench press. Usually there's a small weep hole at the bottom of the pump bearing to indicate water leakage past the bearing seal. When water begins dripping, bearing failure isn't far away.

Over the life of the engine we can expect to replace fresh- and salt-water hoses, hose clamps, and the larger exhaust hose clamps. The old "sponge" test here is helpful: if the hose easily collapses under finger pressure, then it's time for replacement. Light-duty diesels often employ some odd diameter hoses, so it's a good idea to carry spares. It's usually possible to extend the life of a failing water hose with the judicious use of duct or electrical tape and a few hose clamps. Sometimes a sheet of thin aluminum or copper is helpful. The real McCoy all-stainless heavy-duty hose clamps last almost forever, but they are not so easily found in most chandlery shops. Carry several dozen assorted sizes of hose clamps. Past 10 or15 years, it's worth paying attention to the wire reinforced exhaust hose exiting the exhaust manifold. When the hose fails, the exhaust makes a real mess. The exhaust elbow exiting the exhaust manifold can often be a trouble spot, so carry a spare fitting.

Outfitting the Offshore Cruising Sailboat

Salt water pumps with neoprene flexible impellors can last for hundreds of hours or they can self-destruct in a few minutes when churning up a sandy bottom. Usually it's easier to change the entire pump than to refit a new impellor and gasket. Some owners routinely replace the impellors every 300 hours or so. A handy device to temporarily bypass a failing salt-water pump is to fit a 12-volt salt-water pressure pump with an appropriate hose connection so the electric pump can bypass the mechanical pump. We've used the pass several times on both main engines and gensets, and they work like charms. Of course, some care is needed to turn off the pump when the engines are not working. Otherwise, the pumps will flood the exhaust circuit and flood the engine.

Some ambitious cruisers go whole hog and carry a complete set of engine gaskets in case of a required rebuild in a distant land. These ambitious folk will also pack along a spare high-pressure fuel injection pump, a manual fuel pump assembly, an exhaust manifold, and a complete set of pressure and intake pipes. Hardly anyone ever carries a spare high-pressure fuel injection pump—it's ordinarily the most expensive part of the engine.

Getting parts overseas can be such a hassle that more than a few cruisers engage in a preventative rebuild for an older engine, even though the engine is working fine. Such a rebuild might include replacing the starter motor and solenoids, alternator, pressure fuel lines, injectors, engine hoses, both salt-water and fresh-water pumps, and maybe an engine head gasket as well. While a preventive rebuild is not a trivial outlay, it can be a bargain if the engine fails in a remote place.

Finally, a comprehensive engine tool kit is just as important to successful voyaging as a serious set of engine spares. Even if one is all thumbs, having a comprehensive engine tool kit can be a lifesaver if repairs are required where there's a friendly cruiser nearby. The essential engine tool kit is presented in Fig. 2.4, page 50.

POWER BOAT ENGINE INSTALLATION INSIGHTS

Engine installations in mid-size and larger powerboats are invariably done to a high standard. Examining several such installations can help cruisers understand what constitutes a first-class job. Generally the engine(s) are installed in a separate engine room with good headroom, bright lights, and access all around the engine, including the transmission and shaft log. Large primary switchable filters, big exhaust blowers, electric fuel pumps, electric oil change pumps, and fuel polishers are pretty much standard nowadays. Ordinarily there's good access both below and above the engine, permitting an in-frame rebuild. Given the larger quantities of oil required, often there are tanks for both used and fresh oil.

Fig. 2.5 Reverso Oil Change Installation
An oil change pump installation makes it easy to change genset and engine oil and for quick refilling. The installation can also be configured to change engine transmission fluids as well.

Well-designed engine room installations are important selling points for powerboat builders. After all, engines are the powerboaters' sole means of propulsion. so owners/crews will spend some serious time in maintenance and occasional repair. When visiting boat shows, I've noticed that powerboat displays always have the engine room access door open to visitors. I've yet to experience a boat show sailboat display where the floorboards are lifted to allow inspection of the engine installation. With sailboats, it's the joinery that gets the attention!

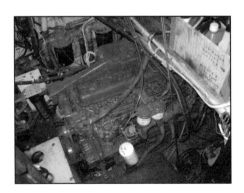

Fig. 2.6 A 135 hp Perkins 6-354 diesel installed in a center cockpit engine room with good access. Keeping the engine clean and well painted makes it easy to spot water and fuel leaks. This engine has a separate sump and electric bilge pump for occasional cleaning. Note the water intake strainer is elevated to the outside water level so that cleaning the filter doesn't flood the engine room. There was enough space to completely rebuild this engine in-frame without removal.

Outfitting the Offshore Cruising Sailboat

One of the real benefits of the well-engineered engine room installations found in powerboats is that engine rebuild is measured in hours of running time, not age of the engine. Most mid-size and larger powerboat engine room installations readily permit in-frame engine rebuilds, which are far less expensive than engine replacements. So it's not unusual for a 20-, 30-, or even a 40-year-old powerboat to have had several in-frame engine rebuilds, as long as parts remain available. Moreover, rebuilding a 200 or even a 300 horsepower powerboat diesel might not cost any more than the removal and reinstallation of a new 40 or 50 horsepower engine in a sailboat. Powerboat engineers and designers take their engines seriously.

Yet another good idea gleaned from inspecting powerboat engine rooms is how they decorate their engines and engine rooms. Sailboat diesels are typically painted red, blue, or grey, while the rest of the installation is simply the boat's hull and cabinetry backside. That's not too cheery. In contrast, powerboat engines often are painted white, as is the entire engine room—floor, ceiling, and walls. Not only is that a nice environment to work in, but it's much easier to detect fluid leaks. Even though the original Detroit Diesels were painted green and the Caterpillars and Cummins yellow, the fashion is to paint the engines white and keep them spotlessly clean.

Understandably, perhaps, powerboat engine room installations take sound insulation far more seriously than do sailboat engine installations. Whereas sailboats commonly install cumbersome generator sound shields to keep the noise down to reasonable levels, most powerboat installations that I've seen rely on good sound insulation throughout the entire engine room to keep down the decibels. On a really good installation it's hard to notice when the gensets are running. In contrast, a sailboat's genset's sound shield prevents regularly taking a look, unless one or more of the covers are removed, which is a real impediment for staying on top of potential trouble before it occurs.

In a word, sailboat owners and crews have a good deal to learn from observing powerboat engine installations. Many of their standard practices can be copied, *e.g.* electric fuel pumps, engine oil change systems, fuel polishing systems, big exhaust systems, and so on. While sailboat cruisers may feel reluctant to ask powerboat owners and crews if they can inspect their engine rooms, I've invariably found a positive response. I find some new ideas from dozens of such visits. When it comes to engine installations, sailboat builders are centuries behind our powerboat brethren.

Fig. 2.7 Genset Installation
Yanmar 8kw diesel genset installed on a shelf above the engine in a center
cockpit engine room makes for easy servicing and removal when it's time for a
replacement. Gensets are best left uncovered with a sound shield to allow easy
access for service and spotting water and fuel leaks.

Outfitting the Offshore Cruising Sailboat

Fig. 3.1 Basic Anchor Gear Inventory

Stout double bow roller
Heavy-duty windlass
2 plough anchors on double bow roller with preventors
2 Hi-test chain rodes for primary and secondary anchors
Rated stainless shackles
Chain snubbers with chain claws or chain hooks and line
Stout bow cleats
2 nylon spare rodes
Spare anchors, *e.g.* Danforth, Fisherman
Spare rated shackles
Spare solenoids, foot switches and motor for electric windlass

3

GROUND TACKLE

It may seem odd to begin a discussion of essential cruising equipment with anchors. After all, all boats have at least one anchor and there's no shortage of tall tales of cruisers sailing to the ends of the earth and making do with just a single anchor. Most times we enjoy secure anchorages where the principal peril is more likely to be another boat dragging anchor rather than unpredictable heavy weather. Yet cruisers often spend one-half or more of their time at anchor, and there invariably are times where quick deployment of serious anchor gear protects both boat and crew from dragging ashore or worse.

Proper anchor gear is all about being fully prepared. Any well equipped cruising boat should be able to weather an unexpected serious storm with the anchor gear carried aboard. It may not happen very often, but resetting a dragging anchor(s) during a major blow is a frightful experience. With the right anchor gear, even surviving a tropical storm in protected waters is doable, although not for the faint of heart.

Proper anchor gear resembles insurance. Because of cost, many cruisers do not carry replacement hull insurance when going far afield. But most cruisers carry a serious anchor gear inventory. Over time that inventory often becomes larger with a better appreciation of the importance of being prepared for serious weather. It's rare to meet a cruiser who ever considers having too much anchor gear aboard.

There's a considerable amount of gear involved in creating a proper anchor inventory. And while the expense can be considerable, once purchased, anchor gear is quite durable and not subject to obsolescence, as is much modern cruising gear. After the engine, rig, and electronics, the anchor inventory may be the most costly gear onboard. Anchor gear is a great leveler. Much the same gear is needed on a 40-year-old fixer-upper as with a gold plate, brand new boat of the same length and tonnage.

The primary purpose of anchor gear is to hold the boat securely to the bottom in just about all conditions. Ordinarily the requirements for such duty are fairly modest. But any cruising boat worth its varnish will surely sooner or later encounter conditions where stout anchor gear deployment is required at a moment's notice. The onboard equipment should allow the anchor gear to be retrieved under uncertain or difficult conditions by any member of the crew, not just the one(s) with the most muscles.

Long experience has shown that many more cruising boats are lost when anchored or moored in heavy weather than are lost at sea. In part this reflects that the largest part of the cruising adventure is typically spent at anchor rather than under sail. In part this reflects that when difficult weather hits there usually is no safe harbor readily available. And in part it reflects that many cruisers go to great lengths to avoid horrific weather and thus are ill-prepared when it arrives. After all, weight is always a consideration in cruising boats. Storm-ready anchor gear is heavy stuff that has to be carried around all the time "just in case."

Well-thought-out anchor arrangements send a strong signal that the owners are serious cruisers—or at least have dreams of serious offshore cruising. Sailors always like to stroll the docks looking for new ideas, so well-laid-out anchor gear sends a good message. Over the years, more than a few of our friendships have started with the phrase, "I like your anchoring arrangements." It's a good ice-breaker.

A proper anchor gear arrangement for a well-found cruising boat—independent of length, value, or pedigree—consists of a double bow roller, two stout anchors on rollers, appropriate chain and nylon rodes, several chain hooks, heavy-duty shackles, at least two spare anchors and rodes, and a windlass, preferably an electric one, robust enough to set out and retrieve the anchors and rode in adverse conditions. However, a small, light cruiser with a robust crew may prefer mostly nylon rode and forgo the windlass.

All in all, such an inventory may well weigh several hundred pounds for a reasonably sized cruising boat. It could easily cost several thousand dollars, especially if a powerful electric windlass is installed. For a mid-sized or larger boat, a proper anchor inventory, including an electric windlass, could easily approach five figures. Except for several spare anchors and rodes stored below where they serve as additional ballast, the entire anchor equipment inventory is on the bow, ready for deployment.

Of course, many make do with just a single anchor and bow roller or just keep one anchor secured to the deck. But then if conditions warrant and they need additional anchors and rodes it becomes a "perils of Pauline" affair to retrieve the needed anchors and rodes from below-deck stowage and assemble the gear on a rolling deck. Doing this once, late at night in a thunderstorm, provides a convincing argument to be better prepared the next time.

A two-anchor inventory (sufficiently stout) on a double bow roller should serve to meet just about all the usual anchoring requirements. Ordinarily the stout primary anchor should serve for the 50- to 60-mile gusts a nasty thunderstorm may bring. That may seem overly ambitious, but long experience suggests that it's far better to routinely set out heavy anchor gear that can take a thunderstorm in stride rather than have to rise to the occasion every time the weather turns nasty, or have to rush back to the boat from shore to set another anchor when threatening weather appears. Robust anchor gear allows the crew to venture ashore with a high probability that the boat will be found right where she was anchored.

The argument for having two anchors on their bow rollers is that when really heavy weather arises, the crew should be able to both quickly and easily deploy a second anchor in a V formation. That saves precious minutes lost below decks hunting for additional anchors and rodes and then assembling anchor and rodes under duress. With a second anchor on its roller ready for deployment, it's usually a straightforward matter of using the engine to move forward several hundred feet in an arc away from the primary anchor and then falling back into the secure V formation. Note that in the double bow roller set-up, the primary anchor does almost all the work. But when more holding horsepower is needed, the second anchor and rode is there on the bow roller at the ready.

Serious cruising boats always used to carry a "hurricane anchor," weighing upwards of 75 or 100 pounds, used when the end was in sight. Such anchors typically slept away for years on end in the bilge. While it was comforting to know that they were aboard when conditions for their use might warrant, it was almost impossible to carry them topsides, deploy them, and then retrieve them afterwards.

Long experience has shown that two readily available anchors set in a V will almost always have greater holding power than a single larger anchor dragged up for duty at the last minute. It's easy to understand why. During any real blow, wind and seas are rarely steady. The boat moves back and forth. With the V anchor formation one anchor is almost always holding firmly. When it's not possible to set out anchors in a V formation or not possible to set out the second anchor independently, an alternative is using two anchors in tandem. Setting out two anchors, one right behind the other, markedly improves holding power. However, that takes some advance preparation and it does bet all of one's horses on just one anchor rode.

Outfitting the Offshore Cruising Sailboat

As a practical matter, for most cruising boats the upper limit of anchors set on bow rollers is 50 to 60 pounds. Even these big fellows are challenging to set in place at the dock. Carrying a similar size anchor from below in a rolling sea is really a two-man job—and two able men, at that—that carries a fair chance of damaging the woodwork below. Most cruisers will do well enough with a pair of 30- to 45-pound anchors set on bow rollers with several different, but similar size anchors below in reserve. Two stout anchors appropriate to the size and weight of the boat mounted on double anchors is the basic requirement for getting the job done safely, with the least fuss.

DOUBLE BOW ROLLERS

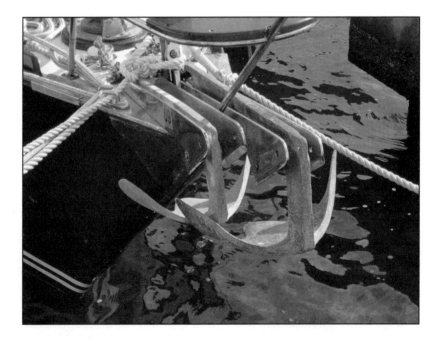

Fig. 3.2

Double bow rollers are indispensable. They facilitate immediate setting out and retrieval of anchors, and prevent bow damage. Years ago, modest-sized cruisers with strong crews seldom used bow rollers. Back then, one or more Danforth or fluke-type anchors were simply secured to the deck at the bow with rodes attached, or sometimes stored on the cabin top just aft the mast.

Dropping the anchor literally meant picking the anchor off the deck and carefully dropping it away from the bows securing the rode through the bow chock. Even experienced cruisers acquired some anchor scars.

The big advantage of double bow rollers, ungainly as they may appear to the novice, is that both anchors are immediately available to be set without delay, even in unpleasant weather. Ordinarily, anchors can be retrieved and held in place without damaging the boat by banging into the topsides as they are brought aboard—even when the boat is pitching up and down. The double bow roller is often a dead giveaway about whether the boat is a serious cruising vessel or whether the owners just have dreams.

Until fairly recently, most new boats did not come from the factory with double bow rollers or even any bow rollers. It's easy to see why. They're ungainly and disturb the rising sheer lines of the boat. Far and away the largest sailboat market is for the charter industry. There, one modest-sized bow roller or just a bow fitting is considered sufficient. After all, charterers seek pleasant locations with pleasant weather and usually avoid unpleasant weather. Second, even boats for non-charter uses are designed for coastal sailing. Here, too, a single bow roller or bow fitting is sufficient because safe harbors are usually available. Many harbors, especially in New England, are so chock full of mooring balls that one can make an extended summer cruise and rarely set anchor.

So in purchasing an older boat, it's likely that the bow roller will have to be installed or the bow modified. It may cost $1,000 or more to build and install a double bow roller out of ³⁄₁₆" or ¼" stainless steel plate. Since in a good blow a medium-size cruising boat can impose several thousand pounds of force upon the anchor rode, both the bow roller itself and the below-deck back-up plates must be stout.

Sometimes one can economize with an off-the-shelf single bow roller. We installed a supposed heavy-duty bow roller constructed of ³⁄₁₆" stainless installed with ⅜" bolts on our 11-ton, 45-foot ketch. While anchored in Onset Harbor during Hurricane Bob several decades ago, we discovered the limitations of our off-the-shelf "heavy-duty" bow anchor. The solution was easy enough: go up a size to ¼" stainless steel and have a beefy one fabricated from scratch by a competent metalworker. It's important to have a sturdy axle bolt of at least ⅜" diameter holding the roller. Typically a plastic roller similar to those used for boat trailers is employed. If one has time and the roller is large enough in diameter, it's a good idea to file a curved groove in the middle to help ease the chain rode aboard. With nylon rode that's not necessary.

Another good idea is to have a bolt, say ⅜", above the top of the roller. This prevents the rode from jumping out of the roller when the bow is jumping up and down. With larger boats using all chain rodes, that may not be necessary, but it's a good safety device when under way, since the upper bolt helps keep the anchor in place when the bow dives into head seas. It also helps to have bow rollers of unequal length. Usually the larger anchor is stowed to port, the smaller one to starboard. Arranged properly, the anchors will not bang together when stowed.

You need a way to secure the anchor to the deck immediately aft of the bow rollers. That's often done with a line attached to a bow cleat. We've used a snap shackle attached to a deck plate. In heavy seas, anchors have a curious way of departing from their bow rollers even when the rodes are pulled tight, so having a safety is prudent.

On occasion, stern rollers are seen on boats in the Caribbean. Here the idea is to set out, by dinghy, a fairly light Danforth anchor to set the axis of the boat perpendicular to the incoming swells. Even a large boat will roll unpleasantly if anchored perpendicular to modest 3- to 5-foot swells. In fact, watching an entire anchorage rolling back and forth under such conditions can provide some useful clues about the initial stability of different boats. Few facets of sailing life are more unpleasant than spending time in an anchorage trying to roll your toerails under each swell.

In sum, the double bow roller facilitates deploying and retrieving anchors without delay and without heroics.

ANCHORS

Fig. 3.3 Two large Bruce anchors (110 and 60 lbs.) in a sturdy double bow roller attached to 400 and 200 lengths of 3/8" hi-test chain combined with an Ideal windlass have proved a reliable heavy weather anchoring system for this 35-ton cutter.

While there is no one perfect anchor, plough types remain the favorite among cruisers. These include the venerable CQR, Bruce, and Delta anchors. All have a long shank and a plough arrangement that allows the anchor to dive deep in the seabed. The CQR is hinged; the Bruce and Delta are one piece. These anchors fit nicely on double bow rollers. When properly set in a suitable seabed, they have impressive holding power. A great virtue of plough-type anchors is that they tend to reset themselves fairly quickly when the pull from the anchor rode changes direction.

The second most common anchor is the Danforth, with its broad flukes. Sometimes these are called lightweight anchors. Danforths are popular the world over among fishing fleets. They're especially common on powerboats where it's convenient to store them on deck. Since Danforth's original patent ran out, these anchors have been widely copied in terms of design, but typically not to the original robust specifications. Often they are now less sturdily made than the originals, using soft steel that can readily bend under moderate load.

Even high-quality modern Danforths made from high tensile aluminum can suffer damage. We have a modern 55-pound Danforth type with bent flukes, made by a well-known firm. To be sure, it's large, lightweight with the latest alloys, doesn't corrode, comes apart neatly, and is quite expensive. It's great in sandy bottoms. But it would not be our first choice as a storm anchor, even though it's advertised as suitable for a 60- to 70-foot boat.

The very best Danforth-type anchors I've seen for cruising boats are those made during WWII. They're about 33 pounds and they disassemble. Their stout iron stocks are heavy enough to use as sledge hammers.

For their weight and size, the robustly built Danforths have amazing holding power, especially when used in sandy bottoms. The problem is that a 50- or 60-pound Danforth is unwieldy to carry around the deck and retrieve. Danforth-types do not lend themselves to storage on bow rollers, though it's not uncommon to see Bahama-bound cruisers with both a plough and Danforth anchor on their separate bow rollers.

The third most common anchor is the old standby fisherman-type anchor with broad flukes set perpendicular to the long stock. The fisherman requires disassembly to be conveniently stowed, and it needs to be fairly large to work well. With its wide flukes it is challenging to hoist aboard without damaging the bows. Also, when the boat is swinging at anchor, chain can sometimes turn around a fluke or stock and dislodge the anchor. But in a rocky or heavy grass bottom, nothing works better than a fisherman type. The big flukes, once set firmly in the bottom, have enormous holding power. Old-time fishermen would have nothing else aboard. Of course, they do not bury like modern plough-type anchors and so are not suitable for all occasions.

Several generations of New England cruisers obtained sturdy replicas of Hershoff fisherman designs from a master builder of aluminum sailing craft, Paul Luke in Boothbay Harbor, Maine. His son Frank still makes them available. These Luke fisherman anchors come apart into three pieces and stow nicely. Even a 100-pounder becomes feasible when broken into three parts. I carried a 75-pounder for years and used it several times. I can still remember, when I purchased it, Paul Luke, almost 80 at the time, carrying the beast over his shoulders from his shed down to the docks without any effort.

There's no shortage of tables detailing the proper size anchor needed for a particular size boat. Every authorized cruising or seamanship guide has one. But these tables are less useful than they might first appear. Typically they're constructed in terms of the holding power of specific anchors in known conditions subject to specific wind loads, depths, and the steady pull of a steam tug. Conditions are not so tidy in the real world where the condition of the sea bottom is unknown, the wind shifts, and behold, there are real seas running. And crews and skippers make mistakes.

Rather than relying on tables, you're better off observing what sits on the bows of serious cruisers. The basic requirements are anchors that stay in one piece when abused, are easy to set and retrieve, have sufficient weight, and bury into the sea bottom. Some of the new designs are impressive feats of engineering using CAD software. But cruisers are a conservative lot. It's unlikely that any of the newer designs will displace the basic trio of plough, Danforth, and fisherman types. These have their well-known merits and defects; every properly outfitted cruising boat should have at least one of each type.

Even accomplished cruisers lose an anchor or two, whether from carelessness or bad fortune. And there will be times when one or more bozos drag through an anchorage and foul everyone's anchor. Also, it's wise to cast off quickly in a remote anchorage when suddenly visited by questionable characters in black.

In the age of sail, carrying a good supply of anchors was the order of the day. It wasn't at all unusual for the rode to be cut or the chain to be let run out if a sudden squall came up or an enemy vessel appeared unexpectedly. When posted to a harbor or a coast for an extended time, it was common to arrange a temporary mooring buoy with several anchors. When heavy weather set in, ships left the temporary sea buoy and stood out to sea, as Richard Dana described in *Two Years Before the Mast*.

The bare cruiser minimums are two robust anchors carried on bow rollers, a larger storm anchor such as a fisherman, and a smaller Danforth or fluke-type anchor. The Danforth is especially useful carried in a dinghy with a long nylon rode to assist kedging when grounded in shallow water and also to keep the stern perpendicular to incoming swells when exposed. The prudent cruiser will carry one or two spare anchors as well. Bringing our 45 ketch from the West Coast to the East Coast several decades ago, we started out with nine anchors. Not all of them survived the trip.

Plough anchors depend upon their weight to properly set, and for practical purposes 30 pounds is the smallest size commonly used. For a 30-foot boat, under most conditions that should be more than adequate. The benefit of going up a size in weight is improved ability to quickly dig deep into the seabed. Going up in size, a 60-pound plough anchor is sufficient for a 50-foot boat under most conditions. For a 60-foot boat (double the displacement of a 50-footer) we'd need a 110- to 120-pound plough. Once in the 100-pound-plus range, plough anchors set quickly.

With a fairly decent seabed in a protected harbor, these recommendations should allow boats to withstand 50 to 60 knots sustained wind, the outer limits of most thunderstorms. No doubt some readers will view the 50- to 60-knot requirement for the primary anchor as overly ambitious. But long experience has been an important teacher. Once sustained winds are in the 30-knot range, seas of 3 to 4 feet can be expected even in a protected anchorage. Most cruiser engines aren't powerful enough to do much more than keep the bow pointed into the wind when it's blowing 30 knots. So as a practical matter, when its blowing 30 knots and the main anchor is dragging, it may be challenging to set out a second anchor and hold successfully on both anchors.

In theory it may seem prudent to only carry a primary anchor that's good for expected conditions. After all, why carry that unnecessary weight at the bow? But in practice, when the anchor that's adequate for 95 or even 99 percent of the time proves unsuitable, it may just not be possible to set out a second anchor.

All too often, once the wind begins to howl, one sees crews looking anxiously at the fleet wondering whether nearby boats are going to drag. Typically a prudent crew stays alert in the cockpit ready to start the engine. When the wind howls at night, flashlights are walking from cockpit to bow, just checking the anchor. Rather than worry, it's better to have set out a primary anchor that can secure the boat in heavy weather. Maybe that's overkill, but it does make for more pleasant cruising.

Anchors can be expensive, but there is no reason to purchase only new ones. Over the years I've purchased quite a number of anchors from surplus marine shops in harbors with a commercial fishing fleet. Most every dredger or trawler at one time or another picks up an abandoned anchor. An enormous number of anchors were built during WWII and many can still be found at surplus shops. So it pays to go wandering when ashore. Among the very best are the folding fisherman-type anchors weighing about 65 pounds carried by flying boats.

Even for a 30-foot boat, the weight of a well-considered anchor inventory is fairly modest—about 125 to 165 pounds. That would include 35- and 30-pound plough types at the bow carried in bow rollers and 30- to 50-pound take-apart Danforth and fisherman anchors. For a 50-foot boat the weight of the basic anchor inventory increases to about 250 pounds, *e.g.* 50- and 40-pound plough types at the bow and 50- to 60-pound take-apart Danforth and fisherman types. Notice that the weight of the total anchor inventory just about doubles between 30- and 50-foot boats, but the displacement of a 50-foot boat is likely four times that of the 30-footer.

For a larger boat, say 60 feet, the basic anchor inventory again doubles to between 300 and 400 pounds. A basic inventory would include 120- and 60-pound plough types at the bow and several 65- to 80-pound or heavier take-apart fisherman and Danforth types. Larger boats often have some really big boys stowed deep in the bilge for when the end of days is in sight.

Cruisers new to the game often are reluctant to size up when outfitting their anchor inventories, being concerned about weight at the bows. To be sure, weight at the bows is always a concern since it adds to the boat's pitching motion. However, while the difference between a 35- and 45-pound plough anchor at the bow is fairly modest, it can make a substantial difference in taking an early set at the seabed. As a rule, heavier anchors always set earlier than lighter ones and tend to dig deeper.

Moreover, the weight of the anchors at the bow isn't the only consideration. Typically, the chain rodes of a well-found cruising boat will weigh more than the anchors. Consider a 35- to 40-footer carrying perhaps 75 to 80 pounds of anchors at the bows. A 200-foot length of ⁵⁄₁₆" chain weighs about 200 pounds. For a 60-footer the minimum chain inventory is two 200-foot lengths of ⅜" high tensile chain, about 600 pounds. That's almost twice the weight of the plough-type anchors carried on the bow.

The virtues of setting up a suitable inventory of anchors, chain and nylon rodes, and windlass are that it's quite durable and lasts for years and years, and it isn't subject to technological innovation. Unless one is heavily into electronic navigation aids, the anchor inventory is apt to be the third most expensive part of refitting. But anchors are the cruising person's best friend: They are the only cruising gear not waiting to be outdated by newer technology.

SHACKLES

Anchor shackles rarely get the respect they deserve. Countless boats have come to grief on the beach from flimsy anchor shackles. Walk down any dock and you'll likely find more than a few examples of anchors and chain secured by inexpensive galvanized shackles of uncertain heritage. With anchor shackles, only the best is good enough. Rated stainless steel anchor shackles are well worth their $20 to $30 cost.

The only shackles worth having are those that are rated for a given load; otherwise, the shackle is invariably the weak link of the anchor system. Given the cost/ importance of the anchor and chain/rode, having a weak link is false economy, indeed. Proper shackles must match the load rating of the chain or nylon rode.

Ordinarily two shackles are required to connect the anchor with its chain rode or leader ahead of the nylon rode. First is a large shackle with a half-inch or larger pin that goes through the eye of the anchor. Second is a smaller shackle connecting this anchor shackle with the chain. The size of this second shackle is dictated by the chain's opening, or belly. Common practice is to use the same size shackle as chain. However, high-test chain is several times stronger than the usual galvanized iron shackles, so it's false economy to use the galvanized, no matter how inexpensive. Actually the shackle can be one size larger than the chain, i.e. ⁷⁄₁₆" shackles with ⅜" chain. Wichard (France) is a well-known hardware manufacturer who makes rated stainless steel shackles. They're not inexpensive, but they have ratings just about equal to the ratings of high-test galvanized steel chain from a reliable manufacturer.

Matters are less tidy for the primary shackle connecting the anchor. Here the common choice is to secure a large shackle of uncertain parentage that "looks big enough." But size can be deceptive. The only large shackle to use is one rated for heavy lifting. Typically these red-colored, OSHA-rated shackles are available from wholesale equipment supply houses. They are considerably more costly than the Far East specials. Since these rated shackles are usually not galvanized, they need be kept painted or replaced periodically.

Sometimes chain needs to be spliced. Various connecting links are available; however, to the author's best knowledge, none has the same working load characteristics as the same size high-test chain. So whenever possible, it's best to use chain without connecting links. When you're forced to work with connected chain, it's a good idea to weave flexible lines between the adjacent links to provide additional support. Even better, fasten the largest stainless steel wire loops that can be put through the chain loops. The wires can be connected with Nicropress fittings or even stainless steel U clamps. As a general rule, combining lengths of chain with chain links almost always compromises the strength and integrity of the chain. Don't do it: used chain always finds a function somewhere.

Common practice is to secure the screw pins of the shackles with a vice grip and twist tight. Better practice is to lightly grease the pin threads and use a one- to two-foot length of thin stainless steel wire and then seize the eye of the shackle pin to the body of the shackle itself. Make half a dozen loops, then twist the ends together and tuck them away.

Seizing shackle pins is much more reliable than simply tightening the pin. A sturdy needle nose pliers and a pair of nippers make light work of pulling the seizing wire tight. Upon leaving a long anchorage, cruisers often find that when the anchor and its rode are retrieved, the seizing needs attention. Sometimes it has actually broken away and the pin is loose. Given the working of the anchor in the seabed, it's easy to understand why seizing need attention.

CHAIN AND NYLON RODES

It's long been standard practice for distance cruisers anchoring in unfamiliar waters to use all-chain rodes—at least for their primary anchors. Chain is strong and it's tough. It's relatively immune to damage from being dragged across a seabed strewn with rocks and coral.

And when long lengths are let out, chain has a catenary effect: the pull on the anchor embedded in the sea floor remains horizontal, while the force of the rising and falling boat is transferred to the chain. Chain is also easy and convenient to stow in a narrow space and readily lends itself to convenient retrieval with a windlass.

Fig. 3.4 Chain vs. Nylon Rodes

Chain Pro
catenary effect
mfg. to known standards
known load characteristics
durability
ease of stowing
withstands being dragged over rocks
"talks" when dragged
link length gives current strength

Nylon Pro
low cost
stretches under load
easily retrieved by hand
easily cleaned

Chain Con
expensive
heavy
requires windlass to retrieve
difficult to clean

Nylon Con
chafes easily
easily damaged when dragged over rocks
damaged by U.V. exposure
degrades with age
load strength known only when new
mfg. standards variable, not marked
requires chain leaders behind anchors

Alas, chain does not last forever, but with reasonable care should give 5 to 10 years' service, especially if the chain locker is washed out periodically with fresh water and the chain is fully inspected during haul-out.

The major argument against chain in favor of conventional 3-strand nylon rode is that chain is heavy, it requires a windlass, and it's expensive. But even small cruisers will use substantial chain leaders—typically one foot per length of boat— attached to the anchors, followed by nylon rode. Many cruisers will use all chain rodes for anchors stored on bow rollers. Others will use a chain leader and an attached nylon rode on the secondary anchor to save weight. It's also common to use chain leaders with nylon rodes on spare rodes and for rodes used when kedging.

One of the arguments against chain is that it takes a strong back to haul it in by hand, and often a second set of hands to stow it below. Nowadays electric windlasses are widely used, so one person can easily retrieve and set out chain almost effortlessly. Occasionally one sees a hand-lever-operated windlass on smaller to mid-sized boats. These usually work satisfactorily. It just takes longer.

Sometimes one sees a third anchor rode alternative, stainless steel cable, operating on a hydraulic reel windlass on larger boats. These systems are used on submarines and on some fishing boats. These neat-looking arrangements are very space efficient, but they require considerable care in their use and for most purposes are not practical on cruising sailboats.

The most common type of chain is called "proof coil," with fairly long links made of fairly low tensile strength steel. This is the standard industrial chain used in warehouses and shipping. However, the only chain worth using in cruising boats is high-test or high-tensile galvanized steel chain made by reputable American, British, or German manufacturers. Such chain is roughly twice as strong for a given size as proof coil. Each link of high-test chain is appropriately marked, e.g. G-40. High-test chain is immensely strong; its links will noticeably deform well before it breaks.

You can readily determine if chain was subject to unusual strain: Measure the length of a single link of chain against a known standard for that size and type. We once measured a 200-foot length of ⅜" high-test chain that held a 45-foot ketch during a major hurricane and found it had stretched about 10 percent. We estimated the loads on the chain at between 5 to 6,000 pounds or about one-third of its rated break load. Once links are deformed by large loads, the remaining strength of the chain is noticeably diminished, so it's good practice to replace chain that's been subject to high loads.

The usual sizes for cruising boats are either ⁵⁄₁₆" or ⅜", with breaking loads of about 10,000 and 16,000 pounds, respectively, and working loads half those figures. For boats 40 feet and under, ⁵⁄₁₆" high-test chain is usually strong enough to weather a major blow. Larger boats up to about 60 feet use ⅜" high-test. Generally one can be fairly confident when using high-test chain rodes of appropriate size and length in good condition that the chain will be strong enough to weather the loads imposed by a major storm—or even a hurricane, when several rodes are used.

High-test chain from reputable manufacturers is expensive. Currently ⁵⁄₁₆" and ⅜" high-test costs between 3 and 4 dollars a foot, sold in either half-barrels (200 feet) or full barrels (400 feet).

Chain is also heavy. For example, ⁵⁄₁₆" high-test weighs about one pound per foot, and ⅜" high-test weighs about 1.5 pounds per foot. So a 200-foot length of ⁵⁄₁₆" high-test weighs about 200 pounds, and a similar length of

⅜" high-test weighs about 300 pounds. Those are substantial weights to be carried in the bows of moderate-sized cruising boats. Where two equal 200-foot lengths are carried, the chain weights become quite substantial, indeed. A common practice is to use a shorter length of chain as a leader for the second anchor, say 50 feet, and then connect a long nylon rode. Or if 200 feet of chain is used for the secondary anchor, place just 50 feet in the chain locker and then stow the remainder farther aft in the boat by means of a horizontal chain pipe.

For larger cruising boats in the 50- to 60-foot range, it's common practice to carry two lengths of 200 feet of ⅜" chain, about 600 pounds. Many large cruisers with 7 foot or deeper drafts routinely carry a 400-foot length of primary chain. That means carrying almost a half-ton load of chain. Together with several anchors and a large, heavy windlass, a deep draft 60-foot cruiser can easily carry a ton of anchor gear, plus perhaps another 500 or 600 pounds of spare anchors and rodes.

Under the CCA design rules, boats had shorter waterlines for a given length, with long, spoon-shaped bows. So the chain and the windlass were placed farther back than is common today. Keeping the chain and the windlass back from the bow reduces the boat's moment of inertia and makes for a softer pitching motion. Sometimes the chain was carried on deck all the way back to the mast and then led down below through a chain pipe. Modern designs with their nearly plumb-shaped (vertical) bows and long waterlines typically require the chain and the windlass to be placed quite near the bow.

The usual rule of thumb is to use a 5:1 scope with chain, thus 200 feet should be sufficient for 40-foot depths. However, the last 10 feet or so remains in the chain locker and then one has to account for the height of the bow above the water, usually 4 to 6 feet. So as a practical matter, 200 feet of chain is good for 30- to 35-foot depths. In heavy weather a longer scope, such as 7:1 or even 10:1, is used. So 200 feet of chain is ordinarily adequate for depths of 20 to 25 feet.

Most cruisers on the East Coast of the United States and Bahamas can get by with just 200 feet of chain. The only times when 400 feet might be needed for 40- to 50-foot depths would be during storm conditions. Larger cruisers, say 50 to 60 feet, often carry 400 feet of chain for their primary anchor, but they are big enough to accommodate the additional weight.

As we've mentioned, one great virtue of chain lies in its catenary effect caused by its substantial weight and its resistance to being dragged along an uncertain bottom. In all but really serious weather, some portion of the chain will lie along the seabed, pulling the anchor horizontally and thereby encouraging the anchor to drive or dive into the seabed. However, most of the chain assumes the shape of a gentle curve, so as the boat rises and falls with the sea, the sheer weight of the chain softens the wave action. When 400 feet of chain are let out, the catenary effect becomes quite powerful; it's especially helpful in softening the effect of serious swells.

Another great advantage of chain, aside from its durability and great strength, is that when the boat moves about at anchor, chain often "talks" to those inside the boat, especially to crews inside the forward V berths. Sometimes the talking chain gives early warning of stronger winds. Sometimes the first notice you'll have of another boat dragging anchor is when the chains intertwine and start grinding away at each other.

Chain takes a lot of abuse, from scuffing along the bottom of a rock-strewn seabed to sitting in a dank locker drenched in corrosive seawater. Over time even the very best made chain will lose its galvanized coating and begin to rust. If left undisturbed for months or even a few years, the rusting chain will actually weld itself into a stiff, unyielding heap of metal.

Surveyors often ignore the chain locker or avoid stretching out the entire chain when the boat is hauled for both measurement and inspection. However, for large yachts, especially those maintained in a "class certification," the entire chain inventory is always removed and inspected during periodic surveys. This is wise practice, because chain that looks quite OK on top can be sitting on a pile of rusted junk.

Keeping chain clean is a nuisance, especially when anchoring in muddy bottoms. As the mud dries, the smell of decaying detritus wafts into the boat even when the chain locker is separated from the rest of the boat with a bulkhead. Ugh. In the olden days buckets were used to wash off the incoming chain, 6 feet at a time, especially the part near the anchor where the mud really has had time to attach itself as the anchor buried itself into the seabed. Sometimes moving the chain up and down with the windlass can do a pretty good job of cleaning off the offensive materials. On occasion it's time to take out the long-handled brush.

If budget and temperament permit, the best solution is to fit a high-pressure salt-water pump, hose, and nozzle, and make the chain whistle-clean as it is retrieved. Keeping one's balance holding onto the salt-water pressure hose while stepping on and off the windlass foot switch as the bow is heaving up and down can be exciting. A strong salt-water pressure hose on deck is also helpful for cleaning up occasional messes from too-friendly birds or from fish-cleaning. Some elegant yachts have fixed salt-water pressure pipes at the bow that automatically clean the anchor chain as it's retrieved. That's a neat installation. No wet hands.

Changing wind and tide invariably cause the chain to twist over time, and depending on the size and characteristics of one's windlass, twisted chain can jam it. So it's helpful once in a while to let the chain out in deep water on a calm day and let it unwind. Some cruisers use a chain swivel device for this purpose. But the load ratings of these devices (expensive as they are) are usually well below the rating of the high-test chain itself. And even when these chain swivels are rated equal to the chain, they can fail when subjected to side loads and shocks.

It's the old story of avoiding the weakest link. High-quality chain swivels usually use some type of Allen machine screws to attach the swivel to the chain at one end and then a shackle to the anchor at the other. These Allen machine screws have to be secured with some type of sealant, and potentially can unscrew themselves under load. All things considered, the tried and true method of using two load-rated anchor shackles—one large and one smaller just behind—provides some useful flexibility and security at low cost. Since anchor swivels cost several hundred dollars each, that money can be better spent elsewhere—buying more chain or another anchor.

In pleasant conditions when anchoring in shallow water the chain can be let out with the load carried by the windlass itself. However, when there is any serious load on the chain, standard practice is to set out a pair of chain hooks with 20 to 30 feet of ⅜" line that is then fastened to the bow cleats. In this way, the load on the chain is transferred to strong points on the bow rather than to the windlass itself. Hopefully the bow cleats will have sizeable aluminum or stainless steel "strong back" plates.

Sometimes one sees a chain lock device mounted between the windlass and bow roller. The idea is to lock the chain and take the strain off the windlass. It's not a bad idea, but it adds more gear to the already cluttered bow deck. Besides, you'll still need chain hooks to temper the strain on the chain, and then chain locks become redundant. Such chain locks are often found on larger craft where the chain is heavy enough so the catenary effect takes care of occasional shock loads, and the windlasses themselves are heavy pieces of industrial machinery weighing hundreds if not thousands of pounds.

With some careful planning, some portion of the chain can be kept at some distance from the bow through the use of horizontal tubes. Modern designs, with their nearly plumb stems and narrow entrances, are particularly sensitive to anchor gear at the bow of the boat. So a useful strategy can be to place just 100 feet of chain or so in the chain locker and then carry the remainder of the rode several feet behind, using a chain pipe. This is especially helpful when carrying 400 feet of chain.

It's good practice to tie the bitter end with ⅜" line between the stout eye bolt and the last several links of the chain. Then if the chain has to be run out to the seabed during an emergency—dragging anchor or pirates (real or imagined)—it's relatively easy to cut the chain. The only way to cut chain in an emergency is with an electric grinder. Even with a sturdy hacksaw and new blades it takes forever to cut high-tensile chain, which is why it's such wonderful material.

And if you do have to cut it, don't worry: shorter pieces of chain have their useful purposes as well. Chain is often used to assist in typing up dinghies where theft is common or where "borrowing" is a local custom. Sometimes chain is useful tying up to a piling, especially in storm conditions, since the chain can ride up and down with the tidal surge. Some marinas, especially those in the Hawaiian Islands, require loops of chain around dock cleats to counter chafing from the ever-present surge. Chain has also been used to repair broken rigging stays and to assist in removing an engine in remote locations. And a short length swung around the head might convince an unwelcome "visitor" to seek opportunities elsewhere. So a bucket of short lengths of chain has its purposes.

Eventually the end of the chain exposed to the elements just behind the anchor ages and begins to rust. Then it's time to end-over-end the chain, exposing a fresh new end—the former bitter end—or to cut back several feet with an electric grinder. In bygone eras it was often possible to re-galvanize the chain. Alas, that seems more difficult these days. One of the arguments for ordering more than the standard 200-foot (half barrel) length of chain is the ability to cut off the rusted short ends as they appear.

One of the major improvements in anchor locker design is a locker that can be accessed through the deck just behind the bows. That gives one a fighting chance of untangling chain when the boat has had a rough passage and the chain moves around. It also lets you see how much chain remains and facilitates cleaning the chain occasionally with fresh water and airing out the locker itself. In older designs the chain locker usually needs be entered from below decks forward of the V berth. That can be inconvenient.

The best anchor locker installation divides the chain locker vertically in half into port and starboard sections just behind the bow. That helps keep the chain separated when you hit rough seas. It's especially important to attach the bitter end to a stout eyebolt. Just about every cruiser lets the chain run out too swiftly at one time or another, and the momentum of a fast-running chain rode is something to behold. Wear boat shoes when doing anchor duty, since a carefully applied foot can sometimes save the entire chain from going overboard. More than a few cruisers have been hurt from chain rushing to exit the chain locker, so sturdy shoes and heavy gloves are essential.

Carrying chain in the forward sail and/or chain lockers isn't all there is to the chain business. Recall our recommendation for at least two additional spare anchors. These, too, will need separate rodes. So some smaller lengths of chain, typically a foot or so per length of boat, will be needed, perhaps half as much for the rode used with the kedging anchor. These shorter pieces of chain and their nylon rodes can be stowed below where they can be accessed quickly when needed.

Before leaving our discussion of chain, a few words about nylon anchor rode. For smaller or very lightweight cruisers, nylon rodes have an important weight advantage over chain. Where nylon rodes are preferred, the usual practice calls for a chain leader (one foot per boat length) attached to the anchor, followed by the nylon rode. Even cruising boats that use all chain rodes will carry spare rodes of nylon, and of course nylon is the preferred rode for use with a kedging anchor. Heavy lengths of nylon can also be used when tying to a mooring and for towing.

When it comes to choices in size of 3-strand nylon anchor rode, it's usually between ½", ⅝" and ¾". While ⅜" may be strong enough for smaller boats, it tends to kink and combine into tangles. Larger sizes are less prone to tangles and kinks. Nylon is pretty strong while it's intact and kept from the sun and heat. For example, 1" nylon will hold almost 20,000 pounds when new.

But as with everything, there's a downside. One of the major worries about using nylon rode in a real blow is preventing chafe where the line comes over the bow roller or through the bow chock. Friction can cause the line to overheat and fail as the line is moving back and forth over the bow roller or through the bow chock. The usual remedy is to use a length of vinyl tubing and/or canvas wrappings over the chafe point.

Also, nylon degrades under sunlight and is subject to chafing both on the seabed and through bow and/or anchor chocks. For most cruisers these drawbacks overshadow the benefits of stretch. It's also more difficult to stow, in most circumstances. When left out in the sun it becomes stiff and hard. Braided nylon rodes are much easier to coil, if considerably more expensive than the old dependable 3-strand variety. However, making a splice in braided nylon is a chore. Most folks can learn to make a suitable eye splice in 3-strand nylon without difficulty.

Nylon is also much more difficult to handle with either hand or electric windlasses. For example, most modern windlasses allow chain to run out quickly and retrieve chain hands-free with control by foot switches alone. Some windlass manufacturers have attempted to mitigate the shortcomings of nylon by making wildcats that can handle both. In the author's experience these do not work well. Moreover, they involve a special splice through the chain link that not only weakens the rode but shortens its life.

Another difficulty arises from the required use of thimbles that permit the joining of the nylon rode with an eye splice and the chain leader. When thimbles are too thin they tend to elongate and put undue strain on the eye splice. Best bet is to use heavy stainless steel thimbles.

Since nylon degrades over time, it's best to use a larger size than needed. It's false economy to keep nylon anchor rode more than 10 years or so. It may be strong enough or it may not be, but it's difficult to tell from surface inspection. Nylon rode that's been used can often be softened somewhat by washing or soaking in fresh water and mild detergent.

Where nylon rode really shines is when used as a kedging anchor rode. Here the practice is to bring the dinghy to the bow, drop in kedging anchor— typically a Danforth type of 20 to 30 pounds or so, with perhaps a small chain leader—and the entire nylon rode. Then the anchor is dropped from the dinghy where appropriate and the nylon rode is taken by dinghy to the stern chock and thence to a convenient winch. Then it's "haul away, Joe" to kedge the boat back into deeper water.

WINDLASSES

An electric windlass is typically the most costly item in a well-found cruiser's anchor equipment inventory. Windlasses have a hard life, so it's good economy over the long haul to buy one that's larger and more robust than might be needed. Buy from a well-known manufacturer that can provide future repair service and spare parts. That advice might seem like overkill, but the market for used windlasses is pretty thin. With windlasses, what you see is usually what you get: large size usually means robust gear trains and large motors. A robust windlass properly sized for the boat can often last the life of the boat.

The venerable Ideal Windlass Co. of Greenwich, Rhode Island has for generations made bronze icons that hark back to an earlier industrial age. These bronze behemoths last forever, can be readily rebuilt, and are easily disassembled. Because of their size, weight, and initial expense, Ideal Windlasses are something of an upscale item for larger sail and powerboats, but they are durable and can pull with prodigious power when called upon.

Most smaller and mid-size cruisers use modern lightweight windlasses weighing about 50 pounds. These are typically built with aluminum bodies and lightweight electric motors and can apply 500 to 1,000 pounds of force for limited periods. Intelligently used and well maintained, these modern windlasses can be quite effective.

While electric windlasses are a convenience for smaller cruising boats, for larger boats they are necessities. After all, several hundred feet of chain and the anchor itself can easily weigh 400 to 500 pounds. Hauling in that size load by hand is more than a strong back can handle. And it's no picnic using the emergency hand-operated crank or lever. More than a few cruisers faced with retrieving the anchor in heavy weather with a recalcitrant windlass have simply let the whole mess go overboard. So monies spent on purchasing a heavy-duty, reliable windlass are well spent.

Nowadays hand-operated lever windlasses are occasionally seen on smaller and sometimes on traditionally minded mid-size boats. While some venerable designs are still available, e.g. the Simpson Lawrence "Tiger," they all suffer from the same disadvantage—they are just too slow, especially in low gear.

Electric windlasses come in two varieties, vertical and horizontal. The vertical ones are most commonly installed with just the business end—the chain wildcat and capstan—above deck. They take up the least deck space and can usually be installed close to the bow, two important advantages. They also keep the motor below deck, away from sea water.

Capstans are useful for docking and also for retrieving nylon rodes. Against these advantages vertical windlasses have several limitations. To work manually they require a winch handle—not a pleasant prospect on one's knees in heavy weather under a rolling deck. Also, they usually require a separate handle to let the chain fall free. And when they are installed near the bow they can be a bear to remove for repairs.

Horizontal windlasses, the more traditional design, are usually seen on larger boats. They are sizeable T-shaped affairs with a chain wildcat and capstan at either ends of the T and the motor behind in the fore and aft direction. Some larger horizontal windlasses have chain wildcats on both ends, making it easy to control each anchor's chain rode independently. The better-made ones have separate levers that allow each chain wildcat to run out when required, often a useful feature when it's important to anchor in a tight space. Not surprisingly, horizontal windlasses with double wildcats and separate run out levers can cost as much as a fair-sized dinghy and motor.

Horizontal windlasses take up much more deck space than vertical ones and usually have to be installed at some distance back from the bow. However, the installations are usually easier, as is removal, since there is no protruding motor below decks. An important advantage of a horizontal windlass is that it can usually be operated quite effectively by hand, while standing, using a long lever arm. In other words, it's fully functional as a manual windlass. That can be an important advantage when the electric motor gives up the ghost. Since the motor is above deck, the chances for water intrusion are greater. Unless the boat is 50 feet or greater, a horizontal windlass often looks out of place.

Windlasses have holes in the deck where the chain, guided by "strippers" adjacent to the chain wildcats, falls into the chain locker below. In order to work properly there needs to be 12 to 18 inches of freefall. However, in most chain lockers with vertical windlass installations near the bow, there's insufficient free-fall space, so as chain is retrieved it piles up in a pyramid and then jams the windlass above. Some boats have 3-inch pipes that encourage the chain to move aft into a deeper portion of the chain locker. In any event, it's important for the windlass operator to pay careful attention.

Salt water is the nemesis of electric windlasses. That's why large cruisers and commercial boats usually prefer hydraulic windlasses powered off the generator. The vertical electric windlass does have the important advantage of housing the motor below deck. But that doesn't completely isolate the motor from an occasional dousing when the bows go under water. And there are limits on how large a below-decks motor can be. After all, it has to be removed for repair from time to time.

Electric motors used in horizontal windlasses need special installation attention to keep their connection studs from corroding. Solenoids are especially prone to corrosion from salt water. It's helpful to wrap the solenoids with plastic to keep the salt water from corroding the terminals. Periodically coating windlass and solenoid terminals and cable ends with protective sprays is a good idea.

The Achilles heel of electric windlasses is their electric motors. Lightweight windlasses use small, modern automobile starter motors, while the older designs use starter motors commonly found in trucks and commercial vehicles. While both types can put out lots of torque when engaged, easily drawing 100 amps or more, the problem is that 12-volt electric motors heat up noticeably under heavy load.

So with the same size heavy load, a small windlass motor will heat up much faster than a much larger motor drawing the same current. The end result is that the larger starter motors tend to last longer even when abused. Placing one's hand on the windlass motor after it's been running under load for 5 minutes, nicely makes the point. So it's best to run the windlass for 15 to 30 seconds at a time, giving the motor some time to cool down and dissipate all those BTUs rather than keep the pedal to the metal.

Large commercial-type starter motors used in the larger cruisers have another advantage. They can usually be rebuilt at modest cost at any conventional auto/truck electrical repair shop. Typically, replacing the bearings at each end, cleaning up the commutator, and replacing the brushes is all that's needed, unless a ham-fisted operator has burned out the windings. In contrast, the smaller motors often found in imported windlasses may require special components not so easily found in the local shop.

The best solution when upgrading to a larger windlass is to upgrade the electric cables to 1/0 or 2/0 size welding cable to the battery distribution bus (see Chapter 8) rather than putting a separate battery forward. Use neoprene welding cable rather than the usual marine battery cable. To be sure, 30 or 40 feet or so of 1/0 or 2/0 welding cable will easily cost several hundred dollars, but that's only a fraction of the cost of a serious, heavy-duty windlass designed for the long haul. The other part of the windlass upgrading installation calls for a heavy-duty 100+ amp alternator for the diesel engine, especially an alternator that can put out 30 to 40 amps just above engine idle speed, if one hasn't already been installed. Without an alternator that puts out big amps at idle speed, it's easy to run down the batteries, even with the engine on, when setting out and weighing the anchor in difficult situations.

Other than checking the oil in the gearbox, the only basic service for windlasses is occasionally (once a year or so) removing the power leads to the windlass, cleaning them bright, then refastening and spraying on preventive or using old-fashioned axle grease, which is less costly and more durable. It's often helpful to periodically lift off the capstan/wildcat chain sprocket assembly and lubricate the spindle. Remember, solenoids are service items, as are their rubber switch covers. Carry spare foot switches/covers and solenoids.

What happens when the windlass fails? Using a winch handle in a vertical windlass can be pretty discouraging. A well-proven method uses a chain hook with a line lead to a cockpit winch. (An electric cockpit winch can do double duty as a windlass backup.) The basic procedure is to bring a crew forward in a dinghy, attach a chain hook to the chain at the waterline, and then bring a line over the bow roller to the cockpit winch. It takes some co-ordination, but usually 5 or 6 feet of chain can be retrieved with each set. Of course, it's much easier to do this when the seas and winds are moderate. Otherwise, use the engine judiciously to take the strain off the chain. With good crew, the anchor and chain can be brought aboard in 6-foot segments in about an hour or two. Then it's time to hunt for the spare windlass motor.

A few more notes: Electric windlasses make it easy to send crews up the mast or to haul a dinghy—or even a 50-gallon drum of diesel fuel—aboard with a halyard. But they are not designed as heavy load mooring bits. Experienced cruisers usually set out chain hooks with 15 or 20 feet of braided ⅜" line to carry the anchor and chain load to the heavy-duty bow cleats rather than let the windlass carry the loads directly. Also, windlasses are designed to lift chain and anchor vertically, not to pull the boat forward, though windlasses can help pull a boat close to a dock when needed. All in all, it's good advice to install a really heavy-duty windlass that will last for decades. And don't forget proper maintenance.

4

SAFETY GEAR

Views about safety related gear vary considerably among distance cruisers, reflecting age, experience, crew characteristics, pocketbook, family obligations, confidence in their boat, cruising area, length of voyage, health status, perhaps even faith, and whether they carry insurance. Some trust Poseidon and comply with just the required USCG and/or insurance items. Others take safety very seriously and provision accordingly with a certified ocean-rated liferaft, high-quality life vests and MOB (man overboard) buoys, high seas communication gear, (e.g. EPIRB, SSB, SAT phone), redundant heavy-duty bilge pumps, heavy-duty anchor gear, extensive medical kits, rocket flares, and so on.

Here are our priorities for the essential safety requirements and gear:

1. Staying afloat while repairs can be made
    —redundant independent heavy-duty bilge pumps
    —engine-driven pumps, 12,000 GPH trash pump, 110 v. pumps
2. Staying afloat when the vessel is lost
    —USCG/SOLAS life raft and emergency valise
3. Communication gear to seek assistance
    —electronic: EPIRBs, SAT phone, SSB, VHFs, AIS
    —visual: rocket SOLAS flares, SOLAS smoke flares, mirrors, floating strobe lights, MOB lights/pole
4. Keeping an overboard crew afloat
    —USCG/SOLAS life vests, tethers, harnesses, spare halyards
    —Mustang survival suits
5. Fire control equipment
    —automatic fire extinguisher system in engine room
    —fire extinguishers and CO/CO2 systems
6. Well-equipped EMS type medical kit

Outfitting the Offshore Cruising Sailboat

Some cruisers pay much more attention to their navigation electronics than safety gear on the grounds that careful navigation and prior experience will always keep them from harm's way. Unlike commercial vessels and those subject to periodic inspections by the USCG where safety gear requirements are mandated, blue-water cruisers are free to follow their hearts' delight when it comes to safety gear beyond the minimum regulatory requirements.

Nowhere are safety issues better focused than on life rafts and EPIRBs. More than a few cruisers do not carry rafts and/or EPIRBs, and based on our observations over the years, most cruisers do not regularly certify their life rafts. On the other hand, there are others who take safety quite seriously. We carry 4 EPIRBs: one stowed inside just adjacent to the cockpit stairs, an automatic one on a radar pole, and two personal EPIRBs worn by the watch crew. Altogether this reflects an outlay of several thousand dollars, but EPIRBs have saved thousands of lives and just because one is aboard ship doesn't mean it can be reached in time or will work properly when activated.

Ocean-rated life rafts are far more expensive than EPIRBs and require periodic servicing. Yet many, if not most, cruisers avoid the required periodic certifications, which nowadays cost close to a thousand dollars. Cruisers often purchase life rafts by price points rather than by USCG or SOLAS standards. Similarly, SAT phones are often viewed as luxuries, despite their ability to call for assistance anywhere at any time. Even when it comes to relatively inexpensive items such as flares, some cruisers buy the minimum package every few years. Others buy a dozen parachute SOLAS-grade rocket flares and keep another dozen in reserve.

We learned long ago to be very careful when commenting about safety gear when visiting other cruisers. It's OK to discuss the merits of anchor gear, but try to convince a cruiser who doesn't carry a life raft or avoids certification inspections and you're asking for trouble. We have a dear friend, a retired engineer, who goes on long cruises with his lovely wife on a well-fitted-out boat with all the latest gear. This gentleman steadfastly maintains life rafts are not necessary. He's happy to sail with us; we wouldn't leave port on his vessel.

Interestingly, first-class safety gear requirements for distance voyaging are pretty similar between small and large sailing cruisers. Human nature being what it is, most cruisers first outfit their boats in proper order or until their budgets are depleted, and only then provide safety gear before taking off. Given the considerable cost of first-class safety gear, it's a good idea to initially deduct the cost of safety gear from the acquisition and refit costs, lest the safety gear get shortchanged. Consider $10,000 or so a down payment on one's life and crew.

Safety gear is a critical component of the well-fitted-out cruiser. There are other ways to economize on outfitting a cruising boat; safety gear is not one of them. Even if we're cavalier about our own survival, our crews and our family deserve the best safety gear available. We purchased our first life raft almost 40 years ago from Jim Givens, a lovable genius who first invented a raft with a large self-ballasting underwater bag that would keep the raft upright even in hurricanes. At $3,000 it was the most expensive gear on the boat and broke our budget at a time when a pretty good cruiser could be bought for about $10,000 or so. But it bought peace of mind for two decades and let everyone aboard know that we value their safety.

While much of the installed cruising gear has safety implications, there are several really critical safety areas that stand apart. The first is staying afloat when the hull is damaged. That requires a redundancy of heavy-duty bilge pump systems until repairs can be executed. The second is staying afloat after the boat is lost. That requires an ocean rated life raft kept in compliance. The third is electronic communication gear to seek help/assistance, e.g. EPIRBs, SSB, SAT phone, and VHF. The fourth is individual floatation and man overboard crew recovery gear. The fifth and sixth is a first class medical kit and ample fire extinguishers, including an automatic engine room extinguisher.

Beyond these six critical areas is a large host of commonly installed gear that has safety components. These include horns, hand flares, manual bilge pump, convenience electric bilge pump, seacocks, engine fuel intake and exhaust installations, fuel tank installations, head installations, batteries, wiring, switchboard fuse panels, handhelds, lifelines, stanchions, and so on.

The first essential safety requirement is assistance in staying afloat until hull repairs can be made. That requires a reliable and redundant set of high-capacity, heavy-duty bilge pumps, with adequate alarms, and sufficient to keep up with a serious water inflow, such as the failure of a 1" to 1.5" sea-water intake hose. Heavy-duty bilge pumps are quite different from the conventional light-duty "convenience" pumps designed for occasional dewatering rather than sustained large volume water removal. The required manual bilge pumps are hardly suitable for serious water removal.

Outfitting the Offshore Cruising Sailboat

The emphasis on bilge pump capacity is on redundancy. Two heavy-duty bilge pumps are better than one. But when the incoming sea water rises above the floorboards and shorts out the batteries, one or more backup systems are required. Three back-up bilge pumping systems are commonly available: an engine-driven emergency bilge pump of about 1,500 to 2,000 GPH, a heavy-duty 110-volt pump of about 5,000 GPH run off an installed generator, and a gasoline-driven emergency 12,000 GPH trash pump. These trash pumps, costing about $500, are the only ones likely to keep up with a serious water inflow. They're widely used throughout Asia and Africa in commercial fishing vessels.

The second essential safety requirement is staying afloat after the vessel is lost. Here there is no substitute for a well-equipped ocean-rated life raft inspected periodically, together with a well-equipped abandon-ship valise. A life raft, which requires periodic servicing, is likely the most expensive required safety gear. The usual size accommodates either 4 or 6 persons. Preferably it should be either USCG- or SOLAS-approved, and the raft should be securely mounted in a special container where it's readily accessible. And remember this: spending the money to buy a life raft and then ignoring the periodic servicing requirements is pure folly.

The third essential safety requirement is adequate communication gear to ask for assistance/rescue. Here there are two categories—electronic and visual. In the electronic category the essential list includes EPIRBs, VHF radios, SAT phones, and a SSB transceiver. Every boat should have at least two EPIRBs and VHF radios aboard for redundancy. Along with life rafts, EPIRBs have been the premier lifesaving devices. There's no better way to summon SAR than using a SAT phone with the number punched in. The number for the Atlantic SAR Co-ordinator is 757-398-6231.

In the visual communication category there is a long list of gear that mostly predates the modern electronic age. The essential list includes rocket flares, smoke flares, horns, water dyes, mirrors, SOS flags, rescue floatation buoys with light, a MOB (man overboard pole) with a rescue light, and strobe lights. A dozen SOLAS-approved rocket flares should be part of every abandon-ship bag. Without rescue floatation buoys and an MOB with a strobe light, it's almost impossible to rescue an overboard crew at night in the ocean.

The fourth essential safety requirement is flotation gear. Here the essentials include Type 1 USCG/SOLAS life vests, inflatable vests with harnesses, tethers, and halyards long enough to reach a crew in the water. In colder waters survival is greatly enhanced with Mustang Survival Work suits.

Even with a capable crew, hauling a mate back aboard is a very demanding task, especially at night in heavy weather. The best preparation is a pair of very long spare mainsheet halyards on either side of the mast. These extra long halyards can readily be led to powerful cockpit winches.

The fifth essential safety requirement is a well-equipped medical emergency kit (with instruction manual). Here it's helpful to have the assistance of an emergency physician or trauma nurse to outfit the kit bag. Having a SAT phone or SSB along with emergency medical reference phone numbers can often be crucial to obtaining needed medical information.

The sixth essential safety requirement is an automatic fire extinguishing system in the engine compartment/room, together with suitable fire extinguishers and smoke/CO_2 detectors. Given the presence of both wind and combustible fuels, fire has disastrous consequences on vessels. Without an automatic fire suppression system in the engine room/compartment, the odds are pretty slim that you'll be able to put out a serious fire aboard with the usual assortment of required handheld units.

All in all, this is a lot of expensive gear not related to actual sailing or operating the boat. Yet essential safety gear is what the name implies, ready for the preemptive strike when the unexpected occurs. The ocean-rated life raft and a good quality SSB transceiver each cost about $3,000 plus some related antenna work. A SAT phone and purchased air time is about $1,500. A redundant set of heavy-duty pumps and backup systems can easily cost a thousand dollars, if not twice that. EPIRBs cost between $500 and $1,000. Without much effort, safety gear can easily run $10,000 or more.

That's a large sum, to be sure, for a beginning cruiser's budget. But "stuff" doesn't always happen to the other guy, and most of us—and our crews—have lives worth saving.

KEEPING THE VESSEL AFLOAT

It's a rare cruising boat that doesn't have one or two 12-volt electric bilge pumps and a manual bilge pump aboard, as required by insurance underwriters. But these are usually convenience pumps for occasional water removal, hardly suited to cope with a serious water inflow. What's really required to stay afloat are large-volume, heavy-duty pumps that can work full bore for several hours removing thousands of gallons per hour.

The conventional light-duty bilge pump installations are not designed for serious water removal. Their motors are too small, their exhaust hose diameters are too narrow, and they usually lack a check valve. They are usually connected into a flimsy bilge water level switch with inadequate-sized wire in turn wired into the switchboard rather than into a heavy-duty battery bus.

Manufacturers commonly rate their bilge pump capacities under ideal conditions with zero head without any restrictions and with fully charged batteries. But once a check valve is installed with 4 or 5 feet of vertical lift and 10 to 20 feet of flexible exhaust hose, pump capacities swiftly decline, especially when available battery voltage declines under real world conditions.

For serious dewatering, commercial fishing boats and knowledgeable cruisers use commercially rated Rule 3500 GPH heavy-duty bilge pumps. Even with a check valve and a 5-foot head with 10 to 20 feet of smooth bore exhaust hose, these pumps will push out about 2,000 GPH for extended periods. Their motors are rated for thousands of hours of continuous service under load, provided they're wired with a short run of number 10 insulated marine wire to a heavy-duty bus, with a heavy-duty automatic switch.

Two of these pumps (or their equivalent) is the minimum requirement for offshore cruisers. Three is better; even better is having a spare aboard. Having used them for decades, I can attest that they rarely fail. Since the pumps have leads of only about two or three feet, some care is needed to make waterproof connectors on wires leading to a heavy-duty bus bar. The pumps must be individually fused, and they need individual exhaust lines as well as individual bronze check valves adjacent to the pump in the 1.5" exhaust hoses. These hoses must run high enough inside the boat so that heavy seas will not push water back into the bilge. Typically the bilge pump exhaust hoses exit the stern.

When cruising, it's good practice to wash out the bilge with fresh water once weekly and give the pumps a good workout at exhausting several hundred gallons of fresh water. Cleaning the bilge also keeps the bilge switches clean. Some cruisers rely on the conventional toggle switches. We like the electronic ones used by the Coast Guard and commercial boats. They're more expensive and sensitive to oil and detergent, but they do seem to last forever.

To be sure, it is annoying to be periodically cleaning the contacts. We once were frustrated for several years by the required monthly cleaning of the contacts, until we located an obscure shower drain that had been disconnected for many years that was allowing the waste water to empty into the bilge. After we cleaned out several gallons of accumulated sand and other debris, the contacts have remained clean for months at a time. It's good practice to partially flood the bilge at least once a month and see how long it takes the bilge pumps to remove the flood.

It's important to install bilge pumps at different levels. One pump does the primary pumping, the other is the secondary standby. It's especially important to install the pumps and switches so they can be easily inspected, removed, and replaced. We attach the pumps and switches with hose clamps to a several-foot-long length of 2" x 1/8" aluminum flat molding. In turn, the upper end of the molding is secured to a convenient bilge floor. Every few years we replace the aluminum molding because of corrosion.

Another good feature of a suitable bilge pump installation is an automatic bilge switch with a light easily visible within the boat or within the engine room. Similarly, an automatic water level alarm is easily installed. These electronic devices are inexpensive and it's worth having two. Over the years we've formed the habit common to powerboat operators of taking a look inside the engine room hourly, especially before nightfall, with a flashlight to check the bilge water, leaking engine hoses, and smokes. The best bilge alarms are the eyes and ears.

An engine-driven pump with a manual control is commonly used as a back-up bilge pump on powerboats. While fairly expensive, these pumps usually have only 1" exhaust bores so their capacities are limited to 1,500 to 2,000 GPH. Some cruisers have a T in their engine intake pump lines to serve as an emergency pump. However, these pumps are usually rated at about 500 GPH or so and are very sensitive to debris. They may be a last ditch effort but aren't really up to the task of serious bilge water removal. Running a diesel with a failed or clogged sea water pump for more than a few minutes is really asking for trouble. Without an adequate supply of sea water, the exhaust hose will fry, smoke, and burn, causing unbelievable damage to the boat's interior.

With a generator one has the choice of a large number of industrial-rated high-capacity 110-volt pumps. We use a stainless steel 5,000 GPH one costing several hundred dollars. Even an inexpensive ½ hp sump pump rated at several thousand GPH could be used. One could also use these motors temporarily with an inverter, given a large enough battery bank and that the batteries aren't submerged. Having a heavy-duty pump running off the generator provides a good bilge pumping backup system independent of both batteries and the main propulsion engine, especially when the genset is mounted well above the bilge.

By far the most sensible emergency bilge back-up system, especially in dollar cost for GPH capacity, is a Honda Trash pump. These pumps are simple to operate and require only initial priming to begin quickly pumping tons of water. With a 3 or 4 hp motor (translating into 1.5 to 2 hp in electric motor terms) and lengths of intake and exhaust hoses, these units can remove 10,000 to 12,000 GPH and will usually pull items almost as large as an inch through their hoses. A good Honda pump with suitable intake hose will shoot water some 200 feet.

While these pumps do work on gasoline, they work just fine with the common gas/oil mix used for outboards. With a full tank, the pumps will run for about 45 minutes on a tank of gas. The pumps weigh about 30 pounds and are quite compact, roughly a 2-foot cube.

With deeper pockets one can go upscale and purchase a diesel powered "firefighter's" backpack portable pump. These are several times as expensive, much heavier and larger. Many boatyards and marinas have trash pumps handy for emergency dewatering.

It's a good idea to purchase several 25-foot lengths of heavy walled intake hose when installing a trash pump. The hose may cost as much as the pump itself, but it allows the pump to be run on the boat's stern or aft cabin top with enough hose to reach into the bilge.

STAYING AFLOAT WHEN THE VESSEL IS LOST

Life rafts are critical gear to offshore voyagers, their expense and inconvenience notwithstanding. A good quality ocean raft for 6 people can easily cost $3,000 to $4,000 and over the years its annual or periodic maintenance will easily equal the original cost by several times.

Not all rafts are made to the same standard, as any Certified Repacking Station will attest. But the essential features are large stability bags underneath, double floors, and robust covers. A step up from the standard offshore raft is a USCG- and SOLAS-approved raft.

It's eye-opening to visit a large commercial life raft repacking station to inspect how various life rafts are made and to talk to the service personnel, whose views are often quite different from the pretty presentation in the boating catalogs. Some popular so-called ocean service rafts cannot be serviced or repaired at a commercial repacking station. There is ample reason why USCG and SOLAS rafts are in a class of their own, are heavier, and cost more. Like most, but not all, boating gear, with life rafts you get what you pay for. A top-grade raft can easily last 15 or 20 years, far longer than the lightweight 60-pound wonders.

Buying a less-than-top-notch raft to sit out in the hot tropic sun and then not having it inspected defeats the whole purpose. Gas bottles fail, seams corrode, especially when the raft is sitting in its cradle for years in the tropics. When looking at used boats for sale, invariably you'll find that the raft doesn't have a current certification, a sure sign of either a disinterested owner or a project boat. Having examined or surveyed literally hundreds and hundreds of boats over a 40-year span, I can count the number of times the life raft was in current certification.

Our first raft was in a valise. At the time, that made sense since our budget was extremely tight and the cradle cost several hundred dollars. Moreover, it seemed sensible to stow the raft below and bring it topside only when needed. That it weighed 120 pounds or so and was a bear to lift into the cockpit didn't faze us. Since then we've always stored the life raft within a fiberglass container secured to a purpose-built metal frame securely mounted on deck on the premise that when it's needed, it's really needed and should be instantly accessible by the weakest crew.

The best place to stow a raft is near the stern on an aft cockpit boat or aft of the cockpit on a center cockpit boat, on the grounds that when trouble comes the crew will be in the cockpit, and moving aft is usually easier than moving forward in heavy seas. Even when lying-to in heavy seas, the aft portion of the boat is more likely to remain dry. Besides, most boats have sturdy stern pulpits. On one boat with an especially far back aft cockpit, we had the raft mounted on the aft pulpit. In our view, mounting the life raft on the cabin top just aft the mainmast or even forward of the mast on the deck just makes access harder and makes the raft vulnerable to boarding seas. Consider, also, that most deck brackets for holding the life raft are just mounted with sheet metal screws. Unless they're bolted through deck, one good wave will carry your raft off.

Outfitting the Offshore Cruising Sailboat

When abandoning the boat, one also needs an abandon-ship valise filled with useful items such as rocket flares, smoke flares, mirrors, emergency rations, flashlights, medicines, ship documents, and so forth. Some folks pack in an EPIRB and emergency long-life VHF. We're big on SOLAS parachute rocket flares and SOLAS smoke flares, especially since most commercial raft packers have ample supplies of just barely outdated SOLAS rocket flares. Flares are really a last ditch effort, so it's prudent to have a dozen or more of them. Rocket flares really do light up the heavens.

Our exit plan calls for grabbing the SAT phone, some portable VHFs, the Mustang Survival suits, spare life jackets, strobe lights, and the two abandon-ship bags. The crews are already wearing their life vests attached with strobes, flashlights, knives, and personal EPIRBs. In heavy weather, especially at night, we're not reluctant to bring all this gear up to the enclosed cockpit to keep it handy. It lets everyone know where the gear is stored. We always keep the SAT phone, our ultimate security blanket, within reach. Prior to abandoning the vessel, emergency calls would be sent out via SAT phone to SAR, via SSB, and even VHF and cell if near shore. One never knows who is listening.

COMMUNICATION GEAR

The electronic age has ushered in a formidable array of communication gear. In addition to VHF for short range, SSB, and SAT phone, there's also EPIRBs. Reportedly, calls to SAR via SAT phone are faster than EPIRBs with or without GPS co-ordinates. VHF radios are inexpensive, so redundancy is in order here. EPIRBs range between $500 and $1,000; it's prudent to have at least two. Personal EPIRBs carried on the belt are great comforters. We have four EPIRBs aboard: an automatic one mounted externally on the aft radar pole, one just inside cockpit stairs where anyone can turn it on when needed, and two personal EPIRBs worn by crew on watch in the cockpit. EPIRBs do fail, so redundancy is really useful here.

From an earlier age are non-electronic communications gear including SOLAS rocket flares, SOLAS smoke flares, SOLAS hand flares, signal mirrors, water dyes, SOS flags, and so forth. SOLAS rocket flares can easily last a decade or more, so it's prudent to have at least a dozen or two plus several within their compliance dates as required. Commercial life raft repackers often are only too happy to give away outdated rocket, smoke, and hand SOLAS flares. Just about every maritime nation manufacturers SOLAS rocket flares, so there's considerable variety and it's important to know how to fire them in the dark. Ones made in Germany are the smallest and easiest to use.

KEEPING CREWS AFLOAT

Lifejackets are required gear and it's prudent to have the best available—SOLAS/USCG grade commercial Type 1 jackets each with lights, strobes, and whistles for every crewmember, plus some spares. The whole point of wearing life jackets is to stay afloat in heavy weather, so only the best with the most buoyancy are worth wearing.

Inflatables are much handier to wear, especially if they have harnesses built in. But here, as with life rafts, standards for inflatables vary. Most of us would grab an old-fashioned life jacket when hopping overboard, even if we were wearing inflatables. Several horseshoe buoys with flotation strobe lights and a MOB pole with a strobe light round out the usual deck gear. Some cruisers like the throwing inflatable balls or rings. When going forward, the usual arrangements are harnesses with two tethers attached to jacklines or webbing running fore and aft on either side deck and securely fastened. Using lifelines attached to stanchions is courting disaster.

There is no point in having top-notch life jackets stowed away deep down in the lazarette or some other locker; better practice to have them out in clear view when offshore. In addition to keeping some life jackets handy in the cockpit when offshore, it's also useful to keep one or more powerful searchlights—a portable and one with a 12-volt plug accessible from the cockpit. With searchlights, the golden rule is "bigger is always better." Some of the newer LED portable searchlights will run for several hours and are really worth having.

Short of grounding, unexpectedly taking on large volumes of water, or being run down by a fast-moving freighter, retrieving someone from the water at night, offshore, in heavy weather, is the ultimate nightmare. Even a strong crewmember will be challenged to lift a limp person from the water using a standard halyard winch. Conventional wisdom calls for using a spare genoa or spinnaker halyard, but both of these are forward of the spreaders. So the halyard will be pulling against the spreaders as the boat is moving, which just makes it harder to hoist a crew member. Moreover, genoa or spinnaker halyards are usually just long enough to reach the undersized mast winches.

What are really needed are halyards that set aft of the spreaders so the boat can pick up the crew at the stern while drifting downwind. Extra-long spare mainsail halyards on either side of the aft portion of the mast do nicely here. The halyards must be long enough to reach well into the water to attach to the crew and also be long enough to be led to the much larger cockpit winches. Electric cockpit winches make the job relatively easy. Spare mainsail halyards have other uses as well, such as lifting dinghies, motors, and on occasion 55-gallon drums of diesel in faraway places. In a pinch a spare mainsail halyard can keep the rig in place when the backstay lets go. It can even be used to hoist a heroic crew to free up a jammed halyard while under sail.

Fig. 4.1 A sturdy stern ladder that drops down 3 to 4 feet below the surface can be an important assist to an overboard crew in regaining the safety of the deck.

Over the years we've become somewhat paranoid about the difficulty of retrieving overboard crew, especially at night in heavy seas. Often, overboard

crew are hurt in such circumstances. Old salts claim that being hit by an errant swinging boom has sent more cruising sailors to Fiddlers Green than all
the storms put together. The point here is that even if the overboard crew is
secured, the force required to lift that person is enormous, especially when
the rescuing crew are holding on for their lives.

For many years it's been our standard practice to require anyone going
out of the cockpit to suit up in an inflatable with a harness and two stout safety
straps—even when motoring on calm seas offshore in the bright sunlight looking for dolphins. We also require a backup crew ready to go forward with
similar gear at hand. At night no one goes outside the cockpit unless there is
a critical reason for doing so. And even at night, we light up the decks like a
Christmas tree with overhead spreader and deck lights to keep track of the
crew.

To be sure, these are overly cautious designs. But over the years we've
had more than our share of heroic exploits at sea, and we've had crew get hurt
despite our best efforts. Keeping crew aboard is a matter of having the right
gear and the right attitude.

FIRE EXTINGUISHERS

Most cruisers have the required two or three Coast Guard-approved 10-pound
fire extinguishers aboard. Fire extinguishers are pretty inexpensive, so redundancy is in order. An old rule of thumb is one extinguisher per cabin, but it's
a good idea to have several large ones aboard, especially near the galley and
inside the engine compartment.

While the required portable extinguishers are sufficient to put out a
galley or small electric fire, they are hardly sufficient to put out an engine
fire. That requires an automatic fire extinguisher right in the engine room.
These can cost several hundred dollars for a small engine installation, several
times that for a separate engine room. Most units have a remote switch. A
really first-class installation shuts down the engine when deployed, and also
the genset. Automatic fire extinguisher systems are de rigueur in powerboats, but somehow cruisers often seem reluctant to install such essential
safety devices.

Like life rafts, fire extinguishers need recertification periodically, especially the automatic systems. There is no sense having one aboard unless it's

dependable. If one is really concerned about fire, it's helpful to have a water pressure or salt-water pressure hose set up near the engine, as is common on larger powerboats.

All in all, fire extinguishers are cheap insurance and no one should complain about having too many aboard.

PROPANE STOVES

With increased use of small microwaves, stoves have become less important— except for those who like to cook. Propane stoves on cruising boats have relegated the once-venerable alcohol and kerosene stoves to the museum. When buying a used boat it's good practice to replace just about every facet of the stove installation unless it's been recently redone. A brand new aluminum propane tank with a new electric cut-off switch next to the tank and hoses is a good place to begin. Steel propane tanks belong in the barbecue at the house, not in a sailboat—or any boat, for that matter.

Propane safety solenoid cut-out switches tend to have a limited lifespan of about 5 years or so. If the boat is more than 10 or 15 years old it's helpful to install a new line from the propane tank to the stove and also new flexible line from the tank in the propane locker to the cut-off switch. Just to be safe. Many of the older boats used copper tubing for the propane supply line to the stove and copper tubing tends to become brittle over time, especially at the end fittings. Also, with age the flexible rubber gas line between the gimbaled stove and the gas line needs replacement.

Propane stoves also require replacement. Eventually the burners, heat sensors, and control knobs corrode to the point where hard-to-find replacements are required; then it's time to replace the entire gimbaled stove and oven. It's hard to resist one that's made entirely of stainless steel. New designs allow ignition via batteries, but after a year, it's back to the old-fashioned butane lighter pencil.

Two important features of gimbaled stoves are often overlooked by manufacturers. First, it's important to have a beefy, very secure mounting and locking device so the stove can be secured during heavy weather. Stoves are like batteries in this sense. One wants confidence that they'll stay in place no matter what. An airborne stove in heavy weather can cause considerable damage and/or injury. Most stoves have mounting devices that are easy to install but don't give any real confidence that the stove will remain in its brackets during heavy weather.

Second, it's important to have an array of first-class potholders and enough substantial rails around the edges of the stove. Unless that pot full of pasta is held firmly in place, having a gimbaled stove is just asking for trouble. Most stoves have flimsy potholders, so one often has to make suitable holders out of flat aluminum or stainless stock. Building a 2- or 3-inch rail around the stove top is also a good idea to keep pots off the galley floor.

When invited aboard a blue-water cruiser, I always pay careful attention to how the galley is set up, especially the stove. That often says pages about how the vessel is managed. Every once in a while I cast eyes on one of the older Shipmate gimbaled stoves, whose replacement parts are hard to find. They were heavy, but had really first-class pot holders and high protective rails around the outside.

Our current 4-burner is a not-very-heavy stainless marvel inside and out, but it has terrible pot holders and I had to build a heavy rail around its outside. The electronic ignition worked—for about a year. But everyone admires its stainless steel finish. And I have to admit it is easy to clean.

Finally, remember that propane is explosive. Test your propane locker periodically to make sure that the excess gas really does exit. Usually a simple test with a water hose is all that's required. Some inexpensive household battery-powered CO_2 and smoke detectors around the boat are useful, even when they go off while you're cooking.

VISIBILITY

Being seen at night is a great concern for offshore cruisers. So it makes sense to upgrade the navigation lights with lights suitable for boats 60 feet and larger, under COLREGS. Most older production fiberglass boats have their original navigation lights (under a different COLREGS standard) that are far too small to be practical. Fortunately, upgrading to larger lights is relatively inexpensive. Larger lights mean larger electric outlays, but a tricolor mast light uses just one bulb for the two forward and aft navigation lights. Similarly, a good set of spreader lights can help you alert other vessels when needed. Sails illuminated by spreader or deck lights can often be seen as far as 10 miles on a clear night.

The ultimate nav aid is a strobe light atop the mast, used in emergencies.

Outfitting the Offshore Cruising Sailboat

More than one voyager has sailed across the oceans with the masthead strobe merrily popping off at night, even though such use violates COLREGS. Carry a spare strobe light in the cockpit at night; you'll use it occasionally.

More important than being visible to others is knowing what vessels are nearby, say upwards of three miles or a half-hour's sailing distance. Here there's just no substitute: you need a good radar mounted in the cockpit. Our procedure calls for sweeping the ocean every 10 to 15 minutes, beginning with 12 miles, then 6, and finally 3.

We think it's more important to know what's around us than to place our hopes on being seen by other vessels. We treat all commercial vessels as potential hazards and assume the watchkeepers are off duty. Occasionally, when a commercial vessel is egregiously violating navigation rules, we attempt to make contact with the offending vessel on Channel 16 in hopes that the Coast Guard monitoring system will record our efforts. Our standard procedure is to keep at least a mile between us and any commercial vessel when offshore. If there's a tow involved, we up the safety zone to several miles.

While sailboat radar domes are usually mounted on the mast, we prefer to mount the dome on a well-secured pole at the aft end of the boat for easier maintenance and to avoid the extra weight, extra long cables, and wear and tear on the jib as it slides past the radar. To be sure, mast-mounted radars have longer ranges, but for most purposes radar is a short-range navigation aid. Even so, on a good day our 72-mile, 20-year-old Furuno can often see out to its full range.

Most cruisers have radar reflectors as another standard navigation aid. Usually they're mounted high on the mast on the grounds that, just as with the radome, higher is better. We've tried them all, and despite different manufacturers' claims of superiority, we find the results fairly indifferent to design.

It's instructive to turn on the radar on a quiet day in the anchorage to see just how difficult it is to pick up sailboats. So we keep a small, triangular high-tech reflector mounted just below the radome on a pole to evidence our blue-water seamanship credentials. We've observed that most larger commercial vessels that pick up a smaller boat on radar fail to yield to sailing craft that have the clear right of way. Our general presumption is that fast-moving commercial ships on the ocean pay attention only to other fast-moving commercial ships and to no one else. On the ocean the big gorilla is king of the jungle.

COMPREHENSIVE MEDICAL KITS

Most cruising boats have some sort of modest first aid kit on board. In fact, the USCG requirements for first aid kits for fishing vessels and commercial craft are quite modest. Over the years we've accumulated ever more complex and larger comprehensive medical kits, complete with instruction manuals, courtesy of physicans' assistant (PAs) crews with medical training who feel we should be prepared. PAs usually have 3 or 4 years of formal medical training and extensive trauma experience. We're now prepared for serious medical emergencies, provided we have the right crews aboard.

People do occasionally get hurt on offshore sailing boats, because of falls, cuts, and sometimes even broken bones. Most of these injuries require more extensive attention by trained professionals than can be administered by amateur crews, even when armed with comprehensive medical kits. Several firms specialize in providing emergency medical advice by SAT phone to offshore yachts, so when serious injuries occur, the SAT phone can the ultimate safety device. Commercial vessels routinely use SAT phones for medical assistance when crews are injured. SAT phones are the ultimate safety device.

DINGHIES

Dinghies are not usually thought of as safety gear, but there are times when it's imperative to get to shore: for example, to seek medical aid for an injured crew, to set out another anchor when the main engine is cooked, and so forth. In fact, more than a few boats have been saved by tying their dinghy to their quarter and pushing the big boat with the outboard. It's surprising what a long-shaft 10-hp motor will do as a push boat in quiet waters. Of course, it won't be very effective with some wind and waves, but that's what the sails are for. Even though most dinghies do just fine with short-shaft motors, it's worth considering purchasing a long-shaft motor for its push boat capabilities when called upon to do emergency duty.

Dinghies used to be made of wood, stowed on the cabin top, and rowed by real men. Occasionally a 2-hp was kept on the stern pulpit for the really long trips ashore. Nowadays the ubiquitous inflatable has taken over, with 10- to 15-hp motors as standard equipment.

The big debate with inflatables is whether to have soft or hard bottoms. Soft bottoms stow much more easily, but their performance is more slovenly, even when they're equipped with high pressure floors. Hard bottoms are often stowed on davits with a gaggle of associated hardware, which is asking for trouble. Sooner or later in a real storm a big one will come over the stern and make mincemeat of the dinghy.

Fig. 4.2 Dinghy Cradle
A secure set of cradles for securing a dinghy forward of the mast.

The best place to store a hard-bottom dinghy is on cradles just forward of the mast, providing there's adequate deck space aft the staysail. With lines to the bales of the lifeline stanchions, the dinghy can be secured to survive heavy seas over the bow. It's easy to offload with a spare spinnaker or genoa halyard using the anchor windlass or mast winch. With smaller hard-bottoms many cruisers carry them upside down, thereby allowing the forward hatch to be opened for ventilation. The only drawback to a forward-mounted hard-bottom dinghy stored forward of the mast is that it diminishes visibility.

We resolved the hard- versus soft-bottom dilemma by carrying both.

When anchored we often leave the soft bottom tethered to the stern, which signals that there's crew aboard. The soft-bottom is also helpful on rocky shores, when walking the dog, and when junior wants to spend time ashore by himself. The soft bottom is also an ideal for refinishing teak toerails and cleaning the bottom while afloat in calm waters. The large RIB is carried forward of the mast right side up. It's convenient to store fenders and we keep it well covered. When adequately secured it will withstand sizeable rollers coming in over the bow. After all, its stern is square up against the mast and the mast is well secured.

Two dinghies require two motors, one big and one small. In crowded anchorages near shore just the small motor is used on the large hard bottom RIB. Lifting a 25-hp motor off its stern pulpit mounting is hard work, even with a crane. So unless there's a real need to travel to the next country we generally use the smaller motor. Its fuel tank lasts almost forever.

We've bought our fair share of inflatables over the years. For hard use in the tropics the Caribes are hard to beat, with their large redundant tubes. Perhaps the ultimate inflatables are the 8-man high-tech black ones used by the Navy SEALs. Even used, they cost serious money but do make a statement. Alas, at 14 feet and 250 pounds or so, they are not practical for cruisers.

AUTOMATED INFORMATION SYSTEM (AIS)

Along with EPIRBs, radar, sat phones, and life rafts, AIS are one of the great modern safety innovations for reducing collisions at sea. About 40,000 commercial craft worldwide have such installations that provide other similarly equipped vessels with name, speed, direction, timing of nearest impact, and distance of nearest impact out to about 15 miles.

Over the last year or so the cost of Class B AIS for non-commercial craft has been reduced to where they are affordable—less than $1,000. Software upgrades may be required to show the AIS targets on the chart plotter. Standard Horizon makes a nifty model with a modest-sized stand-alone screen displaying AIS target information along with an integrated VHF for just about $500. It's a "must have" for offshore voyagers.

Outfitting the Offshore Cruising Sailboat

Fig. 5.1 Interior Systems Equipment Installations

Sanitation: marine heads; macerator; waste tanks; plumbing

Potable water system: tanks; manual/pressure pumps; hot water heater;
    plumbing; spigots at heads, galley, showers, aft deck

Salt water system: pressure pumps; outlets at bow, aft deck, galley, heads

Desalinator: 110 or 12 volt

Galley: gimbaled stove, double sink, pressure/manual spigots for fresh and
    salt water

Refrigerator/freezer: compressors; evaporators

Electric system—12 volt: batteries; switchboard; distribution bus; 110 char-
    ger; alternators; outlets; lights; blowers; exhaust fans; circulating fans; in-
    verter; connection boxes, terminal strips, battery switches, fuse buses,
    circuit breaker switches

Electric system—110 volt: switchboard; shore power receptacle; shore power
    cord; inverter; lights; outlets; blowers

Generator

Navigation/communication instruments: SSB; radar; SAT phone; EPIRBs;
    VHFs; depth finder; sailing instruments; GPS; chart plotter; weather fax

5

INTERIOR EQUIPMENT

Modern sailboats carry a bewildering amount of internally fitted equipment. Unless one is pretty ruthless about the must-haves, the total outfitting costs will escalate to utterly unacceptable levels. The old truisms are worth remembering: First, the builder provides only about 30 percent of the boat's value, buying the rest from other vendors; second, even experienced, sharp-eyed cruisers typically wind up buying their boat twice by the time they've outfitted her.

Some gear is absolutely necessary: an autopilot, basic electronic navigation aids, batteries, life raft, life jackets, flares/horn/whistle, and electric circuits and switchboards. Other gear is somewhat optional, depending upon budget and ambition: desalinators, chart plotters, pressure water systems, refrigerators, sailing instruments, and oil-fired heaters for colder climates. Looking back several decades, we realize that our best cruising per dollar and time spent was in boats now considered pretty primitive. We had a good depthfinder; a handheld lead line; an undependable, old-fashioned ship-to-shore radio, a taffrail log, a kerosene heater, a manual fresh-water pump, and a less-than-dependable alcohol stove, a few lights, a horn, two auto-style batteries, some navigation lights, and a manual bilge pump. Our most expensive gear was one of the first offshore life rafts from Jim Givens at a cost of several thousand dollars.

After tending to the major cruising gear—anchors, engine, rig, hull, and deck—owners of newly purchased boats will spend the largest portion of their initial and subsequent refit time and funds on internal gear. Internally, boats are continuous works in progress. With a large enough budget, the mid-size or larger cruiser can install just about all the cruising amenities carried by a similar size powerboat.

In this chapter we briefly discuss some basic features and concerns about refitting the seemingly endless list of internally secured equipment. Even with a large budget, some prudence is required. There are important distinctions between recreational and commercial quality gear, especially for electronics. For example, some gear is truly necessary: a dependable autopilot, commercial quality radar, GPS, SSB, and a first-class electrical system with adequate batteries. But if a genset is fitted, then it's hard to deny the charms of a large desalinator, air conditioning, and large freezer/refrigerator. Most cruisers manage to do well enough without a genset. Over the years we've found that gensets, a/c's, desalinators, and freezer/refrigerators are consumables whose care and attention add measurably to cruising costs.

AUTOPILOT

Modern autopilots have revolutionized cruising. Without one, a small crew faces the unrelenting "tyranny of the wheel." Reliable autopilots make long-distance sailing with a crew of just two normal-size adults a mostly pleasant experience, absent serious weather. Since autopilots are most needed when the going gets rough, it's important to obtain one that's beefy enough for the heavy lifting, one that won't fail when the heavens open up. Even a very modest pilot will adequately steer a 100-foot boat in calm water. Odds are pretty good that the autopilot that comes with the boat will be undersized and have a limited life span, so high on the must-do list is installing a proper autopilot. Two are always better than one and the original pilot can be used for light duty and motoring.

Unfortunately, autopilots are among the very least reliable essential cruising gear. The usual choices are between one mounted to the steering wheel outside in the exposed cockpit with an internal motor drive or belt-mounted drive mounted to the steering wheel, and a much more elaborate one mounted below the cockpit protected from the weather with an electric motor and hydraulic ram driving the rudder quadrant or external pilot arm attached to the rudder post. Below-decks models are considerably more expensive and often challenging to install. But the larger below-deck models are much more powerful, more reliable, and offer the not inconsiderable advantage of providing a steering back-up in case the steering cables or fittings fail. Below-decks models are usually linear hydraulic units with a 12-volt reversible motor and a hydraulic ram attached to the quadrant. These are controlled by a computer module usually mounted below decks amidships tied in to a compass and rudder post indicator.

Over the years we've spent more money on autopilots than any other piece of interior equipment. Pilots work hard out in the ocean and are on continuously for days and even weeks on end. The electric motors used in the linear hydraulic drives have limited life spans and capabilities and are very sensitive to getting wet. Also, the computer modules that control the current inputs to the linear hydraulic drives just aren't designed for extended heavy use. In our experience, once past 30 tons or so it's time to move up a notch with a continuous-duty commercial-grade hydraulic pilot installation designed for rough duty. Off-the-shelf linear hydraulic electric motor installations are certainly attractive in price and reasonably easy to install, but in our long experience they are not commercial grade. So they are common replacement items.

The standard practice for truly long-distance voyagers is to carry a complete back-up linear electric hydraulic pilot or at least a spare computer module. Surveys by the Seven Seas Cruising Association (SSCA) repeatedly show that autopilots are the least reliable major cruising gear. It's easy to see why. Sail a few months and the units accumulate a thousand hours or so, along with several hundred hours of really heavy going. The common experience of long-distance voyagers with medium-size boats is that they are required to hand steer in heavy weather, no matter what the autopilot brochure says.

It can be downright dangerous to have the autopilot motor disengage in heavy weather running before the wind or quarterly seas at hull speed because the boat is not responding fast enough. Once the motor disengages, the units typically lock in position and then the boat broaches quite quickly. We've had this happen enough times so that when the weather is heavy at night we hand steer, no ifs and buts. Sometimes we change course to take the strain off the pilot if the crew is tired. At night it's challenging to judge the waves, and if the wind is blowing hard enough the audible alarms of the autopilots may not be heard. There are only a few places in this book where there are some "thou shall not do"s. This is one of them.

Running before the seas at hull speed on a dark night and depending on the autopilot to track straight is just asking for serious trouble. We learned this the hard way when we allowed a rogue wave to put the mast in the water, injuring a crew. Moreover, running the autopilot motor at full bore inevitably shortens its life. Autopilot motors used in cruising sailboats usually are no bigger than those used in bilge pumps. Normally that's OK because they work in fits and starts, going this way and that, so the current loads are not too great. But once the boat is off course more than the pilot can easily correct, the course computer sends full power to the motor and shuts it down lest the motor overheat its windings. During that time the rudder is hard over 30 to 40 degrees and the boat heads up.

Autopilot motors are not designed for continuous heavy-duty work as is a windlass motor. They are designed for brief intermittent duty alternating direction triggered by the course computer. For example, the largest pilot made by Raymarine for recreational use draws a maximum of 30 amps for intermittent use. But even a small windlass will draw upwards of 75 or 100 amps and grind away for 5 or 10 minutes at that load. The big boys will easily run at twice that amperage. Raymarine recommends number 6 cable for its largest units, but a good size electric windlass needs 1/0 or 2/0 cable to handle the amps. It's really an apples and oranges comparison. Our spare autopilot motor weighs maybe two pounds compared to about 30 pounds for our spare Ideal windlass motor.

Over the years we've tried all sorts of tricks to enhance the performance and longevity of our autopilots. These include very oversize electric cables, short cable runs, and hooking the system directly to a large distribution bus, all with the objective of maintaining ample current and high voltage to the autopilot motor. But even given a truly large battery bank, once the other electric units (navigation lights, plotters, communication and radar gear) kick in, voltage of the battery bank declines as the pilot works.

Autopilot motors have the same issues as conventional bilge pump motors. With a full battery voltage load, such as when the boat is motor-sailing, they work fine, because they are designed to provide full power at a full battery charge voltage. But once the battery bank is drawn down to just 50 or 60 percent, problems begin and the units easily shut down. Most reputable bilge pump manufacturers go to some lengths to state that their rated capacities are based on no head discharge and a fully charged battery. Would that autopilot manufacturers also stated that their capacities are for ideal conditions. In a perfect world, having a dedicated large-capacity battery or bank available solely for the autopilot motor would be helpful. Outside of bilge pumps and autopilots, virtually all the other standard electric operating gear on the boat (save the windlass) can manage with partially discharged batteries.

A hydraulic steering system, used in commercial boats, offers vastly improved dependability over the 12-volt linear hydraulic units used in recreational boats. The flip side is that the commercial hydraulic units require continuously running electric motors and typically offer less "feel" on the steering gear. While the major manufacturers of recreational linear hydraulic drives claim their units are suitable to boats up to 70 feet, in our experience they're limited to boats up to 50 feet or about 20 tons.

Autopilots can inspire false confidence in heavy weather. Once the boat veers off the designated course, the command module shuts off current to the pilot's electric motor and holds the rudder in position. Then if the boat is running before the quarter or off quartering heavy seas, the boat will head up into the wind and broach. We've had this happen so many times that when the pilot is used in heavy weather, the on-watch crew sits behind the wheel ready to take manual control and avoid a broach.

Not infrequently the unit sends the signal "pilot off." In really rough weather, pilots are often just not strong enough to do the job, and hands-on steering or a temporary course change is required. The original pilot control module, which gets the most use, is usually mounted on or near the steering console, where it's exposed to the weather and likely to fail at the most inopportune time. So if the budget allows, it's a good idea to install a second pilot control module below decks at the chart table, where charts and GPS fixes are readily available. A below-decks autopilot control head is a really useful backup, and relative to the cost of the entire autopilot installation it's a fairly minor additional expense.

A few more autopilot wrinkles. It's especially important that the linear hydraulic component be mounted below decks so that it is not subject to any water spray or inundation whatsoever, even when water is sloshing down the decks and seeping (or pouring) into the aft lazarette, as often happens because of faulty or limited hatch seals. An autopilot's electric motor is just not waterproof or even water tolerant and easily fails if it gets wet. We've learned this the hard way with several different units. The autopilot motor must remain dry at all times. To test your installation, open the lazarette or flood the aft deck and get out the pressure water hose. If the pilot motor gets wet, then more waterproofing is required.

Ignore the manufacturer's recommendation and buy the largest pilot that can be installed. In our experience the pilots fail when working hard, not because of simple old age. Larger than necessary pilots will consume more power, but they're likely to last longer—and, more importantly, work when they're really needed. Also, buy extended warranties if available. If the budget won't allow a spare unit, consider purchasing a rebuilt unit if there's some appreciable savings. Typically the computer module fails before the linear hydraulic unit. Also, watch for oil leaks and air bubbles in the hydraulic unit. Once some serious air bubbles enter the system because of oil leaks, removing them at sea is a serious task that requires ample supplies of precious hydraulic oil fluid. Moreover, the leaks rarely seal themselves.

Outfitting the Offshore Cruising Sailboat

Ignore the manufacturer's recommendation on wire size from the battery bus to the computer module and from the module to the linear hydraulic drive. Go with one or two larger sizes so that the pilot module and electric motor are receiving maximum voltage for their designated current loads. Remember that the pilots will be working with less than fully charged batteries, and 12-volt motors are not happy working with low voltage. Pilots work best at their rated voltage, usually 13.5 volts, when the engine's alternator is working.

What about wind vanes? These are at least as expensive as comparable autopilots and involve a major installation. While they have their admirers and are well used for long-distance voyages, much cruising is done in light winds or involves extended motoring. A recommended (though expensive) strategy is to install a wind vane and a below-decks oversize autopilot plus some spare parts.

We've had limited success in smaller boats with the above-decks pilots that either attach to the steering wheel with an internal drive motor or use belts. Even though some voyagers have made remarkable runs with these pilots, they are exposed to the weather and really aren't strong enough for the heavy going when pilots are really needed. In any event, if the above-decks pilot is suitable to the boat, it's a good idea to buy a spare unit and put a plastic freezer bag over the unit when it's not working, in order to keep out the moisture.

An old saw in the cruising business is that with three crewmembers you'll have idle hands so there's no need for an autopilot, since tricks at the wheel keep the crew occupied. That's true enough on long voyages in settled weather when each of the crew is robust, in good spirits, young and healthy, and not suffering *mal de mer*. Our experience is that with three crewmembers, usually two are feeling fine at any given time and there's more than enough to do onboard, so a dependable pilot is a coveted friend. After all, it is nice to sleep on a regular basis, enjoy attractive hot meals, keep the boat orderly, and take care of personal needs. In a word, hand steering should be a pleasurable option, not a mandatory drill.

Of course, there will be times when the pilot fails and it becomes necessary to hand steer for days on end. Our experience is that the effort to steer a given course in heavy weather goes up disproportionately with vessel length and tonnage. And there's an important age factor: Young lads can stand for hours and hours in heavy weather; older folks may find that even an hour is too long. The same point can be observed in the specs routinely given out by autopilot manufacturers. A pilot designated as appropriate for a 60- or 70-foot boat can easily be rated as 10 times more powerful than for a mere 30-footer.

Pilots work much harder on performance-oriented boats—fin keels, space rudders, narrow entries, wide sterns, high aspect rigs—than they do with conventional long keel designs. So when choosing among competing hull possibilities, it's worth thinking about how well each design will adapt to an autopilot. For many years we used an above-decks belt-driven pilot on our CCA centerboard 45-foot ketch. That size boat was well above the manufacturers' recommendation. But we had generally good results, except during heavy weather when the boat would sometimes yaw 20 degrees off course before correcting. Power consumption was minimal, and we always had plenty of spare belts. It's the teeth that wear out.

REFRIGERATION

Close behind the convenience of an autopilot in long-distance cruising is having dependable refrigeration. Actually, it's much more important to have a dependable freezer in which foods can be stored for months on end. Of course, some voyagers insist on eating only what they can catch, but fish are not uniformly distributed among the world's oceans and cutting up freshly caught fish when rolling out in the wild blue ocean is not everyone's cup of tea.

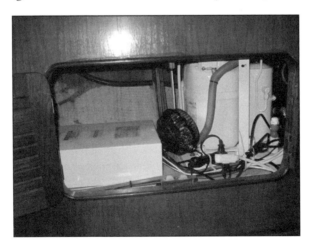

Fig. 5.2 This commercial-grade ½ hp 110-volt compressor with its control unit and condenser is mounted in a well ventilated cabinet and quickly freezes the system's holding plates. The small fan cools the compressor or "can" by about 20 degrees—an important assist in the tropics.

Outfitting the Offshore Cruising Sailboat

Just about every boat has a builder-installed refrigeration box that can be improved with better insulation—using freezer foam—and better seals. The old standby is a plywood box with a fiberglass-covered plywood insert with several inches of foam in between. High-end installations typically use stainless steel interiors, which are easier to clean and have better cold retention properties. Rebuilding a refrigeration box is much harder than it initially looks, since usually the surrounding cabinetry has to be disassembled.

Since size of the refrigerator/freezer units is pretty much dictated by the builder/designer, the basic choices for refit involve refrigeration power supply (12 volt versus 110 volt), using holding plates, air- or water-cooled compressors, integrated or external (motor and compressor separate) and whether to have portable refrigerator or a refrigerator and a freezer. Compressors can also be driven off engines, but those installations usually have an auxiliary 110-volt compressor allowing the unit to be used dockside. These expensive dual installations are usually well beyond the budget of most cruisers. If the budget allows, it's nice to have redundancy—say, a modest-sized auxiliary 12-volt unit in a box primarily cooled with 110-volt power or a backup 12-volt unit in a system primarily cooled with a 12-volt unit.

There is no shortage of 12-volt hermetically sealed units (motor and compressor together in a "can") that will give dependable service provided they are water cooled. Asking a fan-cooled unit to work in the tropics is too demanding since the unit is required to cool down to freezing from 100-degree ambient temperatures, but it can be done as long as power is available. Still, water makes for better heat transfer and water temperature is usually cooler than ambient air. Such units are more expensive, so it's worth buying water-cooled compressors from well-known firms lest the internal tubing succumb early to corrosive sea water.

Holding plates allow the engine's alternator (or alternative sources) to build up a day's reserve, although they make for a much more expensive installation. If possible, install commercial-grade holding plates: they last practically forever and use the highest grade refrigeration components. While holding plates are well-recognized technology, some manufacturers with more efficient 12-volt compressors suggest using 12 volts even in substantial systems, and relying on batteries rather than holding plates. The problem here is that even the best batteries have a limited number of life cycles, and first-class batteries for marine duty are quite expensive. So trying to cut costs by eliminating holding plates and relying on a large battery bank for power storage may be a costly solution.

Holding plates do have the useful feature that when initially cooling the system at dockside or by engine when motor-sailing, considerable "cold" can be readily stored. Most cruisers learn to keep their batteries up as often as they can in order to extend their life spans. Holding plates are especially useful when a boat is stored at a dock in the tropics for months on end. Then when it's time to fill the freezer, the plates can be frozen a day or so ahead of time.

Having used a variety of refrigeration technologies, we continue to favor holding plates. One problem we've encountered is that builders often install undersized holding plates. Two big holding plates are required in a reasonably sized freezer. We've also had good experiences in several installations with a unique European unit sold in the United States by Isotherm. Its efficient compressor is sensitive to available voltage, running full bore when the alternator or battery charger is humming, running at much lower speed off batteries. But for long term use 24/7, nothing beats a commercial-duty ½ hp 110-volt water-cooled compressor. The good ones can easily last a decade, provided first-class water pumps of sufficient capacity are also used and the strainers actively looked after. With a larger budget we would have opted for a dual system that also includes a fan-cooled auxiliary commercial-rated ¼ hp compressor.

There are a number of poor man's aids to improve refrigeration. The best we've found is to use sheets of aluminized sheet foam insulation—say, ¼" to ⅜" thick on the top of the box just under the opening lid and also all around the insides of the box. The basic idea is to reflect the cold. Such inexpensive sheet foam insulation reduces running time as well as moisture on the holding plates. Even better is the same technology using sturdy flexible vinyl protective covers.

Freezers of any substantial size take lots of power, and it's here that 110-volt units with large compressors and many holding plates do the job. A large freezer, along with a desalinator and battery charger, makes a good case for a genset. With the possible exception of the engine, a commercial-grade 110-volt internally-sealed refrigeration unit will likely be the most durable machinery on the boat.

Commercially rated 110-volt refrigeration units can easily last a decade or two with an occasional Freon replenishment, depending on whether they are running intermittently or 24/7. Nonetheless, considering the consequences of freezer failure in distant waters, it's good economy to replace an existing unit if it's beyond 10 years, even if it's running well. It's good practice to purchase a commercial-grade unit, one that's likely to be installed in a large power yacht rather than a recreational unit designed for sailboats.

Any water-cooled refrigeration unit needs spare water pumps. Since refrigeration compressors are really heat pumps, some care must be given to their installation location. Lots of air and ventilation is essential. Even better is a very small, continuously-running fan that runs air across the can, cooling the water-cooled unit. It's amazing how just a small motor can reduce the can's external temperature. Using our favorite diagnostic tool, the venerable temperature gun, we find a small fan cools the outside of the compressor between 20 to 30 degrees when running in the tropics, or from about 120/130 degrees to about 100 ambient degrees.

Another nice touch is a green light indicator that turns on when the compressor is running. All units with external holding plates eventually lose Freon, so occasionally looking at the sight glass for bubbles is part of the drill. Also, the refrigeration controls are set to shut down the compressor when the sea water intake drain packs up with sea life and the reduced salt water inflow is insufficient to cool the compressor. Cleaning out the refrigerator salt water pump sea strainer is one of our cherished weekly rituals and in some places an unpleasant daily necessity.

It's a good idea to arrange the sea water pump to have a conventional male or female 110-volt connection plug on both the sea water pump and the spare pump. Then changing pumps takes but a few moments, provided the sea water pump is easily accessible. We once spent several days rearranging our sea water intake system so we can change the refrigeration pump (and also the A/C and salt water pumps) in just minutes. And we've arranged matters so we can easily push out the nasty critters that once in a while like to live in our sea strainers, *e.g.* eels.

Not to be overlooked by a budget-minded cruiser are the completely portable refrigerator/freezer units working on either 12 or 110 volts. The better quality units (with patented "swing" compressors) are routinely used everywhere in Africa in pickup trucks and by medical care units out in the hinterlands. While on the small size—from one to several cubic feet—they are amazingly efficient and seem to last forever provided they are protected from the rain. We've used one for years as a backup tucked away in the engine room. Even on the hottest days they can hold zero and freeze ice cream—the ultimate test. They're also useful when shopping in an auto to buy frozen food in a distant market. Some cruisers use the better made units as their primary refrigerator/freezer. They usually stow nicely under a dinette table. Even a good size unit costs no more than a thousand dollars or so and is far less costly than a conventional sailboat oriented refrigeration system that can actually cool down and maintain freezer temperatures.

Another alternative for the budget minded is a stand-alone air-cooled commercial ¼ hp compressor driven by a large ¼ hp 12-volt motor. Decades ago these were widely used everywhere, but it takes some doing to find a large enough commercially rated 12-volt motor, and its current draw is large—20 to 30 amps. We used one of these setups for many years decades ago in the Pacific when the budget was tight or nonexistent. Every few years the compressor needed replacement, but they were quite inexpensive.

Still another budget alternative is running a 110-volt refrigeration unit with an inverter off the battery bank to initially start the unit. Then once the compressor is running, switch over to a small gasoline-driven 1,000-watt generator. We also used this "poor man's" setup for many years when large inverters were far more expensive than nowadays. This type of installation requires at least one large 8D battery and occasional engine running to recharge the battery. In mild to moderate weather the portable generator is set up securely on the lazarette and run for a few hours daily.

There was a day when the purr of small gasoline generators was noticeable in any Pacific harbor frequented by cruisers. Standard practice after anchoring away from one's neighbors before setting out in the dinghy for adventures ashore was to fire up the portable generator and let it run for a few hours till it ran out of fuel, taking care of both refrigeration and battery charging. Having a small gasoline generator is still useful for boats without alternative charging systems such as gensets, solar power, or windmills. The trick is always running out of fuel before storing and then making sure to keep the water away.

The downside is that these portable units are inherently noisy and usually quite smelly in their exhaust, so it's important to coordinate refrigeration requirements with missions to the shore. But if the budget is large enough, say $300 or so, it is possible to buy a quite nice upscale 1,000-watt unit that's quiet, fuel efficient, and runs almost forever if well maintained. Even the best of these units requires fairly frequent oil changes.

Still another way of obtaining 110-volt refrigeration offshore without the expense of installing a generator is to purchase an air-cooled single-cylinder diesel genset and mount it on the aft deck under a protective cabinet. Millions of these units are in use worldwide; they can be had for just a few thousand dollars compared to the 10 to 15 thousand dollars required to purchase and install a water-cooled 8 kw generator. The downside is that they are heavy at several hundred pounds, noisy courtesy of their single cylinder designs, do not like rainshowers, and like all diesels, require very clean fuel. Nevertheless, if one is just anchored away for 5 or 6 months in an idyllic tropical harbor, such units can be attractive—especially if a reliable two-cylinder model can be obtained. Refrigeration should not be compromised.

Taking a cue from our sports fisherman friends, there's still another alternative sometimes worth considering. These are externally mounted units 4 to 5 feet wide and perhaps 18 to 24 inches square designed to run either 12 or 110 volts. The better ones can be used as freezers and often can be mounted near the aft pulpit, sometimes as an auxiliary freezer unit.

Some more tips on freezers. First, some type of temperature dial is needed. A fairly recent device is an external digital indicator attached to a very thin flexible flat wire containing the probe. Second, when holding plates are used, the best the compressor can do is to freeze the plates, typically down to 18 degrees as a refrigerator and to zero or lower when used as a freezer. So if the food is not already frozen before it's put into the boat's freezer, it can take days to eventually freeze, especially if it's near the top of the freezer, the warmest part. Ice cream goes down near the bottom along with the meats and fish, while easier-to-freeze chicken and frozen vegetables can be stored at higher levels. Also, freezers work best when they're filled. So if there's space left over, freeze your fruit juice and milk. They'll last for months and months if kept frozen. As the freezer is emptied, it's useful to keep it filled with plastic jugs of water at the bottom, working as additional holding plates.

DESALINATORS

Close behind the comforts of autopilots and refrigeration are desalinators. The basic choices are between modest-sized 12-volt units that run for long periods versus 110-volt units that produce substantial quantities of water with just an hour or two's running time. For boats already equipped with gensets, the 110-volt units are attractive. A 12-volt desalinator costs about as much as a below-decks autopilot. The 110-volt units cost 2 or 3 times as much, but have disproportionately larger capacities.

Desalinators come either in modular form, which aids installation, or completely assembled in a fairly sizeable box, which precludes their installation in anything other than medium and larger boats. Another complication with the 110-volt units is that they can come either manually or electronically controlled. While the latter is initially attractive, typically there are no manual overrides so repairs require factory-certified personnel. That argues for manually controlled units and familiarity with the instruction manuals. Desalinators have lots of parts with various filters and hoses, *e.g.* salt water intake, overboard exhaust, fresh water output, and often pressure water fresh water input for back flushing, plus the pressure water pump, pressure vessels, and various indicators and valves. Setting aside several days or even a week for installation is prudent for a modular installation, given its inventory of filters galore. Desalinator manuals typically make for long reading.

The expensive parts of desalinators are their pressure vessels (long narrow cylinders) and the pressure pumps capable of generating 1,000 psi when forcing sea water through the membranes. Installations require serious attention to the instruction manual, since there are various bits and pieces that leave no margin for incorrect installations. One advantage of the 110-volt units is that the same motor/pressure pump unit is typically used on 15-gallon-per-hour units as ones twice the capacity, say 30 g.p.h. The real difference is that the length/volume of pressure vessels is doubled to achieve larger capacities. In other words, smaller units can usually be upgraded just by adding another pressure vessel.

Care is needed when installing desalinators to make sure that the various parts and controls are easily accessible. One advantage of installations in engine rooms of center cockpit boats is that most desalinator components can be placed together on trays or purpose-built shelves. Also, desalinators require a substantial volume of spares for various types of filters and component rebuilding kits.

Fig. 5.3a and 5.3b
A 20 gph 110-volt modular desalinator installation with the pressure pump on a shelf and the long pressure tube and other components mounted on a bulkhead. Desalinators have lots of parts requiring occasional service, so modular installations facilitate ready access.

When desalinators are left for long periods they must be preserved with chemicals to restrain bacteria growth. In the past this required mixing chemicals, but special filters are now available for this purpose. Many units are now set up so that back-flushing the unit with fresh water for 5 minutes or so every 3 or 4 weeks is sufficient to keep the microbes at bay. Unlike most marine equipment, desalinators tend to be use-dependent and can last for a decade or more before seals on the pressure vessel and pump need to be rebuilt. The big expensive replacement items are the pressure vessels and pressure pumps.

As with autopilots, when purchasing a cruiser the desalinator is a good candidate for replacement. They typically do not come with an "hour meter," and it's challenging to rebuild the larger 110 units in the field. Most surveyors, eyeing the desalinator, will note that it has been pickled or preserved (or assume so), and perhaps briefly run the pressure pump and let it go at that. In cold climates desalinators are usually pickled or taken apart and drained out.

At day's end it takes an outside specialist to properly survey an installed desalinator. Money is probably better spent buying a new pressure vessel and pump and using the existing installation as spares. Desalinator technologies are well established; at last reading there were several dozen builders or assemblers of the 110-volt units. Only a handful of 110-volt desalinators are completely built in-house by long-established manufacturers. On occasion one finds a desalinator put together by a talented amateur.

With a limited budget, the 12-volt units from the well-known builder are an attractive first step. They're easy to upgrade. Life is more complicated for the 110-volt units. With capacities of just a few GPH, the 12-volt units typically run for many hours daily and are noisy, so some consideration must be given to installation. The possibilities for the 110-volt units are far more varied, but they require a substantial genset capacity to start their motors, typically a full horsepower. Since the market for 110-volt desalinators is much larger than for 12-volt units, replacement parts and service are easier to find.

Clearly not every blue-water cruiser needs a desalinator, especially early in the cruising life. Decades ago, a 30- or 50-gallon fresh-water tank with hand pump could prove satisfactory for 3 or 4 weeks for small to medium-size boats, especially if a saltwater pump was fitted at the galley and head. But once pressure water systems are fitted with showers, water consumption rises dramatically and it's easy to justify installing a desalinator. Few boats nowadays fit out salt water pumps in their galleys and heads. In the old days 1 to 2 gallons per crew per day would usually suffice. Our experience is that 4 to 5 gallons per crew per day is more representative of actual use. Not only does water consumption depend upon shower use, but it especially depends on whether a real cook is onboard trying out culinary skills. Some ambitious experienced cooks are not satisfied until all the available pots and pans are used.

More than a few cruisers have gone long distances without a desalinator, making do with 5-gallon water jugs carried on deck and provisions to siphon off rainwater into water tanks. In truth, desalinators are typically used for relatively few voyages over a long sailing career. But the crystal-clear water they produce is almost always superior to tap water available at most dockside facilities, especially in the out islands. However, without special filter arrangements, some care must be exercised before using these modern wonders in commercial harbors with significant diesel oils.

All in all, desalinators are high-valued convenience gear that make it possible for small yachts to travel long distances. Most cruisers requiring desalinators will do well enough with a popular 12-volt unit and lots of spares, paying careful attention to the installation manual. For those with 110-volt gensets already aboard, the capacity advantages of the 110-volt units are attractive.

We've done well enough for many decades in smaller boats with 5-gallon jugs lashed around the decks when needed, along with a household water filter at the galley. Nonetheless, a shower every once in a while offshore—especially in the tropics—is very handy, indeed. Before installing a watermaker, be sure to install a pressure saltwater pump at the galley and head. Those are really essential watersavers.

ELECTRONIC NAVIGATION

Most technologically minded cruisers are fascinated by electronic navigation gear and overspend for the latest and best when other cruising essentials have higher priority. While the boat may come with a long list of installed electronic navigation marvels, most of them will likely be outdated and some will be just junk. So it's attractive to begin with a clean slate. Here the watchword is to purchase just the essential commercial-grade components.

There is a marked quality difference between recreational-grade electronic navigation gear and commercial grade. The latter lasts almost forever and can often be repaired anywhere there is a major fishing fleet. Walk down the docks of any fishing boat fleet and it's easy to pick out Furuno radars that are 10 or 20 years old. They rarely quit. With changing technologies there seems little incentive for recreational electronic manufacturers to invest in making gear suitable for serious offshore marine use.

Fig. 5.4 Cockpit Navigation Cluster
Navigation instruments are increasingly moved outside clustered around the steering pedestal. Here we see a large GPS chart plotter together with autopilot and sailing instruments. A radar display is mounted on the forward cockpit shelf together with a bearing compass. Note the robust hand rail mounted around the pedestal and also one on top of the instrument cluster. (The steering wheel has been temporarily removed for this photo.)

The recreational industry is quickly moving to adopt the commercial standard of importing all relevant information into one screen. That makes for a neater installation and looks impressive at first glance. But one screen puts all the onions in just one bucket. There's no redundancy. Commercial one-screen installations invariably have a backup. Moreover, there's a significant quality difference between the recreational industry and commercial grade electronics. Commercial marine users insist that the gear they buy be repairable by the local marine electronics shop. In contrast, most recreational marine electronics has to be sent back to the factory and replaced with a rebuilt item. The stuff is just not repairable, which is understandable, since next year there's a new model.

The temptation with marine electronics is to overspend the budget. However, the basic items are a VHF, depthfinder, SSB, and radar. Since SSBs are required (usually with backups) on every commercial offshore vessel, the market for SSB is use- and commercially-driven. The SSBs can easily last for decades with occasional channel upgrading. If it's working and not really ancient, the SSB that comes with the boat can usually have an extended future aboard, provided one makes careful inspection of the SSB grounding system and wire lead from the tuner to the SSB antenna typically mounted on the backstay.

RADARS

With radars the story is different. Commercial radars are lifesavers and necessarily robust and long lasting, unlike recreational radars, which are used infrequently except by sport fishermen traveling at high speeds. The major commercial radar brands include Furuno, Raytheon (not Raymarine), Icom and JVC. They can usually be repaired anywhere. Aside from needing to have the magnetron replaced, commercial radars last for decades with minimal, if any, repair.

Experienced navigators consider radar their most valuable tool. Radars serve several purposes. They can reliably identify fast-moving commercial vessels within an hour's sailing time—6/7 miles away. They can identify distant geographical features such as mountains. They can identify live squalls, thunderstorms, and rain showers. They can identify hard-to-see navigation buoys in unfamiliar inlets at night in bad weather. At anchor they can identify uninvited guests at sufficient distance to take corrective action. Radar is especially useful (indeed, a critically important resource) at night on the high seas when a sweep every 10 or 15 minutes locates "company" invisible to the unaided eye.

Outfitting the Offshore Cruising Sailboat

If a boat does come with a radar, it's most likely a recreational unit with the radome mounted at the mast spreaders and the receiver mounted below. That's objectionable on several counts: weight aloft, signal loss through long cable runs, difficulty of service, and difficulty of accessing the receiver in the cockpit where it's needed. Much preferred is a radome on a pole at the stern and a receiver easily visible from the helm, well protected from weather when necessary.

If the budget allows, purchase a new commercial-grade radar with a 3-foot wavelength antenna on an aft pole 10 feet or so above the deck, with the receiver mounted in the cockpit. A 3-foot wavelength radar antenna will cost more than the familiar 18- or 24-inch radome, but it will have much greater resolution, which is the whole purpose of the exercise. Despite the near universal popularity of mast-mounted radar antennas, what's most important is identifying traffic within an hour's sailing time and the ability to see up real close for navigation buoys when the fog sets in.

The importance of a first-grade radar installation cannot be overstated. The greatest danger to cruising boats is being run down offshore by commercial vessels failing to keep appropriate watch. No other navigation tool provides advance notice of impending danger. In short, the radar installation should not be compromised. Buy commercial-grade and be not impressed with the installed recreational-type unit.

A 10-inch receiver screen is the bare minimum. A 12-inch screen commonly found on commercial grade sets is a major improvement. Radars are complicated; to obtain the best results, the manuals need be mastered. Unlike GPS where it's either on or off, radar sets require adjustment at each range for best results, claims for "automatic" to the contrary notwithstanding.

Actually, there's a good argument for having two radars aboard—a shorter range model in the cockpit and a larger range one with the receiver mounted below. The below-decks radar aids the navigator at the chart table and can come in very handy when anchored in a remote place to check on uninvited guests without showing oneself in the cockpit. Putting on the spreader lights after finding an uninvited target nearby will often lead to a visitor's changing course. We speak from some experience.

Fig. 5.5 Cockpit Mounted Radar
Cockpit mounted ICOM 48-mile radar and 6-inch Plastimo compass for taking
bearings allow the watch crew to easily track surrounding vessels at night.

Fig. 5.6 Radars Mounted on Stern Poles
Radar transmitters are best mounted on stern poles to facilitate servicing
and reduce signal loss from long cable runs when mounted high on the mast.
Both units depicted have 4-foot arrays. The left one is a 72-mile Furuno with
a receiver mounted at the chart table, the right unit a 48 mile ICOM with a
receiver mounted in the cockpit. Note that hi-tech radar reflector on the left
radar pole mount.

119

Most cruisers will find the manuals that come with commercial-grade radars to be the most complex manuals of any onboard cruising gear. Radar manuals demand serious study. That's why there are special merchant marine and Navy classifications for qualified "radar operators" and special schools.

Radars are very sensitive to weather conditions and sea states and it does take some serious time and concentration to learn how to read the unit to its maximum advantage. That's especially true when navigating an unfamiliar inlet or anchorage at night in rough weather. Prior to affordable radar, GPS and chart plotters cruisers typically stood off unfamiliar areas at night, especially in bad weather. But with a good radar operator together with a commercial-grade unit, that's often not necessary. We'd much rather trust what we see on the radar screen when making landfall than rely on the chart plotter. All too often the navigation buoys are moved as needed and the plotter is not accurate.

Fig. 5.7 Mast Mounted Radar
Mast mounted radars, being cumbersome, are better fitted on stern poles for off shore sailing.

How far out should the radar see? Actually, once a decision is made to se-lect a commercial-grade radar, that decision is pretty much determined since the available choices typically are 36, 48, and 72 nautical miles. With 3- or 4-foot wavelength antennas, how far the radar sees is a function of power. In terms of power per dollar, the commercial-grade 36- and 48-mile radars will do fine. We use a 48-mile ICOM for the cockpit and a 20-year-old 72 Furuno at the navigation table. The more modern ICOM powers up quickly and is relatively efficient. But the old Furuno is power-hungry and takes a while to tune up properly. Even though both radars have similar sized wavelength antennas, the older Furuno has amazing discrimination. But it does take some fiddling. Even though both radar antennas are set on 10-foot poles (about 14 feet above the water), they have no difficulty seeing the distance. On many occasions the Furuno sees out 70-odd miles of beach when required. That's reassuring.

One more thought. The prudent mariner always assumes that other vessels are not keeping watch, save the US Coast Guard and Navy. Especially at night, radar is the one tool that spots potential trouble. Doing a scan every 15 or 20 minutes keeps the onwatch crew awake and ensures that potential dangers are identified. When changing watches, the first thing the new watch does is to study the radar screen with the assistance of the previous onwatch crew and make sure that all potential hazards are noted. When in doubt there's no harm in trying to make contact with potential hazard vessels by VHF or other means. Sailing at night is often stressful. But once some real comfort is obtained with the boat's radar and its capabilities, the radar becomes the on-duty watch's best friend.

GPS

While well-outfitted cruising boats will have several GPS units aboard, one should be a commercial-quality stand-alone unit, such as one made by Furuno, installed near the chart table. These units with 4-inch screens are not expensive and are fitted out with various alarms. In our experience these units have more robust receivers and better software than the recreational GPS units commonly installed in chart plotters and sailing instruments. It's also helpful to have one or more inexpensive portable GPS nav units as backups. They're a nice safety item when lightning wipes out the electronics and handy on shore and in dinghy exploration. Along with portable GPS, a few portable VHF units come in handy, as does one or more portable EPIRBs.

Chart plotters have dramatically reduced the angst involved in navigation. With a good chart plotter and radar it's possible to enter an unfamiliar inlet at night in heavy weather, something unthinkable for most us without chart plotters. Even offshore, chart plotters are especially convenient selecting routes and calculating distances. Set in "airplane mode," they allow one to sail a perfectly straight line between destinations.

Outfitting the Offshore Cruising Sailboat

While it seems convenient to have a one-screen plotter that can also display the radar and perhaps even sailing instruments, it's much more important to spend the money on a commercial-grade stand-alone plotter, preferably with a 10- or12-inch screen. When the going gets rough, it's far better to have an experienced radar operator focus on the radar screen and the helmsman to focus on the plotter rather than burden the helmsman with both inputs. Interpreting radar screen outputs often requires sustained attention in demanding situations, whereas the information off the plotter is more easily picked up.

Even with a 10- or 12-inch plotter screen there's no advantage in peering into a 5- or 6-inch radar screen. With 20-inch screens commonly found on commercial vessels, it's another story. Besides, their bridges commonly have several sets of watching eyes. Anyway, mounting a 20-inch screen on the steering pedestal is not really feasible. Then there's an argument for redundancy in having a separate radar and chart plotter.

Now, chart plotters are useful tools, but they take out much of the mystery and self-reliance involved in navigation. And they breed a false sense of confidence and dependence. Why bother with a navigator when the helmsman has it all at the wheel?

Would-be voyagers would be well advised to purchase all the requisite paper charts, chart books, cruising guides, and Pilots for a prospective voyage before investing in a chart plotter. Paper chart backups remain a commercial offshore ship's standard requirement. Plotters do fail and are not self-healing. Their internal GPS receivers take "holidays," often when most needed.

The argument for having a complete set of paper charts before charging off to purchase the latest, most up-to-date chart plotter does seem at first glance to be a bit archaic. But it is important to learn the basic navigation tools with paper charts and learn to plot positions by pencil directly on the charts. Moreover, the charts provide a large-area perspective of what to look for in terms of geography. Many experienced cruisers make hourly marks on their paper charts and then keep record sheets of position, course heading, speed, notes of crews on watch, and so forth. With the plotter as the sole reference it's tempting to get lazy and then one day the navigator is unprepared when the trusty plotter is faltering. Working with charts is fun. So by all means purchase a commercial grade plotter, but not until after you've studied the charts.

Still another argument for not wholly relying on the chart plotter typically mounted near the steering console is that if one sails long enough in faraway places the inevitable happens. Stuff disappears. More than one long-distance cruiser has found the externally mounted chart plotter missing. Even when boats are broken into and electronics taken, it's pretty rare to find the paper charts are taken too. Paper charts do not rely on batteries. So they're handy items in the abandon-ship bag as well. The best of all worlds is having duplicate independent chart plotters, one mounted at the compass console, the other at the navigation table. This has been on our wish list for years.

Most boats have a set of sailing instruments including depthfinder, speedometer, wind meter, and wind direction indicator. Except for the latter, meters are fairly inexpensive to buy but are expensive to repair. It's often necessary to replace the set every 5 years or so, to the tune of about $2,000. Consequently, if you can afford it, it's handy to have repeaters or slave units not only at the chart table but also above the navigator's sea berth and the owners berth. Typically meters and their connections are proprietary, so after many years and different brand installations, there's often a rash of sailing instrument wires in the boat.

Of course, not all sailing instruments are required, nor are they all equal. Hands down, the depthfinder is the most important; if the budget permits, a commercial depthfinder is advised. Offshore cruisers often used to purchase a near-shore depthfinder good to about 250/300 feet and a much more expensive offshore one good to about 1,000 feet. Nowadays, with the luxury of inexpensive GPS and moderately expensive chart plotters, most make do with the near shore depthfinder. Most manufacturers now have a temperature indicator in their speedometers, which is handy when sailing through the Gulf Stream, although our old reliable temperature gun works even better.

Depthfinder transducers have limited lives, but if replacement ones are installed low down where the hull is solid glass, using a large tube of silicon to mount them usually works pretty well. Grinding out unusable bronze mounted transducers from the hull when on the hard can be time-consuming work, even when a conventional grinder is available, and expensive if contracted out. Nowadays with cored hulls one may have to experiment with various locations to find solid glass for mounting the transducer. When mounted from the inside of the hull, plastic transducers work fine but bronze still works the best mounted externally. Many (most) builders mount transducers where it's convenient—around mid-ships. But the transducers are most effective when mounted as far as possible forward while still in the water. Since they send out

Outfitting the Offshore Cruising Sailboat

a fairly wide beam, the transducers work well enough even when mounted on hull sides, provided the angles are not too sharp. More than one cruiser has made do with a spare transducer hanging off the stern.

All depthfinders need to be calibrated so one has a really good idea of how much water is actually under the keel. That requires some patience with a handheld old-fashioned lead line. Ideally this requires a level sandy bottom, quiet seas, and the patience to walk around the decks taking some notes. In practice, most cruisers will leave a safety margin of one or more feet lest the keel drag along a rocky or coral bottom. It doesn't take much to do thousands of dollars of damage on an encapsulated keel from sailing in thin waters. When actually sailing, even in 1- or 2-foot seas, the safety margins need be larger. Our experience has been that as the boats become larger and more expensive the depth safety margins become larger. On occasion when walking about in a boatyard one finds an old cruiser with a really chewed-up bottom with stories to match. Repairing such a bottom is perhaps the most unpleasant repair job on a glass boat.

Modern technology has come to depthfinders. Side-scanning look-ahead sonars are the ultimate instrument, though expensive. These are now de rigueur on upscale powerboats and the technology is improving to the point where someday most of us will be able to afford 3-dimensional look-ahead sonars. Having said that, much of the fun in sailing in tropical waters is exploring shallow depths using simple technologies: eyes, lead lines, and an old-fashioned long, marked boat pole.

Even better than the traditional handheld lead line is a 10- or 12-foot-long boat pole (varnished, of course) with one-foot black band gradations. We've used one now for better than three decades. Holding it vertically, it's easy to walk around the decks taking soundings and even checking out depths at low tides while at docks. With a large bronze hook at the end, it's a good tool for hauling in a lobster pot line caught on the prop or rudder. It's also useful for catching errant halyards and all sorts of other practical tasks, especially around docks. To be any real use the pole needs be sturdy, straight-grain oak at least 1.5 inches in diameter so it'll stand up to really heavy use. Once common on every craft, they're now hard to find but far more useful than the rinky-dinky ubiquitous aluminum poles commonly seen everywhere.

Wind direction meters are the most expensive of the commonly found sailing instruments. They can be very handy when sailing at night before the

124

wind. Most sailors soon learn how to judge wind speed without a meter. It's often handy to mount them on the radar pole at the stern rather than at the mast top where they are conventionally mounted. That avoids a long climb towards heaven and often renewing the long wires when changing units. Both wind cups and vanes are fairly delicate and sensitive to errant birds. Reportedly there are new technologies available in which sensors rather than conventional rotating wind cups measure wind speed.

Not to be dismissed in our world of ever-increasing technological electronic marvels are the conventional nonelectronic instruments, *e.g.* compass, temperature and humidity gauge, barometer, and clock. Having several of these old-fashioned instruments around the cabin improves one's comfort level. Keeping an eye on the barometer is a good habit. A recording barometer has long been on our wish list. A remote temperature gauge for the engine room or compartment mounted at or near the helm is a nice safety device. Similarly, it's nice to have a cockpit-mounted temperature and humidity gauge, especially at night. It need not be any more fancy than a ten-dollar unit from Wal-Mart.

A word or two about compasses. The old-fashioned compass hardly gets any real respect anymore. Smaller boats typically have relatively small ones mounted at the helm, larger ones for large boats. Rarely do we find anything larger than 6 inches nowadays. That's a pity. A large, well-mounted and well-gimbaled compass is far easier to see than a digital compass display. Watching the compass needle swing back and forth provides a feel for the boat's motion.

In addition to the obligatory helm-mounted compass, it's a good idea to mount at least one—or better, two—smaller compasses forward on either side of the cockpit where a resting crew can keep tabs on direction. Properly mounted, they're useful to take direction bearings and check on course headings without interfering with the helmsman. They are also good insurance if the main compass fails or is "borrowed."

Despite heroic efforts, with all the electronic gear mounted on our large steering pedestal we've been unable so far to properly adjust our main steering compass so it reads true. In some ways life was better in the old days when a really good compass adjuster could adjust the main steering compass so that it was just about true at every cardinal direction with deviations of no more than a degree or two in between. Even so, once the deviations are memorized we much prefer the old-fashioned compass, especially at night. It's old faithful.

It's also helpful to have one or more compasses down below to keep track of the boat's direction when working at the navigation table, and especially at anchor during a blow. Here just a 3- or 4-inch dial can be sufficient. Being able to look up from one's berth off watch and know the boat's direction can be a real confidence builder.

One more note about compasses. Good ones from reputable builders seem to last forever. Without some protection, the plastic crowns eventually crack and need be replaced. Sometimes the seals leak and the fluid, usually mineral spirits, needs be replaced or topped off. It's always a good idea to protect the compass top when you're not actually cruising. An inexpensive compass in the dinghy and in the survival kit can sometimes be a lifesaver. Even ambling offshore in unfamiliar territory, it's handy to have a pocket explorer compass.

Still another word or two about compasses. The conventional "bearing compass" mounted in a tall box is increasingly becoming a relic in our technological universe. But there was a time when taking compass bearings was a key navigation element. Similarly, the old "box compass" has become a relic. Sometimes they were handed down from one generation to the next. One of the neatest uses for a box compass heirloom is mounting it in the center of the dinette table in the salon, suitably covered by plastic. To those of us who learned to cruise before the age of technological marvels, keeping abreast of compass direction, wind speed, and boat speed was as important as knowing the time.

Newcomers aboard a cruising boat eventually learn how to read and follow the main steering compass. The best crew watch the compass for a few minutes when taking command and then can go for hours and hours just watching the waves while keeping the boat on course. But for some reason it's just difficult for newcomers to learn the importance of using the steering compass to see where one has been. Some skippers even go so far as to mount a "rear view mirror" above the compass to guide newcomers, at least for a while. The point here is that it's important not to mount a bunch of stuff behind the steering compass.

A last word about compasses. With modern chart plotters with built-in GPS, after anchoring it's all too easy to set the "location alarm." That's fine as it goes, but the alarms do not give indications of wind shifts or shifts in the direction of the boat itself. Having compasses here and there about the boat encourages keeping abreast of where the boat is heading and when the headings change. Trouble at anchorages often begins with a change in wind direction, which often occurs subtly. Then even though the anchor has been well set, when the wind suddenly begins to really howl from another direction trouble starts. Even on a pleasant, peaceful day it's a good habit to keep both a weather eye and a compass eye—at least until we have talking and completely failsafe navigation instruments. When inspecting cruisers, the experienced eye looks at the anchor gear, seeks evidence of a good, well-mounted ocean-going life raft, and then, when invited aboard, looks at the compass itself. Quite often the compass tells it all. Some owners become so attached to their main compasses that they remove them from the boat. In some ways the main compass is the true heart of the boat.

In short, sailing instruments are nice, especially when repeaters are mounted at the chart table and in other locations besides the steering console. Hands down, it's the depthfinder that takes top billing and two dependable ones are the usual requirement. Commercial-grade depthfinders can easily last a decade, in our experience, but the recreational variety seem to give up the ghost after several years. Wind meters and wind direction meters are nice to have but are no more durable, in our experience, than depthfinders. Speed-ometers, too, are nice, especially when currents are involved. But normally the GPS will do just fine. Besides a commercial-grade depthfinder and a good, solid, long, properly marked boat pole, the one instrument that is truly essential is a handheld lead line. As for compasses, one can't have too many aboard; over the long haul, really good ones with 6-, 7-, or 8-inch dials are good investments.

PRESSURE WATER

Even though pressure hot and cold fresh water systems are standard features in just about all cruising boats, there is still a good role for a traditional manual hand/foot pump system and a manual or pressure salt water system. Offshore manual fresh water systems conserve water. Pressure saltwater outlets at the galley and heads can substantially reduce fresh water consumption. Not to be overlooked is the traditional rainwater deck fill system that easily drains rain water into the water tanks. All told there are four components of the fresh water system: pressure water, manually available water, pressure/manual available saltwater, and a deck fill arrangement. Few high-end builders incorporate all four components.

In contrast to the traditional manual foot/hand fresh water pumps, every component of a pressure water system is a consumable item. Water hoses, pump, hot water tank, faucets, sump pumps—all need periodic replacement.

Pressure water systems are usually fairly simple in terms of engineering. Most boats have a single water tank, a pressure water pump, hot water tank, shower sump tank or drain, various faucets, ample supplies of plastic hose fittings, and 5/8-inch reinforced clear vinyl water tubing or hose. After 5 to 10 years the vinyl tubing often becomes brittle and requires replacement. Hose clamps, even those stamped "stainless steel" often have short service lives and plastic hose connectors are not immune to breaking apart. When available, the hose connectors made of nylon are superior. In addition to carrying one or more spare water pumps, water hose fittings, and clamps, we always carry a 50-foot reel of the typical size water hose usually installed, ⅝-inch. Any time we need to change a water hose system component or fitting we usually change the associated hose. Reinforced plastic hose used in the hot water section of the pressure water system is especially prone to early failure.

When installing a pressure water system, it's important to resist the temptation towards "bigger is better." Only about 30 psi water pressure is really needed from a pump drawing about 4 amps. Limiting the available water pressure saves both water and the longevity of the pressure water system itself.

Also, shutting off the pressure water system when leaving the boat, even for a few hours, will substantially lengthen its usable service life. But be sure to shut off the hot water tank if it's plugged into a dock. Not every hot water tank has a reliable check valve, so if the pressure water pump is turned off while the tank remains engaged in the 110-volt circuit, the water heater element fails.

Hot water tanks have limited life spans as they frequently rust away in some obscure corner. Often the tanks are too large. Isotherm makes a splendid unit that keeps the water much hotter than usual within the tank but incorporates a mixer valve. That allows a 6- or 8-gallon tank to do the work of one much larger. A class act is to install just 3- or 4-gallon hot water tanks, one for the galley and one for the head. That reduces water consumption waiting for the hot water to arrive. Multiple small hot water tanks are increasingly seen on high-end power boats.

Most builders install a valve to separate the hot and cold pressure water systems and also include a check valve and strainer before the pressure water pump. But very few install cut-off valves before each and every pressure water faucet. Cut-off valves are important,because it's then easy to isolate a leaking faucet at one's convenience. Pressure water systems commonly have hot and cold faucets at the galley, head sink, head shower, and at the stern (for showers). Boats with large water capacities often have fresh water faucets at the bow for cleaning the anchor chain. High-end power boats frequently install two pressure water pumps in parallel with switch valves so it's easy to switch between pumps when one fails. That sensible setup is also used for A/C systems.

Not often installed are fresh and/or salt pressure water faucet outlets in the engine compartment. Each of those is helpful in keeping the bilges clean and sweet-smelling; they also function as a pressure fire hose. Pressure water in the engine compartment is especially useful for occasionally washing off grease dissolver to keep the engine spic and span and to keep the sump under the engine fresh.

The Isotherm unit previously mentioned has a nice reset safety feature. We like hot water heaters with stainless steel covers. Over the years we've learned to trust the experience of fellow cruisers, not the advertisements, when replacing hot water heaters.

Cruisers spending time in colder climates will often install hot water heaters with an engine cooling system circuit. Not only does that provide a more than ample supply of hot water long after the engine is shut down, but the 110-volt heating element in the hot water tank itself can be used as a heating device for the engine. On a cold day that heating can make a substantial difference, but it may take quite a while to heat the engine's fresh water coolant.

In northern climes boats are almost always laid up using potable antifreeze in their water systems. Then in the spring the entire system has to be flushed out with fresh water, while the antifreeze taste lingers on. Much better is the old-fashioned system of using an air compressor to blow out each of the lines. A small air compressor, either 12- or 110-volt, is all that's needed.

Some cruisers go to great lengths to purify their dockside onboard water with various under-counter filtering systems. Over the years we've tried an assortment of such devices and finally found the ideal system: household water purifier pitchers and careful attention where we fill up with water. Generally we draw down the water tanks when away for several weeks or a month or two. Only on rare occasions have we found it necessary to add some bleach to the water. Generally the best water dockside comes from small isolated places using deep artesian wells, the worst from big city marinas.

Another good tip is to replace the dockside water hose every couple of years, no matter how good it looks. Vinyl degrades over time. And, never, repeat never, take water aboard with a water hose available from the fuel dock or use an unknown hose, such as a green garden hose. The trick in having pleasant tasting and microbe-free water aboard is to be scrupulous about where the water comes from and the hose with which water enters the boat. Water that tastes bad usually is best left alone.

Finally, if there's any doubt about the quality of dockside water, take out the portable salinity indicator accompanying the desalinator. All too often marina water really isn't fit to drink. Sometimes, especially in the Bahamian Islands, there's lots of dissolved limestone in the water. The real skinny about most water available from marinas is that it's far inferior to what comes out of the desalinator. Bottled water is a real lifesaver on a cruising boat in faraway places.

One final tidbit. Part and parcel of the fresh water system is how the "used" fresh water exits the craft. For the galley it's pretty obvious that an overboard drain hose is needed. But many builders carry the drains from the galley sinks and showers into the bilge, where they spew corruption. Much better is a central sump into which empty all fresh-water drains save those from the galley. Then a single pump can excrete the effluents overboard. Another nice touch is installing cut-off valves in the galley and sink drains to avoid back siphoning and smells from an unsavory anchorage.

LIGHTING

One rarely hears complaints that the builder has installed too many interior 12-volt lights. Conventional light fixtures are fairly inexpensive, and it brightens up matters considerably to have light fixtures precisely where they are needed rather than just a few overhead. Every berth needs a reading light. There are ample opportunities to install fixtures that dimly light the interior when offshore at night. Low-intensity red lights are very pleasant to have aboard at night to aid getting around down below.

When retrofitting lights there are various opportunities to improve matters. Having switchable dual-bulb overhead lamps is a nice convenience, as are conveniently placed wall switches. Having lights in food cabinets is handy. Old overhead lights can often be recycled to serve as lights for closets.

Oil lamps still have a useful role in a well-equipped offshore cruiser. Typically a trawler-style lamp is set hanging above the dinette table. At anchor the sweet aroma and glow from a traditional oil lamp can markedly improve the atmosphere. Years ago, oil lamps seemed to last forever. Nowadays they all seem to be imported and need to be replaced every few years either because their thin metal solders are leaking or their varnished copper-looking finishes eventually show their true metal colors, pressed steel. The only oil lamps worth having are ones made out of solid brass or copper.

HEATING

Just about all cruisers head for the tropics, where the living is easy. Nonetheless, many cruisers return to their northern haunts after the cruise and must contend with colder climates. The usual heating devices for cruising in colder climates are coal stoves, pressurized diesel stoves, and electric forced-air diesel furnaces. The latter, which are expensive, function as a hot air heating system putting out upwards of 20,000 BTUs and more, depending on the size of the burner. The coal stoves and pressured diesel (and propane) stoves put out about 10,000 BTU and are sufficient for small to mid-sized boats. Sometimes a diesel-fired stove and oven can also function as a heater. Boats with gensets can use a reverse-cycle air conditioning set, provided the sea water temperature is moderate. Hardly ever seen anymore is the traditional wood-burning fireplace.

Each of these devices has its strong points. In our early years we burned far more diesel and kerosene in our stoves than we did running the engine; we were forever wiping down the boat's interior looking for soot. In many ways, hard anthracite coal is an ideal fuel, though hard to come by nowadays. Forced-air diesel heaters are frequently used by liveaboards in icy climates. But they are expensive and require periodic cleaning. Two smaller units are better than one larger unit. It's worth remembering that thousands of Gloucester fisherman fired up their coal stoves in relatively small sloops before venturing a hundred miles offshore, even in the dead of winter.

Outfitting the Offshore Cruising Sailboat

Staying warm while under way in colder climates is always challenging. After many years of experimentation we learned about Mustang Survival Suits routinely worn by Coast Guard personnel. They're not terribly comfortable but they do keep you warm, even when there's ice on the decks and the wind is howling. Taking them off in a hurry is another matter. They're also a good insurance policy if you're forced to take to the life raft. More than a few times I've wondered, when wearing a Mustang, how the old salts managed their duties high in the rigging or on deck clad in just oilskins and woolens while the snow swirled about.

6

ELECTRIC INSTALLATIONS

For older boats the original electric installations are almost certainly inadequate in terms of numbers of circuits and battery installations. Over the years the original and subsequent owners will have added circuits and electric equipment with varying degrees of expertise. Even the finest yacht electric installations degrade over time because of the moist interior environment. And cruisers nowadays carry much more electric equipment and electronic gear than in years gone by.

So even an older boat with a first-class original installation invariably needs to be upgraded. Such time is well spent, since electric problems are usually the most frequent source of equipment failure. Unfortunately, industry standards for electric installations in older boats were neither rigorous nor consistent. Once again, the contrast with production fiberglass powerboats is illuminating. Generally the good engineering standards applied to engine installation carry over into the engineering of their electric and plumbing installations.

Unlike rig and engine refits, attending to the electric systems primarily involves a sizeable commitment of labor that is well within the skills set of most cruisers. So by and large, refitting the electric system is mostly a substantial commitment of time, rather than money. The only expensive items are batteries/cables and the 110- and 12-volt switchboard panels. Replacing these can run $3,000 to $4,000 at most. Otherwise, the required outlays for wire and cable, connection boxes, and terminals are fairly modest, though sometimes new cabinetry or modifications are required for installation of a larger switchboard panel. Also, the battery boxes usually need upgrading.

Few older boats have the original electric circuit diagrams. Furthermore, most older boats have chunks of obsolete wires and circuits. Odds are good that the battery cables have degraded and need to be replaced and much of the wiring needs attention. Often existing wiring can be used, provided the terminal end fittings are replaced. Running new wires and cables fore and aft is often a real chore since few older boats used plastic conduits in their original construction, and their original switchboards are likely due for replacement.

Boating industry standards for electric installations have improved but remain below those for residential construction, well below those for commercial marine practices, and light years behind U.S. Navy standards. For example, both residential and commercial marine standards require all metal enclosures for switchboards. But boating industry standards just require a front panel switchboard mounted in cabinetry. Similarly, marine industry standards require wire and cable runs in conduit. Boating industry standards allow ample scope for wire and cable runs outside of conduits.

The U.S. Navy has long been recognized as having the highest possible electric installation standards. Even after 3 or 4 decades in harsh environments, the original installations are expected to fully function. The key differences are both installation practices and wire/cable construction requirements. All U.S. Navy wire and cable must be made to detailed mil-spec standards by approved manufacturers. Permanently mounted power cables are typically armored with wire braid, and runs through bulkheads require watertight stuffing tubes. Every cable carries a paper tape indicating date of manufacture, name of manufacturer, and applicable mil-spec. Every reel is subject to comprehensive testing prior to delivery and the reports must be stored for future reference. The point here is that there's ample room to seriously upgrade the electric installations on any older (or newer) sailboat with much better components, thereby ensuring that the installations will perform satisfactorily for many decades. Failures in electric systems are often fiendishly difficult to identify and repair when at sea, so there's every incentive to improve the electric system and make it more reliable. In this chapter we briefly discuss some useful upgrades involving batteries, switchboards, the battery bus, battery cables, connection boxes and battery charging.

BATTERIES

Batteries are the heart and soul of the 12-volt electric system, so it's sensible to have a first-rate installation using commercial grade batteries of adequate capacity (amp hours). Odds are that the existing battery installation is inadequate. Batteries and battery cables are usually prime candidates for replacement, especially the old standard wet lead acid cell and the newer sealed AGMs. The former are cheaper and can take more abuse at the expense of required periodic maintenance. The latter are more expensive, maintenance free, can usually take higher charging currents, and hold charges longer. Moreover, the sealed batteries can be placed just about anywhere—even on their sides.

In the good old days, heavy-duty commercial-grade lead and acid batteries lasted as long as a decade if you always maintained the distilled water levels, kept their tops free of acid, avoided very deep frequent discharges, and kept them properly charged.

Besides replacing and/or expanding the battery bank, it's also important to replace all the original automotive-type battery cables with either 1/0 or 2/0 neoprene welding cable. Not only are these much larger than the original battery cables (typically number 2 or 4 cables with plastic jackets), but welding cables are very flexible and with their neoprene jackets last virtually forever—even underwater. These are the cables used in heavy-duty mining and commercial marine applications. Because of their much larger size conductor and jacket construction, welding cables are considerably more expensive than the commonly used marine battery cables, but they offer impressive advantages in durability and performance.

Furthermore, it's important to both mechanically crimp and solder (with a propane torch) the connection lugs at either end. With thousands of strands, the solder has no trouble penetrating each one of the conductors and ensuring an unusually tight fit to the cable lug fittings, thereby preventing corrosion due to moisture. The automotive-style battery cables frequently used in marine applications typically have just a dozen or so copper strands under a plastic coated jacket. When these are crimped mechanically, even using a hydraulic press, contact between the bare copper wires and the terminal end is incomplete. When soldering battery cable ends to welding cable you need a fairly low flame propane torch and a good supply of small diameter rosin core solder. The solder needs to blow out past the end of the battery terminal. That makes a bulletproof connection.

The reason for replacing the battery cables and all other heavy load cables with much larger sizes—cables to the windlass, autopilot, SSB, and switchboards—is to allow large current flows without any appreciable voltage drop. A good test when cranking the engine is to connect the battery banks and see whether there's any appreciable dimming of interior lights. Or put a volt/ohm meter on the circuit and see if there's an appreciable voltage drop. Adequate current flow to the starter motors of both engine and windlass extends their life and makes them function as designed. Even with a 20-, 30-, or 40-foot run using 1/0 or 2/0 welding cable, there shouldn't be any appreciable voltage drop under serious load. Using extra large battery cables ensures that the full voltage and current capacity of the battery bank is available to all the heavy amp loads: engine starter, distribution bus, and electric switchboard—even to an electric windlass and electric winches.

How large a battery bank should be installed? Our suggestion is to size the battery installation in terms of worst-case scenario, *e.g.* when the diesel injection system is airbound and the engine needs to be cranked over for extended periods, or when the alternator fails. The usual recommendation is for either a 4D or 8D (200 to 220 amps) battery for engine starting, independent of engine size. This size battery will easily start a 500 or 600 hp diesel engine in good condition without protest, but with a small diesel it should stand and deliver when the going gets tough.

Another advantage of the 4D and 8D batteries is that they're widely used in commercial installations for over-the-road and stationary generators, so they're relatively inexpensive for their amp hours and made to high standards. The one drawback is that they're fairly heavy, but that can be overcome by installing two 100-amp commercial-grade batteries, although that costs more, takes up more space, and requires additional battery cables.

The size of the house battery bank is more problematic. It depends on equipment installations and how the boat is used. An autopilot forced to keep a hard-mouthed cruiser on course will wear down the house bank fairly quickly. At a minimum, the house battery bank should be at least as large as the engine battery so it can serve emergency duty when required.

The real issue here is that batteries have limited "duty cycles" and degrade when frequently brought below 50 percent charges. While a 200-amp-hour battery sounds impressive, its optimum drawdown is only about 100 amp hours. Most cruisers will need at least a 400-ampere-hour battery bank for the house side. That means installing 4 or more 100-amp-hour batteries in parallel or several 4 or 8D batteries. Unless there's high-use 12-volt circuits, that should be sufficient for a week or so. A good rule of thumb is to install a house bank large enough to handle reoccurring loads for a week. Of course, if 12-volt refrigeration systems are installed, more frequent engine charging would be needed.

Batteries last longer if they are installed some distance from the vibrating diesel in cool, dry locations. With 1/0 or 2/0 size battery cables, the batteries can be installed just about anywhere on the boat. It's good practice to use sturdy battery boxes and arrange matters so the batteries will remain in place when the mast "kisses" the water. It's also good practice to refrain from placing the batteries deep in the bilge where they'll improve the boat's ballast/displacement ratio. When lead acid batteries get submerged they usually cannot be restored. Moreover, installing the batteries in the bilge makes maintenance such as keeping the cable connections clean, dry, and free of corrosion just that much harder.

Battery cable ends corrode in the presence of moisture, so it's good practice to liberally apply the cable ends with protective spray until a good thick film has built up. Sprays made for this purpose typically are dark red in color. We used to use axle grease or petroleum jelly. Also, it's good practice when installing new battery cables to label them—red for positive, black for negative—using colored electricians' tape. Even better is to use waterproof identification tags indicating where the connections lead to.

Make sure the connectors to the battery and battery switch are snug tight and covered with insulation, i.e. rubber topped boots. Actually it's an industry requirement (often ignored by surveyors) to cover each and every high amperage electric cable connector—battery terminal ends, connections to distribution buses, alternator connections, and even engine solenoid connections—with rubber boots.

It's good practice to secure sturdy covers over the battery boxes. The boxes themselves are best when carefully constructed with heavy marine plywood that's been epoxied inside and out. The commonly used plastic battery boxes don't make the grade. The right way to install battery boxes is to secure the boxes to the boat's structure and then secure the tops of the battery boxes to the battery boxes themselves with either strong straps or webbing or even bolts. Then when the mast hits the water or the boat turns turtle, the battery boxes will remain in place.

It's worth remembering that when the batteries are worn down so the engine won't start, all is not lost. Reconnecting a pair of batteries in series (rather than in parallel) raises the output voltage well above 12 volts, and in a pinch that just might be sufficient to power the starter motor. Another trick is to carry a very long—20 to 30 feet or so—set of larger conductor battery cables in order to give or receive a boost from a nearby boat. Finally, a portable lead acid emergency starting battery can come in handy. Usually when the engine and house batteries are unable to provide sufficient juice for the starter, some additional juice from the emergency battery pack is all that's needed to produce sufficient amperage and voltage to crank the starter motor.

Several thousand dollars or more can easily be spent replacing the existing battery installation and the battery cables, but these are monies well spent. Like most items aboard, batteries are consumables. Careful attention to the proper feeding (if needed) and maintenance of batteries yields big dividends. Moreover, batteries are apt to be horrendously expensive in faraway places. Consequently, in some parts of the world it's common practice to rebuild the large lead acid batteries by cutting off the top, installing new plates, and then sealing the battery up again so it's good as new.

Our suggestion when purchasing a new boat is to replace the batteries and their cables/connectors with known brand AGMs and rebuild the battery boxes. That's just good insurance. Owners frequently paint their hulls to encourage a quick sale, but it's not often they replace batteries.

DISTRIBUTION BUS

A well-designed electric system usually feeds positive leads from both the house and engine battery banks through a battery switch that feeds into a distribution bus to handle the heavy power loads, *e.g.* engine, switchboard, SSB, and so forth. In a well-designed system, either or both batteries can serve either house or engine requirements. The battery switch for the engine start circuit allows either the engine or house batteries to energize the starter circuit. The house battery connects with the distribution bus, which in turns connects to the engine start switch for use when needed. The distribution bus is usually a thick piece of plated copper about 8 to 10 inches long by about ¾ inches wide with a dozen or so ⁵⁄₁₆" diameter protruding bolts for wire and cable connections, all mounted on an insulated pad. Ideally the bus is covered by a removable plastic or rubber insulated cover. Two buses are needed, one each for the positive and negative legs of the circuit.

The distribution bus, a critical component for a well engineered electric system, should be mounted in a convenient, easily accessible place. The bus serves four critical functions. First, it powers up the switchboard for a host of generally low-amp circuits. Second, it powers up a variety of high amp load circuits, such as windlass, autopilot, SSB, refrigeration, etc., through the use of solenoids with connector switches at the switchboard. Third, it allows direct connection for key voltage-dependent critical components, such as bilge pumps. Fourth, the distribution bus is the correct place to connect feeds from the engine alternator and also the battery chargers. Also, the bus has available connectors for future high load installations and is readily available for testing replacement items such as a pressure water or bilge pump.

Fig. 6.1 Bilge Switches and Distribution Bus
This illustration shows four bilge pump switches—engine, shower sump, and two bilge pumps—each connected to the distribution buses (middle right side). The wiring could be neater and the distribution buses should be covered with protective panels. Connecting the bilge pumps directly from the distribution buses rather than the switchboard (in turn connected to the batteries) gives the pumps maximum current and voltage.

Quite often in older boats with only modest electric systems, the switchboard is called to serve also as a power distribution bus. But when redoing the electric circuitry it's important to build in separate distribution buses for both positive and negative leads and then leave plenty of room for future circuit attachments. These buses need to be beefy terminals capable of handling several hundred amps each, with heavy connection posts that can handle heavy cables. The buses themselves should be installed where they're easy to access. If the solenoids at the switchboard for the windlass pack up, it may be possible to temporarily set up a bypass circuit with a heavy-duty jumper cable.

Still another use of the distribution bus is to wire up critical engine room components such as bilge pumps rather than routing them through the switchboard. In our current boat we have four separate engine room heavy-duty bilge pumps wired directly to the distribution bus, with appropriate switches and fuses. Since the pumps' capacities are voltage-dependent, we want maximum voltage available to the pumps through the shortest possible cable runs. Using oversize battery cables ensures that the voltage at the distribution bus is the same as at the battery terminals.

With a large inverter—say, 2,500 watts—it's a good idea to wire it directly through a standard battery switch to one or more of the house batteries, rather than connect the inverter to the distribution bus. That's because the inverter is likely to draw 100 to 150 amps of battery power for extended periods. Also, having a separately installed battery switch ensures that the inverter can be kept off unless it's actually needed. For smaller inverters where the amperage draw is far more modest, then connections to the distribution bus with suitable remotes for the inverter are satisfactory.

Still another advantage of a convenient distribution bus is that the batteries can be installed out of the way in secure locations. With proper sized battery cables, the full capacity of the batteries is brought directly where needed. So if you need to give a fellow cruiser a battery boost, you can connect to the distribution bus rather than to the generally inaccessible batteries themselves.

Distribution buses are standard practice for commercial marine installations. They make life easier when upgrading existing and future high-amp circuits. Furthermore, buses allow the use of individual wall-mounted heavy-duty circuit breakers for high-amp circuits such as autopilots and windlasses.

In sum, when redoing or upgrading the electric system, it's a good idea to install a separate distribution bus for positive and negative leads from the battery and then supply power to all requirements throughout the boat from those buses. Sometimes an older but inadequate switchboard panel can be readapted by creating a separate distribution bus to handle the really heavy loads. All too often one sees a batch of negative wires attached to the engine block. This is poor practice. Invariably the connections corrode and the engine is not supplied with all available battery power.

SWITCHBOARDS

Fig. 6.2 Switchboard Panel
This large 12 volt and 110 volt AC switchboard with voltage and amperage meters is conveniently located at the chart table and contains a remote genset start and inverter switches plus several cigarette lighter type receptacles. Note the handy compass.

Switchboards are large panels with mini-circuit breaker switches allowing activation of individual circuits throughout the boat. Normally the switchboard is divided into two components: a smaller panel on the left-hand side for 110-volt circuits and a much larger section on the right for controlling various 12-volt circuits. Switchboards often have amperage and voltage meters for the 12-volt and 110-volt circuits.

The switchboards receive their 12-volt power from the positive and negative distribution buses or from the batteries directly. The 110-volt power is fed through the shore power cable connection mounted on the boat. The 110-volt power feed from the shore power cable should be fed to a separate set of circuit breakers for both the positive and negative leads at the point where the circuit breakers are mounted between the shore power connection on the boat and the 110-volt switchboard panel. This is an industry requirement. There should thus be two places for shutting off the 110-volt power inside the boat—at the switchboard and at the circuit breaker between the shore power receptacle installed on the boat and the switchboard itself. This provides re dundancy in the positive 110-volt feed, and also provides a circuit breaker for the negative feed, which is usually not installed at the switchboard itself.

Common practice on recreational boats is to install separate ground bus connections for the 12-volt and 110-volt circuits so that only the positive leads in each circuit are controlled by fuses or circuit breaker switches. Commercial and U.S. Navy practice is to fuse both positive and negative sides of each circuit for safety as a backup. That way, if the positive circuit breaker fails, or if for some reason the circuit is completed by another available ground lead, there's always an available circuit breaker on the negative side to open the circuit.

Older switchboards with just a handful of circuits are good candidates for replacement with much larger, modern boards. Circuit breakers, especially the mini-breakers, should be considered consumable items, so some spares are recommended. Sometimes one finds switchboards with fuses rather than the more modern mini-circuit breakers. Since fuses take up more space than the mini-breakers and look old-fashioned, that's another argument for updating the switchboard.

Typically the 110-volt switchboard has a half dozen or so circuits, while the 12-volt switchboard has a dozen or more. In a large, well-found cruiser the switchboards may be veritable works of art taking up a sizeable bulkhead. Switchboards are most often found close to the navigation center. While analog meters are fine for the 110-volt circuit board, it's handy to have digital meters for both voltage and amperage flow for the usually much larger 12-volt switchboard.

Besides having a nearby light to illuminate the switchboard, it's also handy to have several female cigarette plug-style receivers to handle charging devices for cell and SAT phones, portable VHF radios, and small inverters to power the computer. While it is possible to hand-build a suitable switchboard, the monies are well spent for a manufactured one that meets the desired space and circuit requirements with appropriate meters and so on.

When replacing or upgrading the switchboard, also upgrade the connecting wires with appropriate sized tinned flexible wires with suitable insulation jackets and crimped ring connectors. Putting the switchboard on a hinge makes it easier to work on the backside of the switchboard. Sometimes there's an opportunity to mount a protective Plexiglas cover over the switchboard.

Switchboards handling 110-volt circuits need special attention. Usual practice in recreational marine installations is just to mount the panel in the faceplate of wood cabinetry, but ideally the 110-volt switchboards should be completely mounted in a separate metal container, as is standard practice in residential and commercial marine use. Mount master circuit breakers for each section of the switchboard in addition to the required one for the 110-volt power feeds coming into the boat from the shore power cable.

When upgrading the 12- and 110-volt switchboards, it's good practice to build in capacity for extra circuits. This is especially true for boats that will spend considerable time powered to a dock or fitted with a generator. Beyond the usual duplex outlets are circuits needed for a hot water tank, battery charger, desalinator, refrigeration, A/C, and so on. Circuit breakers, especially the mini-breakers typically mounted on switchboards, can fail or simply wear out, so have some spares.

CONNECTION BOXES

Common practice is to feed several 12-volt circuits from the main switchboard and then use open terminal or connection plates, which are just two separate strips of copper with screws mounted on an insulated plastic plate, to connect several circuits. Typically these plates are mounted in an out-of-the-way place inside an accessible cabinet. Since the terminal plate is not sealed from access, there's always a danger that it could be short-circuited and start a fire.

A much better practice is to use fully enclosed connection boxes (plastic or metal) throughout the boat rather than just terminal plates. These connection boxes have the terminal plates built inside the box, with suitable fixtures to allow wire and or cable entries. Even better is to use watertight non-corrosive connection boxes following standard commercial marine practice. At the very least, the exposed terminal strips should be carefully covered with insulating electrical tape. Covered connection boxes are required for 110-volt circuits, so it makes good practice to use them for 12-volt circuits as well.

It's especially important to use non-corrosive watertight connection boxes in areas subject to moisture, such as at the base of the mast or the bow. The usual practice is for mast wires to have no more than a foot or two of wire at their ends; consequently, wire connectors are needed deep down in the bilge. Much better when rewiring the mast is to have 4 or 5 feet of wire at the bottom of the mast so the mast wires can be connected inside a watertight connection box mounted high up in the bilge. Coating the connections with moisture-repellent spray also helps. Only 110-volt duplex receptacles with GFI grounds should be used. A standard comment on surveyor reports is the absence of GFI receptacles.

SHORE POWER CABLES

Nowadays 30 amp power is pretty much standard for dockside power access. Standard cables are 50 feet long. It's good practice to carry a spare cable with spare connectors. Industrial-duty connectors are typically less expensive than those in the marine store. Running a few electric heaters from the dock on a cold day can make mincemeat of the cable connector ends, particularly the male connector at the dock box. Actually some serious monies can be saved by purchasing standard #10 3-wire black neoprene flexible cable from a local electrical supply store rather than the much more expensive colored marine cables sold in boating supply houses. And don't be fooled into purchasing rubber insulated power cables. They may look and feel the same, but there's a world of difference in their durability and water resistance and the cost differential is about 100 percent.

Where air conditioners are fitted, the choices are either a second 30-amp cable with its assorted connection hardware or a 50-amp cable with a reconfigured switchboard. Typically the 50-amp service brings in two separate 110-volt leads and the switchboard is appropriately wired. Marine colored 50-amp cables, typically #8 4-conductor cables, can cost upwards of $600, so it's more economical to upgrade using a second 30-amp cable. As a general rule, the best installation uses a separate 30-amp shore power cable to power the A/Cs if fitted, and in any event to use two separate 30-amp cables rather than one 50-amp. Electric charges for long-term dockside storage are considerably less with 30 amps.

ELECTRIC WIRE AND CABLE

Wire and cable used for 110-volt circuits in recreational boats usually meets UL residential standards for 600-volt service, but there's no UL requirement for either tinned or flexible conductors. Typically the 110-volt sizes use either #16 or #14 with #8 or #10 wires connecting the switchboard to the power cable receptacle mounted outside the deck. When repowering 110-volt circuits inside the boat, it's best to stick with only #14 wire rather than the #16 often found in older boats. Use tinned flexible marine cable from a known manufacturer when replacing wires. If possible, 110-volt wires should be run in plastic conduits or in well-secured, dry locations.

In contrast to the 110-volt cable designed to carry 600 volts, there is no industry standard for the 12-volt wire and cable. Look for tinned flexible wires designed for marine use and rated for at least 300 volts. Moreover, older (and newer) boats often have single conductor wires carrying 12 volts in various places. That's just asking for trouble, because electric wires are subject to chafe in marine environments. Over time, the insulation becomes brittle and subject to moisture. A good rule of thumb is to use only 600-volt-rated tinned and flexible dual conductor marine wire from a known and reputable manufacturer for both 12- and 110-volt circuits.

Wire and cable should be kept out of the bilge and away from moisture. Over time the insulation will absorb moisture and can deteriorate in the presence of oil and diesel fuel. It's also good practice to use ample supplies of pull ties to hold runs of wire and cable together. That lessens chances of chafing. Whenever possible, secure wires and cables to the structure of the boat. Even small movements, over time, can eventually rub through the insulation.

When undertaking substantial electric wire and cable upgrades, it's good practice to test wires and cables with a volt/ohm meter for continuity before final installing action. Unlike mil-spec U.S. Navy electric wire and cable, there's no commercial requirement for the manufacturer to inspect each reel of wire and cable. Also, remember that plastics age, so purchase fresh reels of wire and cable and make sure that it meets U.L. requirements.

When installing or making new runs of wire and cable inside the boat, it's good practice to leave some extra wire and cable at each end of the circuit. That way, if a terminal or connection fails, there's ample new wire or cable available.

Excluding specialized wires for electronic installations, the indispensable wire and cables are several reels of tinned flexible duplex (2 conductor), 600-volt-rated, in sizes #14, #12, and #10. Note that in a pinch one can always double up duplex wire to get the next size larger wire single conductor by using two runs of #14 for #12 or even #10. It's also helpful to have a reel of #8 wire for connections to the distribution bus. As a general rule, #16 duplex should be avoided because of insulation concerns. Finally, wire and cable is relatively inexpensive compared to its importance, so when purchasing, caveat emptor.

BATTERY CHARGING

Batteries last longer if they are kept at or close to their designed charges, typically 12.5 to 12.6 volts, depending upon temperature and battery construction. When voyaging, engine-driven alternators have been the primary source of charging; when at the dock or with access to a generator, 110-volt battery chargers are the choice. Low cost 100-amp commercial heavy duty alternators with fully enclosed internal regulators can provide 30 to 40 amps at fast idle, so there's no reason not to have one aboard—plus a spare, including belts. While not as fully enclosed as the much more expensive "marine" alternators, they last practically forever if kept reasonably dry. And they are purposely designed to generate high amps at low speed indefinitely in a hot environment.

It's useful to have two separate battery chargers aboard: a 40-amp model suitable for usual dockside use that can handle each battery bank separately, and a 100-amp charger associated with a large inverter—say, 1,500 or 2,000 watts. Inverters are handy devices to have aboard; they normally come with a large battery charger at little or no extra cost. Occasionally it's necessary to put in a large charge to the battery bank within a short time. The large chargers are also handy with an installed generator running several hours a day to keep the freezer plates frozen. A large charger running several hours a day driven by the genset can usually replace the amps drawn by the hardworking autopilot over the previous 24 hours. Chargers do occasionally fail, so it's helpful to have a spare aboard.

Increasingly on the cruising circuit one sees two alternative sources of battery charging being used: solar panels and windmills. Reportedly the windmills are less reliable than the solar panels. They are certainly noisy, and on occasion can cause injury. Solar panels are by far the more interesting development. The basic problem here is that with current technology, fairly large surface areas need to be accessed and the panels themselves must be securely fastened against heavy winds.

Solar panels are ideal for boats moored or anchored for long periods in tropical climes. We know of one cruiser who mounted a large array atop a solid mid-cockpit roof covering a center cockpit feeding into a dozen golf cart batteries. It was sufficient to run the 12-volt electrics but the total cost equaled that of a small generator. No doubt with improved technology, flexible solar panels mounted on top of cockpit covers (biminis) will become increasingly viable options for charging batteries. As best we can determine, alternators will be the method of choice for the foreseeable future, pending some major improvements in technology and lower costs for flexible solar panel installations.

Not often seen in typical-sized cruising sailboats but commonly seen in larger vessels is a 110-volt generator belted to the main engine. With a regulator that is independent of engine speed, these units can put out enough power for a large inverter/charger to put 100 amps into the battery bank at a fast engine idle. So running the diesel at fast idle not only quickly charges the battery bank, but also provides power for 110-volt circuits such as the freezer and desalinator. And since the power draw is several horsepower, there's sufficient load on the engine. Unfortunately, these installations are fairly expensive.

Keeping a portable 1,000-watt 110-volt gasoline generator aboard can also be handy in emergencies. It's powerful enough to keep a 40-amp battery charger humming. Sometimes one sees an engine-driven 12-volt alternator generator that directly feeds the battery bank. And more than a few cruisers spending extended time anchored in the tropics opt for a small single-cylinder air-cooled 110-volt diesel generator kept on the aft deck. If kept dry and well maintained, these noisy beasts can last for years.

Not often seen any more are trolling alternators, whose small, elongated propeller turns a flexible shaft attached to a modest-sized alternator mounted on the stern rail. While these do work, their outputs are small but the propellers are attractive to large fish.

THE ELECTRIC TOOL KIT

With an ohm/volt meter and a well-fitted-out tool kit, a wide variety of electric projects can be handled by almost any cruiser, albeit with some practice. Most electric wire work in cruising boats involves fitting ring terminal connections on wire ends. To do the job right requires a professional-grade terminal crimper, a professional-grade wire stripper, a lineman's pliers, a large supply of both insulated ring and male/female connectors from a reputable manufacturer, a dozen rolls of electrician's tape, and a soldering iron with rosin core solder. It takes some practice to correctly crimp wire terminals. Professionals pride themselves on just doing one crimp. We always do two crimps, and for really important circuits such as bilge pumps, we solder the terminals after crimping. And we always use electrician's tape over the terminals as backup insulation.

Outfitting the Offshore Cruising Sailboat

Suggestions for the electric tool kit are listed in Figure 6.3, below.

Fig. 6.3 Basic Electric Kit

Several volt ohm meters
Clamp-on amp meter
Professional grade solderless connector crimp pliers
Lineman's wire and cable cutters
Electrician's knife
Dozen rolls of electrician's tape
Solder gun and several ounces of rosin core solder
Boxes of insulated ring connectors Nos. 10/12, 14/16, 18/20
Boxes of insulated male and female connectors Nos. 10/12, 14/16, 18/20
Boxes of insulated splice connecting terminals Nos. 10, 12, 14, 16
Supply of No. 4, 6, and 8 insulated ring terminals
Variety of terminal strip connection plates
Covered junction boxes with terminal connectors inside
Reel of 14/2 marine flexible tinned 600 volt rated electric wire
Reel of 12/2 marine flexible tinned 600 volt rated electric wire
Reel of 10/2 marine flexible tinned 600 volt rated electric wire
Large quantity of plastic cable ties, 6 inches and 12 inches
Set of small screwdrivers and pliers
Half a dozen test wires with alligator clips
Box nylon plastic cable tie wall mounts
Several LED flashlights
Trouble light
Box of BUS fuses
Box of mini-fuses
Spare circuit breakers in various sizes
Spare 12v. cigarette lighter receptacle
Spare 12v. bulbs, various sizes/types
Circuit tester

Outfitting the Offshore Cruising Sailboat

Fig. 7.1 Potential Hull Trouble Spots

Corrosion in rudder inner frame and wet core
Rudder post bearings
Worn/corroded rudder pintles and gudgeons
External keel attachment (especially with iron keels)
Bulkhead attachments to inner hull and deck
Bulkhead delamination/decay, especially below floorboards
Floor frame delamination/decay
Decks with wet, spongy cores
Deck fittings not properly thru-bolted and backed with metal plates
Flexible decks
Leaking hull/deck joint
Chain plate corrosion
Improper grounding of chain plates and mast to hull ground plate
Corroded thru-hull fittings
Wet cores around thru-hull fittings
Hull flexes when lifted in travelift and/or when subjected to sailing loads
Extensive gel coat crazing, especially in deck stress areas
Dirty, oily bilges
Mast plate installation
Leaking seals around port lights and deck hatches
Cutlass bearings, propellor struts, and shaft log

7

THE HULL

While the advent of fiberglass (or RFP—reinforced fiberglass plastic) has greatly expanded the ease with which the designer's vision can be realized, cruising boats built 50 years ago are quite similar to those built today. The major external design innovations have been expanding the waterline length, width, and depth of the hull; widening the aft sections; separating the rudder from the keel; and increasing the sail area with taller masts, often with shrouds set inboard. Altogether these innovations have produced faster boats with significantly greater interior volume. On deck, cabin houses have been more recessed, while cockpits have been made considerably larger, wider, and longer. A forward anchor locker has become commonplace.

But whether these innovations make for significantly superior blue-water cruisers is often debated. Most offshore cruisers put a premium on comfortable motion, stability, ability to sail to weather, balanced helm, and easy tracking over speed. Even with these modern design innovations, a sailor familiar with an early 1960s or 1970s fiberglass production cruiser would likely have no difficulty sailing a more modern counterpart. More noticeable than the design changes and lighter weight hulls would be the increase in sailing conveniences—electric windlass, self-tailing winches, autopilot, chartplotter, VHF, SSB, showers, and so forth—that most of us take for granted.

While modern designers have emphasized speed with plumb stems, longer waterlines, much wider sterns, taller rigs, more sail capacity, higher righting moments, and reduced displacement, these useful innovations usually result in boats that are far less comfortable when lying abeam during heavy weather/seas. Our experience has been that the older CCA designs with their soft ends, shorter waterlines, fuller keels, and lower aspect rigs lie abeam to weather much more comfortably than modern designs with their sharp bows, wide sterns, and deep fin keels. Lying abeam to take a "time out" has lost favor in the quest for improved cruising performance. But it's a real lifesaver for two-person crews on long passages when nasty weather sets in.

CCA HULL DESIGNS

Fig. 7.2a   **CCA Hull**   *Fig. 7.2b*

With their long overhangs, the traditional CCA designs are not only graceful but well regarded as comfortable sailors, though not as fast as modern designs with longer waterlines.

Fig. 7.3a   *Another CCA Hull Design*   *Fig. 7.3b*

This CCA hull design has a deeper keel and a near vertical rudder attached to the keel, affording good directional stability. These arrangements are far less demanding on the autopilot than fin keels and separate rudders.

Early fiberglass production sailboats in the 1960s and 1970s typically followed the design parameters established by the Cruising Club of America measurement rules. These rules tended to produce similar looking and quite attractive hulls with long overhangs. By today's standards the CCA hulls are quite narrow, with low aspect rigs. CCA rules defined what most of us recognize as the "traditional yacht." For a given overall length, long overhangs reduce the waterline length, and it's the waterline length that primarily determines hull speed and the set of permissible interior accommodations. In terms of volume, a modern 30-foot boat has just about the same interior volume of a 40-footer early production fiberglass boat designed under CCA rules.

While CCA designs may mostly appeal to the traditionalist, they do have some important advantages for offshore cruising. And since they're out of favor, they can sometimes be purchased very reasonably. They do have some impressive offshore qualities inasmuch as their designs evolved over many, many decades with incremental changes and improvements.

Most offshore cruising is done in following or quartering seas for the obvious reason that sailing to windward against seas and wind is just difficult, unpleasant work. When running with seas and winds, the CCA designs are in their element as their narrow sterns softly break the seas as they pass beneath the boat. In contrast, modern designs with wide, broad, and near-vertical sterns have a squirrely motion when running before the seas. Similarly, the CCA designs do not pound when going to weather with their spoon-like bows. In contrast, modern designs, with their narrow, sharp, pointed, near-vertical bows, have a much rougher entrance. CCA designs, by virtue of their lower volumes and freeboards, are also wetter going to weather and usually have smaller cockpits.

Sooner or later every offshore voyager will hit bottom. Here is where the older CCA designs with their longer keels, often with attached rudders, have a great advantage. The impact load from the grounding is extended over a much longer keel section, which in turn distributes the impact to a larger portion of the hull. In contrast, fin keel boats, even from the best builders, are especially susceptible to internal frame damage when running aground.

Fig. 7.4a   *Deep Fin Keels*   *Fig. 7.4b*
Deep fin keels are fine on the race circuit but not for offshore cruisers. Grounding in a deep fin keeled boat can make for a really bad day.

CCA designs also accommodate centerboards more easily by virtue of their longish keels; more than a few early production CCA rule fiberglass boats had centerboards. While centerboards are certainly attractive for shoal waters, in our experience they are problematic for offshore use. Older designs from custom builders often used heavy metal centerboard foils—typically bronze with robust hydraulic lifting gear—which were costly to build. However, most builders used light fiberglass boards with internal metal weights weighing not more than a hundred pounds or so. While the boards certainly improve weatherly performance, in light to moderate winds and seas the boards are usually tucked away when running and usually bang around in their keel slots when under way.

Running aground with a lightweight board often means breaking the board. Some designs require hauling the boat to repair or replace the centerboards. With others it's necessary to dive under the boat to reattach a new wire pennant. For all their shoal draft advantages, in our experience centerboards are costly to maintain and to replace if the original design is not available. We broke so many boards over the years that we finally gave in and carried a spare board tucked under a long berth.

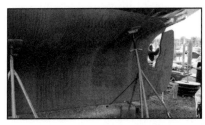 

Fig. 7.5a   **Full Length Keels**   *Fig. 7.5b*

Full length keels with attached rudders have long been popular offshore cruising designs with good directional stability and ample protection for the rudder. They are less attractive for the race circuit.

Fig. 7.6a   **Sharp Bow and Broad Stern**   *Fig. 7.6b*

Fine bows and broad, wide open sterns make for fast boats but not for comfortable offshore cruising. The bows lack necessary forward buoyancy in a sea way and the broad sterns make for unpleasant motion in following and quartering seas.

Fig. 7.7 Full Keel with Attached Rudder and Tiller
These oldtimers had impressive tracking with well-protected rudders. This
traditional design evolved over centuries into a superb hull form. The small
cut-out for the prop means only a small auxiliary was fitted.

Fig. 7.8 Iron Keel with Wings
Iron keels should be avoided—they don't hold paint very well. These flat wings
are unlikely to improve sailing performance. Grounding with this winged fin
keel could make for an unpleasant day.

Fig. 7.9a   *Imaginative Keels*   *Fig. 7.9b*
Some keel designs best stay close to shore.

Fig. 7.10a   *Spaceship Keels*   *Fig. 7.10b*
Some sailboat keel designs show real imagination! But these are not for off-shore cruising.

PROBLEM AREAS (SEE FIG. 7.1, PAGE 150)

Excluding design innovations, perhaps the greatest concern for would-be pur-chasers of older used fiberglass cruisers should be hull construction and con-dition, especially the decks. Here there are six major areas for investigation. First: has the hull itself been compromised by water migration? Second: does the deck structure—the most frequently encountered problem area—have a wet core or lack the required rigidity? Third: do the plywood bulkheads that provide rigidity to the hull structure remain well attached to the hull and underside of the deck? Fourth: are the chainplates free of corrosion and structurally well designed to carry the loads of the rig? Fifth: was the hull deck joint properly engineered and does it remain intact? Sixth: does the rudder's internal metal reinforcement structure remain free of corrosion and are the rudder post bearing supports and quadrant fully serviceable? Also, for centerboard boats, are the centerboard lift mechanism and the centerboard itself serviceable and properly engineered?

Early fiberglass production models employed solid fiberglass hulls that by today's standards are overbuilt and excessively heavy. A good example is the famous 28-foot Pearson Triton, built to almost tank-like specifications. Over time, designers and engineers realized that composite hulls with either balsa or foam (Airex) cores were sufficiently stiff, considerably lighter, and less costly to produce. More recent innovations include vacuum bagging and the use of exotic reinforcement fibers such as carbon to provide additional rigidity and strength. Also, the use of inner hull liners bonded with outer hulls has produced strong, lightweight hulls.

Solid fiberglass hulls can take considerable abuse, are easy to repair, and have attractions for the long-distance cruiser. Their primary maintenance concerns are surface blisters; usually these are cosmetic rather than structural issues. In contrast, the more modern lightweight cored hulls are susceptible to water penetration of the core, especially around through-hull fittings, and are far more costly to repair. Most cruising sailboats built over the past two to three decades have used cored hulls, to save both cost and weight. Recall that fiberglass resin, the expensive part of fiberglass, is a petroleum derivative sensitive to crude oil prices. End-grain balsa cores were used early on, along with PVC or foam cores. Each has its supporters and detractors. While cored hulls have become dominant, they do require a considerably higher build standard than solid glass hulls, particularly in the installation of the cores to avoid voids. With cored hulls it's important to have solid glass used in areas for through-hull fittings and in high-stress areas such as for chainplates, the stem and stern areas, the rudder post, and along the keel.

Actually, the term "cored hull" is a misnomer, since a substantial portion of a cored hull uses solid glass in the bottom area supporting the encapsulated keel, at the bow, and near the hull/deck joint area. Also, there's solid glass in the areas where through-hull fittings and rudder post are secured. Larger boats are often built in two separate parts and then glassed together with solid glass, so a foot or more on each side of the centerline is solid glass.

Some detractors claim that cored boats will always become wet cored boats, "It's just a matter of time." It is true that cored boats are susceptible to water migration in the case of accident or inferior build or a through-hull fitting installed just through the cored area. And it is true that over time, both solid fiberglass and cored boats left in the water year round tend to gain water weight. Yet perspective is needed. Water migration in cored hulls tends to be localized if detected in a timely fashion. While repairs are expensive, it's fairly unusual for a soggy-cored hull to be declared unusable. Tens of thousands of cored hulls afloat year-round in southern climes remain afloat even if they gain an inch or two of draft from localized water migration.

Cored hulls with substantial water migration in their cores can cause problems when hauled in northern climes, when freezing temperatures can cause the water to expand. Using a plastic hammer and tapping the hull can readily detect voids, as can the skilled use of a moisture meter by a surveyor. Many, if not most, older cored boats will have some voids or evidence of localized moisture penetration. So the issue is not the presence of some water migration into the core but whether it is serious enough to reconsider the boat.

While hulls are easily surveyed, inspecting the keel is more difficult. Early producers fully encapsulated the lead keel into the hull itself. That's fine if it was properly engineered with a keel supporting structure and if there has been no moisture penetration. Later on, less costly iron keels were often externally attached to the hull, especially by Far East builders. That technique causes corrosion problems with regard to the keel bolts and water migration between the top of the keel and the fiberglass hull. Even when the keel bolts are exposed inside the hull, it's usually not possible to remove the bolts from the iron core for inspection. As a rule, boats with external iron keels should not be considered unless their keel bolts can be readily removed for inspection.

Higher quality builders often used external lead-mounted keels with substantial metal support cases inside the hull. Such keels can usually be separated from advantage of incurring far less damage from rough groundings. However, if the external keel is a deep-fin keel and the boat is moving at some speed, the damage from a grounding caused by the lever effect inside the boat can be quite awesome.

Most production cruisers used fully encapsulated lead keels. If they were properly engineered and have not been abused by grounding, these work out fine. Again, the proviso concerns deep chord fin keels. In some respects the older CCA designs, with their longish keels fully encapsulated in fiberglass can take considerable abuse from grounding, since the long keel (low chord) structure itself acts like an I beam. Generally an externally moderate chord-mounted lead keel offers the best protection from damage upon grounding. Unlike external iron keels, external lead keels typically hold their bottom paint reasonably well.

Virtually all fiberglass production hulls eventually get surface blisters as water seepage creates an acid that pushes out or inflates the surface gel coat—especially those wet-stored for a decade or more in warm waters. As a practical matter, blisters have become much less a problem with improved build control, knowledge of their origins, and the use of vinylester rather than polyester resins. While blisters can be disconcerting to the prospective buyer, it's rare that a hull has sufficient blisters to comprise its integrity or hull strength. Blisters, which are largely a cosmetic problem, are well within the capabilities of almost all boat owners to keep under control. The basic approach is to grind them out, carefully wash and let dry, then fill with either polyester or epoxy putty, let dry, and fair into the surrounding hull.

Grinding out and repairing blisters is nasty work requiring a good face-mask and protective gear. But it can be done with good lighting at night, even in hot climes. Drying out the blister-prone areas is important to prevent repeats. It takes considerable care and the use of long feather boards to hide the repair. Even so, a 40-foot boat with several dozen blisters can be tackled within a few days of good weather and robust spirits. One advantage of a solid glass hull with blisters over its cored cousin is that one doesn't have to be so concerned about grinding into the inner core.

Early on it was discovered that a coat of epoxy in place of the original polyester gel coat was more impermeable to water penetration. Some enterprising chaps figured out how to shave the gel coat off the entire hull and then apply three or four layers of epoxy. If the naked hull is left to dry for several weeks or months (often inside a tent), the new epoxy outer coating can then serve as an effective barrier to water migration—often up to a decade or more.

Having ground out our fair share of blisters over the decades, our advice is to let the "pros" do the job. Unless one is really skilled with a grinder and a bear for punishment, the end result will look pretty awful. With some practice it's pretty easy to sight the hard hulls that have had an amateur "epoxy bottom treatment." Their hulls are no longer fair as a result of inexpert grinding. Boats with "wavy bottoms" are suspect, since it's unclear just how much fiberglass remains.

At day's end, blisters are part of owning a fiberglass boat. For boats in southern waters hauled every couple of years or so, the appearance of several or even a dozen blisters should not be alarming. Similarly, when purchasing a new or used boat, just as with pressure spray cleaning the bottom when hauled and putting on several coats of bottom paint, an occasional blister repair is part of the game. A competent surveyor should be asked to render judgment on the importance of visible blisters.

BULKHEADS, CHAINPLATES, AND MAST STEPS

Independent of whether the hulls are solid or cored, fiberglass hulls are fairly flexible and are stiffened with plywood internal bulkhead reinforcements. Over time the bulkheads can tear away from the hull and underneath portion of the deck when the hull loses stiffness from an increasingly soggy deck or from heavy use offshore or from abuse when hauled. Bulkhead panels that have separated from the hull forward of the mast usually indicate heavy offshore use.

Unfortunately, bulkhead/hull attachments are often difficult to inspect and require dismantling some interior cabinetry. They are especially challenging to inspect when interior hull liners are used. Nonetheless, careful attention is required to the bulkhead-to-hull attachments when surveying the boat. Bulkhead/hull separations compromise the structural integrity of the hull.

Reattaching these panels to the hull is a tedious process. After several decades of hard use we had to reattach the athwartships plywood support panels on one entire side of our early 1970s solid glass-hulled ketch. The tedious job required grinding away the original glass fastening support before relaying new fiberglass support. The point, of course, is that while older solid glass hull designs are remarkably durable, the bulkhead attachments that provide hull rigidity may require attention over time.

With older boats or boats that have seen hard service, inspecting each of the three chainplates on either side of the mast is essential. Some surveyors inspect just one chainplate, but to be on the safe side all need inspection. Where's there's been substantial water migration from the deck, the metal fittings underneath the deck may have seriously corroded. Similarly, if there are cracks in the supporting fiberglass and plywood foundation structure, it's time for repairs.

Unfortunately, it's costly to inspect chainplates in most boats because you must remove wood paneling. Typically the cost for removal is paid by the prospective purchaser—and that cost may well equal the cost of haul out and survey. But it's money well spent. No one wants to go to sea and have the rig fail.

There's considerable variation in chainplate engineering among production boat builders, and the builder's reputation based on the visible part of the interiors may not really indicate the care and attention given to chainplates hidden by cabinetry. High-end builders go to great lengths to build metal structures or frames to carry the loads upon the chainplates, which are then fiberglassed to the hull sides over a fairly wide area. Most builders create the chainplate attachments out of plywood and fiberglass structures, which are then built inward from the hull in a vertical direction. Stainless steel tangs bolted to the under-deck structures then protrude from the deck upwards to attach to the rigging.

Not surprisingly, standards employed in chainplate installation vary. Without physically inspecting the chainplate supporting structures and associated hull areas, there's no way of determining the adequacy of the chainplate installation. Some cruisers physically inspect their chainplates after lengthy voyages. While chainplate inspection is optional when surveying small and mid-size cruisers, it's usually mandatory for large cruisers.

Like chainplates, the construction of mast steps varies considerably among builders. Some installations are works of art with heavy aluminum structures likely to last almost forever despite the corrosive effects of salt water. Others are barely adequate weldments. In addition to the metal supports is the fiberglass structure to which the mast step is bolted. Usually the mast step support area is heavily fiberglassed. Particular attention is needed for boats where the hull is built in two halves and then joined together. While inspecting the mast step does require unstepping the mast, it often provides useful information about the build quality and hull maintenance.

Sometimes the bottom end of the aluminum mast is heavily corroded from water in the bottom of the mast. Some builders fail to drill water exit holes (weep holes) an inch or so from the bottom of the mast, a simple remedy to prevent water build-up inside the bottom of the mast. On older boats where the mast has been stepped for decades or more, it's good practice to remove the mast and to inspect the mast step and the inside of the mast near the foot, to look for corrosion. Without a secure and sturdy mast step weldment and underlying mast step structure, the rig's integrity is compromised. One indication of better build quality is a mast step whose placement is adjustable.

RUDDERS AND STEERING GEAR

Rudders in fiberglass boats have conventionally been made with a fiberglass skin over a foam core with a metal framework attached to the metal rudder post. Such construction is usually adequately strong in terms of the designated loads when the boat is originally built, but water migration encourages corrosion of the metal framework. While careful use of the moisture meter and phenol hammer can determine the presence of water migration, other than by removing and X-raying the rudder there is no straightforward procedure for determining whether water migration has seriously corroded the metal web framework. Without X-rays there's typically no alternative other than to grind off the fiberglass covering, remove the core, and inspect the metal core framework directly.

Usually it's cost effective to simply make a new rudder if the phenol hammer and/or moisture meter indicate that the core is waterlogged, or if water simply leaks out of the bottom of the rudder when the boat is hauled. In any event, when the boat is hauled it's a good idea to trace out on paper/plastic the design of the rudder and save the tracing in case the rudder subsequently has to be replaced. Chances are the replacement rudder will be better made than the original one if the internal webbing is made with high-grade stainless steel and solid rudder posts are used.

On older boats, removing the rudder is often advised so you can inspect the rudder post, the rudder post bearings, the rudder post hull seal, the bronze quadrant, and the pintles and gudgeons. Cruising sailboats usually have bronze quadrants bolted on top of the rudder post, which allows for attachment of steering cables and/or an autopilot control arm. More than a few early production sailboats built in the Far East installed locally made quadrants of uncertain quality. It's a good idea to replace quadrants of uncertain manufacture with those of a recognized domestic builder, *e.g.* Edson. Similarly, it's useful to inspect and replace, if necessary, bronze sheaves in the steering system and the steering cables.

It's advisable to periodically replace the stainless steel flexible wire used in wire and quadrant steering systems, so it's prudent to carry a replacement length of steering cable together with the necessary tools and fittings. High-end manufacturers often install a manual steering system that attaches to the steering post. Then if the quadrant or stainless steel cables fail, the craft can be steered manually with the assistance of block and tackle. Or if an autopilot is fitted with a steering arm attached directly to the quadrant, the pilot can also serve as a backup steering system.

Fig. 7.11a
Spade rudders, widely used in race boats, put their entire loads on the rudder post. For offshore work a skeg mounted rudder is much preferred when using a fin keel.

Fig. 7.11b
A hi-tech charter / coastal cruiser features narrow vertical stem, wide stern with double wheels, 7/8 rig, sweptback spreaders, no forward lower shroud, fin keel, no forestay, and spade rudder—not good characteristics for an offshore cutter.

Rudder designs have changed considerably over the post-War period. Many CCA-designed boats had rudders attached to the end of the keel. Later on, with the separation of the rudder from the keel, spade rudders and also rudders with partial skegs were introduced. Spade rudders impose heavy loads on the rudder post, since the entire rudder load is borne by the post. The best arrangement is for the rudder post inside the hull to be supported by two rudder bearings, one mounted just inside the hull and the topmost one mounted just underside the deck. Generally rudders with partial skegs are more resilient to heavy rudder loading than fin keels, since the skeg itself bears a considerable portion of the load. Most cruisers favor rudders with partial skegs.

DECKS

The most common problems encountered when surveying older fiberglass production hulls are their deck structures. Deck structures function as an I beam,
providing rigidity to the hull along with the internal support of bulkheads. When
decks become soggy with moisture, the hull loses its essential rigidity. Once the
hull begins to flex, the rig is compromised and the supporting bulkheads tend to
separate from the hull. Eventually the hull is not fit for sea duty.

Perhaps in no other aspect of hull construction do we find such varia-
tions of quality and engineering prowess than in deck construction. In part
that reflects the learning curve associated with building production fiberglass
sailboats. In part it reflects the very labor-intensive nature of building and
assembling deck components to a high standard. Early on, some builders, especially those in the Far East, built decks simply by using plywood—or even
solid wood—and then laying on fiberglass. That works fine until the underlying wood becomes wet and rot sets in. Later, actual fiberglass molds were
developed to create the deck structures using inner cores.

Fig. 7.12 **Celebration** *is a powerful, double head sail 35-ton cutter that has
actively sailed the Caribbean and Atlantic Ocean for two decades. Note how
the designer put the volume into the hull, not the cabin structures, so the
ports are fairly small. The sturdy all-weather enclosure over the center cockpit
creates a de facto pilot house and keeps the crew dry and comfortable even in
freezing weather. It has withstood green water over the entire boat and 50/60
knot winds for extended periods.*

Years ago, plywood and/or solid wood were used as the core material. Eventually core materials were standardized with the far superior end-grain balsa or plastic foam. However, in the various high-stress deck areas the builders still used plywood. High-end builders used solid glass in these high stress areas—the much preferred solution. Quite often, whether the hull became waterlogged was dependent upon how the various deck fittings were attached. Here again, the higher-quality builders used machine screws through-bolted into solid glass cores with suitable aluminum or stainless steel backing plates; however, many builders were content with just using self-tapping stainless screws without backing plates and plywood cores around the high-stress deck gear areas.

You can often observe the original build quality of a boat simply by inspecting how the deck fittings were attached. Even if the deck is judged sufficiently free of moisture by the surveyor, it's a good idea to through-bolt all deck fittings with stainless steel machine screws using appropriate backing plates. That helps insure a deck free from leaks when the heavens open up or water sloshes along the decks. To be sure, refastening deck fittings is a tedious and labor-intensive task often requiring a helper below. But decks do not cure themselves, and leaks play havoc with the interior furnishings and installed equipment.

Soggy or moisture-laden decks can be repaired, though costs are often prohibitive and it's best done when the boat is under cover. Given the ample supply of used production fiberglass sailboats at attractive prices, it's best to reject boats with wet deck cores. A flexing hull invariably opens up leaks in hatches and ports. Unchecked, eventually the interior bulkheads begin to detach.

Some builders for the charter trade, e.g. CSY, used solid fiberglass decks and these boats have proved both durable and in demand. Similarly Gulfstar, the major early builder of boats for the charter trade, used mostly solid glass decks and extra heavy cores for cabin tops. In particular, the 150 Gulfstar 50 center-cockpit designs that opened up the early charter boat business used 1½" balsa deck cores and were robustly built by any standard.

Another concern for decks is the presence of hairline stress fractures. Usually these are cosmetic rather than structural concerns, but they are tedious to repair. The usual method is routing them out with a high speed grinder, filling in the voids, fiberglassing, and then painting over the entire deck or cabin-top affected areas. Some builders used improper cures or too much resin in their gel coats, so their decks were more prone to stress cracks than others. When the decks and cabin tops of an older fiberglass production boat have been repainted, it's a fairly good bet that some attention was paid to deck cracks. Just how carefully the repairs were done often isn't known until the boat is sailed hard.

In our experience, surveyors usually do not give enough time and energies towards carefully inspecting the decks. It's not hard to see why: it requires lots of time and effort on one's hands and knees sounding the decks with the phenol hammer and moving the moisture meter here and there. Before calling in the surveyor, we highly recommend purchasing a moisture meter for about $150 to $200 and doing a preliminary deck survey yourself. It's not rocket science. While it's rare to find a boat whose deck is completely free of moisture, decks with moisture problems will be easily identified.

A temporary fix to stress cracks that we've used over the years is to fill them with a highly viscous penetrating epoxy such as Captain Trolley's sealer, one of our favorite maintenance products. We use the sealer for stress cracks, window seals, and around all deck fittings several times a year. It's especially good around chainplates. Not only does the sealer penetrate, but it also retains some flexibility and dries clear. Routine use of a deck sealer around all deck fittings will help ensure that the boat's interior remains bone dry during an all-day tropical downpour.

Over the years we've spent more time, energy, and money caring for the deck than the hull. In part that's because it takes some very serious engineering to build a really bulletproof deck. The deck is the one place where all the stresses and strains placed upon the hull by the rig become visible. Even on the best-built fiberglass boats, the decks work underneath one's feet during heavy weather, so carefully surveying the decks merits very careful attention.

Walking the decks while the boat is at rest to see if they flex really doesn't tell you how the decks function when the rig is loaded under sail. Unfortunately, it's a rare buyer that insists (at his own expense) that the surveyor take the boat out for a serious sail during the "sea trial" to find out the true condition of the deck structure.

Fig. 7.14 Modern Charter Boat
The open, wide stern with double steering pedestals is not a good candidate for offshore sailing.

Fig. 7.15 Small Cruiser
This modern double head sail full cruiser fitted out with a bowsprit and club footed staysail is a capable cruiser. But the stern dinghy davits are only for coastal work. Note that no bow roller has been fitted.

Fig. 7.16a   *A Pair of Full-Keel Ketches*   *Fig. 7.16b*

A pair of full keel ketches, one an aft cockpit, the other a center cockpit.

Fig. 7.17a   *A Gold Plater*   *Fig. 7.17b*

Lots of varnish, fancy fittings, big Dorades and teak decks in this "Gold Plater." One doesn't often see Gold Platers on the offshore cruising circuit—too much upkeep.

8

THE COCKPIT

Most of the action in a cruising sailboat—piloting and sail handling—takes place in the cockpit. While every cruising boat has a cockpit, there is much more to its design and location than appears at first glance. Cockpit location influences interior accommodation, engine installation, and the ability to protect the crew offshore against the elements. Cockpit design merits careful attention to make sure that it meets the personal requirements and comfort of the crew. A cockpit suitable for a coastal cruiser will differ markedly from one designed for the offshore voyager.

Basically, sailboat cockpits have two locations: the centuries-old traditional aft cockpit design and the more modern center-cockpit arrangement often found in boats longer than 40 feet. The traditional aft cockpit has the best location in the boat in terms of easiest sea motion, least amount of spray from the bow, easy access to sheets and winches, comfortable helmsman position, and access to large cockpit lockers below for storing gear. Not only do aft cockpit designs look better, but they're usually more fun to sail and seem natural. Almost everyone learns how to sail in small aft cockpit boats. With the steering console just over the rudder post, traditional wire and quadrant steering setups are much easier to install and more sensitive than the more complicated center-cockpit steering installations.

Traditional cruising boat designers typically created small "deep blue-water" cockpits focusing on protecting the crew in heavy weather. High seat backs all around plus a bridge deck forward in the cockpit plus high cockpit coamings off the deck offered good protection from the seas. There was special concern about being pooped from an errant stern wave. When filled with water, the cockpit was expected to drain quickly. Often there was a dockside test to see how quickly the water-filled cockpit drained and whether the cockpit floor could support the weight when filled with seawater. Cockpit lockers were expected to remain watertight.

To modern eyes these small, deep cockpits with high seat backs seem out of place or even odd or boxy. All too often the modern seat backs are fairly low, tapering in height from the aft coach roof toward the stern deck. And there may not be any protection at all behind the helmsman. Modern aft cockpits are considerably larger than their traditional counterparts, with plenty of space to stretch out. Moreover, the steering console has replaced the ubiquitous tiller. It's rare to see a modern design incorporate the traditional steering box with an Edson worm gear inside riding on top of the steering post. Some modern designs even use side-by-side steering consoles in very wide aft sections. And sometimes the steering console itself is a virtual navigation center with chart plotters, radar, and navigation instruments. The nav station is now out in the cockpit.

Aft cockpit designs, traditional or modern, do have some drawbacks, at least compared to modern center-cockpit designs. First, engine installations are usually placed deep in the bilge under the cockpit stairs with limited access requiring removal of woodwork. Second, they preclude comfortable accommodations in the aft portion of the vessel. And third, by virtue of being long and narrow they usually preclude effective protection from the weather.

From a traditional perspective these weren't serious limitations at all. Engines were considered auxiliaries, to be used in calm waters and not regarded as terribly dependable. Fuel tanks were quite small. Accommodations were viewed in terms of proper sea berths, either in the salon or tucked away under the cockpit seat in a challenging "quarter berth." Who ever went to sea in a double berth? As for protection—well, maybe a dodger, but oilskins were pretty dependable. In days before gensets, A/C, refrigeration, autopilots, watermakers, and so forth, the traditional aft cockpit cruising designs required real "salts."

Modern center-cockpit designs have some attractive features. They usually allow a dedicated engine room below the cockpit and in larger boats the engine room has stand-up head room, a real plum. With a passageway underneath the center cockpit seat(s), it's possible to offer a standup aft cabin double berth arrangement, often with an additional head. That allows some real privacy from the forward accommodations. And the center cockpit itself allows, albeit at considerable effort and expense, for the installation of a robust all-weather enclosure.

Alas, there are some limitations to these features. To take full advantage of the walkway under center cockpit seat(s), more freeboard is required so the center-cockpit boats sit higher out of the water in something of a "whale" effect. Steering is much less fun, since half the boat is behind the helmsman. It's harder to see the sails from a center cockpit and much more difficult to furl the mainsail using conventional arrangements. Sitting high out of the water is not for everyone. And the larger center cockpit itself is far less cozy and comfortable, especially for the helmsman.

Moreover, a double berth in the aft cabin is only really usable in port or at anchor, not when running before a quarterly sea. So for a given boat length, one usually has better sea berths in an aft cockpit design. Having a dedicated engine room is handy, but it's hard to avoid the temptation to install all the usual powerboat comforts, and then you become the boat's engineer rather than her captain. And unless the boat is really large, say 60 feet or so, it's really difficult to design adequate height passageways and cockpit seatbacks. Even with these acknowledged drawbacks, the ability to construct an all-weather protective enclosure around the center cockpit can be a game-changer for experienced cruisers, especially of advancing age.

Cockpit designs and locations are cast in fiberglass. So one really needs to decide ahead of time which design best suits the intended use of the boat prior to purchase. That's not only a function of prior experience and personal preference, but also a function of age. The joys of sailing in an aft cockpit boat often give way to the comfort conveniences of a center cockpit boat with advancing age. Advocates of aft cockpit design wouldn't be happy in the other and vice-versa.

Most cruising sailors begin their careers in aft cockpit designs. Those just starting on their cruising adventures will likely purchase an aft cockpit design not only because of budget considerations, but because much the largest supply of available 30- to 40-foot cruising boats are aft cockpit designs. No one ever races a center cockpit design.

For subsequent purchases the decisions are more complex. The inventory of boats for sale markedly declines with increasing size, and most 50-foot and larger cruising designs are apt to be center cockpits. However, there continues to be demand for larger aft cockpit boats in both charter fleets and by individual cruisers.

Which cockpit design is better? For sheer enjoyment of sailing, being snuggled up on the lee side of the aft cockpit with one hand gently touching the wheel, the other hand dipping into the water, the aft cockpit experience can't be matched. Steering is much easier, since one overlooks the entire length of the boat and the sails are visible to the helmsman. Often the boat feels like an extension of one's body. Indeed, the experience can be so pleasant that hours can go by while you're locked into the same position. Steering an aft cockpit boat with a sensitive, well-balanced helm in light and moderate seas is one of life's real enduring pleasures.

In contrast, the sailing experience aboard the center-cockpit boat is often far less invigorating, since you are perched higher above the seas. Half the boat is in front, half in back. The wide cockpit takes far more effort to brace oneself behind the wheel when the boat is leaning. And working the jib sheets and winches while kneeling on the cockpit seat can be strenuous.

The strong point for center-cockpit designs is their comfort: a larger cockpit, for the quiet times; generous aft cabin accommodations; a large engine room below; and the possibility of equipping the boat with a fully enclosed cockpit structure to protect against the elements.

Fig. 8.1 Comparison of Aft and Center Cockpit Designs

Aft Cockpits	*Center Cockpits*
Advantages	**Advantages**
All sails easily visible	*Aft cabin, head, and engine room*
Easier sail handling	*Larger galley*
More pleasant motion	*Larger cockpit*
Seems natural	*Allows complete cockpit enclosure*
Easier to raise/stow mainsail	*More interior room*
Easier to install solid boom vang	*More stowage on aft deck*
Can stow dinghy behind mast	*Allows stowage on aft cabin top*
Easier to install boom preventer	*Pilot house effect*
May not need genoa turning blocks	
Comfortable seat backs	
Can brace foot on opposite seat	
Space for cockpit lockers	
Allows quarterberths	
Disadvantages	**Disadvantages**
Usually precludes aft cabins	*Low cockpit seat backs*
All-weather enclosures difficult	*More difficult sail handling*
Reduces interior space	*Harder to install solid boom vang*
Difficult engine access	*Can't brace feet*
	Can't stow dinghy behind mast
	More difficult to raise/stow mainsail

AFT COCKPITS

Managing a sailboat from the stern seems natural with the sails easily visible and both the entire boat and the seas ahead of us. Racing sailboats invariably are conned from the stern, as are all small boats, where most of us receive our first exposure to the delights of the wind. Aft is where the rudder works and traditionally that's where the helmsman worked the tiller. Even with the attractions of center cockpit designs in larger boats and the advent of cruising multihulls for the foreseeable future, aft cockpit cruising designs will prevail.

Traditional aft cockpits with their deep cockpits and high seat backs all around have a host of important advantages in terms of sail handling, protection from the seas, and comfort under sail. They usually allow carrying a dinghy securely on the coach roof just behind the mast and simplify installation of steering gear, boom vangs, and the boom preventer. In a well-designed low freeboard aft cockpit boat, as the boat leans into the wind it's often possible to put one's hand into the water—a nice touch on a moonlit night or even during a blistering hot day. With all lines within easy reach of the helmsman, traditional aft cockpit designs come close to making the vessel an extension of the soul.

Alas, there are some minor drawbacks to aft cockpit placement. None is really critical. Whether one or more are sufficient to tip preferences to a center cockpit for blue-water voyaging is a matter of personal preference.

a) First, the diesel exhaust is close by, just a few feet from the helmsman. So motoring on calm waters under a blistering sun can be quite unpleasant, as can motor-sailing aft or off the wind in a gentle breeze.

b) Second, the long, narrow, aft cockpit makes it quite difficult to arrange a full cockpit enclosure to insulate the crew from foul weather, heavy winds, and more importantly, cold temperatures. That may not be important to near shore cruisers, but for longer runs, especially in colder climates, a cockpit that can be enclosed when conditions warrant greatly improves sailing comfort and extends the sailing season.

c) Third, for a given boat length, aft cockpits usually seat fewer crew than in the larger center cockpits. That's not an important consideration in smaller boats, but when five or six crew are seated in an aft cockpit it's pretty much shoulder to shoulder.

d) Fourth, aft cockpit designs usually preclude standup aft cabin arrangements so pleasant to have in port. But aft cockpit designs usually have better sea berths in the salon and in quarter berths.

c) Fifth, aft cockpit designs usually require the boat's engine to be placed under the cockpit stairs, where access is difficult and removal of woodwork is required. Center-cockpit boats offer the advantages of an accessible, dedicated engine room.

Aft cockpits come in three basic varieties—the older U-shaped designs, the more modern T-shaped designs, and the modern double-wide cockpit with adjacent steering pedestals. U-shaped cockpits are surrounded by high seat backs both fore and aft and across the aft portion of the cockpit. A tiller was usually fitted aft, or less frequently a helmsman's box with a steering worm gear underneath. Traditional aft cockpit designs often look strange to modern eyes. They're both smaller than we're used to and the seatbacks are very much higher. There's no doubt that the crew really sits in the cockpit, and that the cockpit is designed to keep the crew protected from harm's way.

The T-shaped design opens up the fore and aft side cockpit seats on either side of the steering console, allowing the helmsman not only to walk easily around the pedestal, but more importantly, to easily access the sheet winches on the cockpit coamings without having to kneel on the cockpit seats. The full body weight can be worked into the winch if necessary. Since considerable space is taken up from the fore and aft side cockpit seats, the T-shaped cockpit design usually isn't employed in small boats. Even in mid-size boats a T-shaped cockpit may not leave enough room to really stretch out.

One important advantage of both U-shaped and T-shaped cockpits is that the fore and aft cockpit seats are close enough so that they can be used as a foot brace when the boat heels. More recent designs have greatly widened the cockpit along with the aft hull portions so that two side-by-side steering pedestals can be fitted. In these designs the crew can no longer brace their feet on the opposite cockpit seat. That may be of no consequence when sailing in light conditions when chartering or coastal cruising, but when the helmsman puts the rail under, a good brace is really appreciated. Some sailboats have rails on the cockpit sole to brace when heeling. Having a cockpit wide enough to hold a square dance is fine in port, but not offshore.

The double-wide cockpits with adjacent steering pedestals allow a cockpit just about as large as a center cockpit. They also open up the aft accommodation to include limited headroom berths below. For example, mid-size charter boats 40 to 45 feet and up often have twin double berths under the double-wide cockpit. Some double-wide cockpits open up the aft end of the cockpit as well, giving better access to the swim ladders and fishing. The double steering pedestals give a better sight line when steering to windward, but at the expense of a secure cockpit.

Another fairly recent race-boat-inspired innovation pushes the helmsman all the way aft against the backstay. This increases the interior accommodations volume for a given size boat by pushing the cockpit to the extreme aft portion of the boat at the expense of lazarette storage. Some designs go one step further and dispense with the aft cockpit seatback altogether. Lifelines across the stern keep the helmsman inside the cockpit. Most cruisers bypass these race-inspired advantages of double-wide cockpits, extreme aft cockpit positions, or opened-up cockpit floor sterns in favor of security when sailing in heavy seas.

Although the older U-shaped cockpit with a tiller is rarely seen today except on smaller boats, the wheel-based steering box mounted on top of the steering post using an Edson worm gear still survives. When conditions warranted the helmsman could sit atop the steering box, which was mounted for better visibility. Sometimes a helmsman chair was actually installed on top of the steering box on high-end boats, allowing full visibility. More usually the helmsman sat beside the steering box with feet comfortably raised on the fore and aft side bench and body resting securely amidst the surrounding high seat backs and steering box.

My first cruising boat was a 36-foot wood Dickerson ketch with a steering box and specially retrofitted 18-inch-high cockpit backrests kept bright with ribbon-striped African mahogany all around the entire cockpit. With a cushion or two, one was securely wedged into a comfortable seat and could remain so for days on end. Long tricks at the wheel were standard features of sailing in well-thought-out cockpits before autopilots. With suitably high back rests, the crews were secure in the cockpit even if an occasional wave upended the boat, putting her toerails in the water.

While there are more than a few designers who create really useable aft cockpits, all too often the basic design requirements are subordinate to design aesthetics. To modern eyes, cockpits with high backrests all around look out of place. Modern designs often take their cues from the coach roof, typically no more than 12 inches above the side decks, and then reduce the seatback design as the seatbacks extend towards the stern. That gives the boat a nice side profile but makes for an uncomfortable cockpit. Many cruisers accept that arrangement simply because it's so frequently encountered. The only antidote is to seek out a traditional design where the cockpit was really intended to protect the crew under all conditions and where the designer actually spent time cruising offshore away from the office.

Most designers have more success in raising the cockpit floor high enough so that it drains properly even in the unlikely instance of being pooped from a stern wave. Once the cockpit floor is set, then in boats with low freeboard there's not much room left for suitably high seatbacks. In the old days it was common at survey time to have a 2-inch gas-driven water pump fill up the cockpit to see if it drained properly and test whether the cockpit stowage lockers under the seats remained watertight. That's not often seen anymore. Few marinas nowadays have 2-inch pumps anyway. But they're common on fishboats everywhere.

Cockpit seat back height might seem like a minor wrinkle. But adequate height for cockpit seat backs is one of the most critical design comfort requirements for distance voyaging. Without it, sitting in the cockpit for long periods can be quite uncomfortable. Even though there may be adequate sea berths below decks, the off-watch crew often inhabit the cockpit where the air is fresh and the horizon visible. A really good cockpit with high seatbacks makes for a happy crew that's much less likely to get seasick.

Modern cockpit designs often sacrifice cockpit lockers for opened-up accommodations below decks. Before the age of Dacron and roller furling gear, it was commonplace to go to sea with a varied sail wardrobe with spares, especially for the mainsail. Sometimes a special suit of delivery sails was made for the larger boats. Cockpit locker space for sails and sail handling gear was considered essential, as was the lazarette, where anchor line, spare anchors, a deflated rubber boat, and other gear was stowed. Many traditional cockpit designs allowed a lithe crew to climb down through the cockpit lockers and explore the engine transmission and the space under the cockpit floor. Nowadays every inch is used for accommodations.

Aft cockpits greatly facilitate line handling. Typically the mainsheet is attached from the aft boom end down to the deck just behind the helmsman with either a set of double tackle blocks to either outboard side of the aft deck, or more commonly to a mainsheet traveler just aft the helmsman. Some boats with a racing jaunt place the mainsheet traveler forward of the steering pedestal. That's handy for the helmsman and crew, but it reduces scarce fore and aft cockpit seating space. Aft cockpits usually allow the jib sheets to run directly from cars on deck track right to the winches without turning blocks, as with conventional center cockpit arrangements. More than a few turning blocks have torn loose during heavy weather, sometimes with disastrous results.

Aft cockpit designs really shine when it's time to furl the mainsail using simple, uncomplicated systems. Typically there's a fairly long coach roof on which to stand to get the bulk of the sail under control. Then the cockpit seats are used for the final effort. In contrast, center cockpit designs typically require long sail battens and complicated covers or mast furling systems.

When checking out an aft cockpit design, always make sure that crew can stand up in the cockpit without getting their heads bashed by an unseen boom swinging across the cockpit. Some designers like to improve stability at the expense of a low boom.

It's easy to understand why the aft cockpit design persisted for centuries and has a bright future. It looks right, feels right, facilitates sail control, and takes place in the most comfortable portion of the boat. The major drawback nowadays is from an accommodations perspective. Aft cockpits are not space efficient in a world when six berths in a 30-foot world cruiser are not uncommon. Moreover, they do not easily lend themselves to sheltering the crew from the elements. Nor do they permit a dedicated engine room. Aside from these considerations, an aft cockpit has much to recommend it, provided the designer understood the importance of proper seatback design. In a word, the advantages of an aft cockpit are so formidable that beginning cruisers should concentrate their searches on boats with such designs.

CENTER COCKPITS

Center cockpit arrangements are relatively modern innovations that are more spatially efficient compared to an aft cockpit arrangement for a given boat size. Additionally they usually have greater freeboard, so for a given length boat, center cockpit designs have more interior volume. Center cockpit designs offer increased interior accommodation by virtue of an aft cabin/head arrangement and a dedicated engine room below the center cockpit. An additional feature is that center cockpits lend themselves to constructing a completely weather-resistant enclosure, although at considerable expense. These advantages have encouraged the popularity of center cockpit designs for cruising boats in the 40-plus-foot range.

In order to fully realize the benefits of the center cockpit design, the boat's freeboard height is usually increased. Increased freeboard permits a convenient passageway under one (or both) of the center cockpit's seats from the salon to the aft cabin. Since the space under the cockpit seats is used for the passageway, there is no space left over for a conventional cockpit locker. And since it's important to raise the seats as high as possible to permit passageway underneath, cockpit seatback height is sacrificed. Adequately high cockpit seats in center cockpit designs are usually found only in boats 50 feet and greater and often not until boat length is 60 feet.

An aft accommodation with a double berth (or twin single berths outboard) together with standup room and an accompanying private head has certainly increased the attractiveness of the cruising lifestyle. Being able to separate the sleeping quarters fore and aft is a major increase in comfort, especially when children or hired crew are aboard. And it's nice to have a hatch overhead and ports on all three sides. However, such accommodations are usable primarily at anchor or in port or under very mild sea conditions. When the boat is running in blue water, aft cabin arrangements are not any more usable than the traditional forward V-berth arrangement.

In medium-size center-cockpit boats the usual arrangement is for just one passageway under the cockpit seats with the galley outboard. The remaining area is usually dedicated to an engine room. Above 60 feet it's possible to have passageways on either side of the engine room, one of which is usually used for a captain's cabin offering a secure sea berth, the other as part of the galley or as a stand-up engine room. But such large vessels were primarily built for the charter trade and are rarely found on the market at reasonable prices except when they are truly worn out beyond redemption.

One of the limitations of medium-size center-cockpit arrangements is that sea berths are usually limited to the outboard berths in the salon. Neither the aft cabin nor the forward V cabins are suitable in heavy weather. In contrast, aft cockpit arrangements often have one or more quarterberths tucked under the cockpit seats that are suitable for sea berths. So as a practical matter, aft cockpit boats can boast four sea berths, two of which are available on either tack. In contrast, the medium-size center-cockpit design will have sea berths only outboard in the salon. This difference helps explain why aft cockpit designs are more suitable for ocean racing with large crews, and why center-cockpit vessels appeal to those in retirement. Without good sea berths, voyages are apt to be short.

The advantages of a dedicated engine room appeal to many cruisers. Medium-size center-cockpit designs typically have a dedicated engine space, perhaps 4 by 6 feet, with about 4-foot headroom. That affords all-around access to the engine together with space for a genset and the usual comfort mechanicals—hot water, water desalinator, A/C and refrigeration systems—and their assorted pumps, in addition to convenient access to bilge pumps and, sometimes, batteries.

Besides space for the various mechanical comfort installations, dedicated engine rooms offer two important advantages: First, when working in the engine room, the rest of the boat is left undisturbed and other crew can follow their normal activities; second, it's relatively straightforward to remove a damaged engine for repair or replacement at reasonable cost.

Two experienced mechanics usually need a day to remove or reposition an engine in a center-cockpit engine room. Unless the engine has thrown a rod and damaged the block, it can be repaired economically almost forever. Indeed, some mid-size and larger center-cockpit designs have enough space to allow a complete engine rebuild right in the boat. They have enough headroom so the engine can be lifted up to remove the pan and disassemble the main components for rebuild. Sometimes it's economical to cut a large hatch in the center-cockpit floor and simply hoist the engine out using the boom and a chain lift. In contrast, engine removal for an aft cockpit boat is invariably a major undertaking.

Similarly, center-cockpit designs facilitate removal and replacement of the genset. Normally the genset in a center-cockpit design is installed on a shelf inside the engine room with sufficient space to readily disassemble the head when needed. Two strong fellows can usually carry even an 8kw genset out of the engine room. When generator engines fail (a matter of time), it's usually not economically feasible to rebuild most small generator diesels. The usual fix is to purchase and install another engine for the generator—assuming that the builder (or assembler) has one readily available.

So one of the real advantages of center-cockpit designs is that they reduce the eventual cost of genset replacement. With a 40- to 50-foot center-cockpit boat, an inspired crew can remove and replace the genset from within the engine room within a day or two. We've done that more than a few times. Gensets, as described elsewhere, are wonderful conveniences, but they truly are the Achilles Heel of most cruising sailboats. (And, if truth be known, most powerboats.)

Yet another benefit is that it's usually possible to carefully insulate a dedicated engine room so one doesn't have to shout over the diesel when motoring. Sometimes there's enough room to put a sound shield over the genset so that it barely purrs.

The third major center-cockpit design advantage, besides aft accommodations and dedicated engine room, is the ability to install an all-weather enclosure over the sizeable center cockpit itself. To save money, most cruisers get by with just a forward dodger and a collapsible bimini overhead, following their aft cockpit counterparts. But with sufficient determination and at considerable cost it is possible to construct a robust all-weather enclosure that will handily stand up to 40 to 50 knots, be completely waterproof, and allow operation of the boat from inside the cockpit in just about all conditions. Such enclosures greatly expand the sailing season and make it possible to voyage in near or below freezing temperatures with an occasional assist from a diesel heater and Mustang survival suits. We describe the details of such enclosures in a separate section later on.

While large center cockpits are delightful at rest in port when half a dozen crew and guests have more than ample room to stretch out, matters are more complicated when sailing blue water. Center cockpits have some significant limitations for offshore sailing.

First, the cockpit seats are so far apart that the opposite seats cannot be used for support when the boat is heeling. More than a few cruisers have been thrown across the cockpit and injured, lacking such support.

Second, cockpit seatbacks are invariably too low, since the center-cockpit floor and seats have to be raised to allow for passage between cabins under the seat. This is one of the real limitations of center-cockpit designs. Not until the boat is 60 feet or longer is there enough room to provide good side backrests. More often than not the most comfortable position in a center-cockpit boat during rough weather is on the deck.

Third, the helmsman is disadvantaged on several counts. Usually there are only minimal or no backrests running athawrtships along the aft end of the cockpit. And when reaching for the jib winches on the cockpit coamings the helmsman (and crew) has to kneel on the cockpit seats. Furthermore, owing to the large size of the cockpit, the helmsman will likely need a sturdy guard around the pedestal for support.

Fourth, since the cockpit is forward just behind the mast, there may be challenges when installing boom vangs and boom preventers. And there's no room to install a small dinghy aft the mast. However, many cruisers like to stow the dinghy forward of the mast over the forward hatch, both for protection and to allow ventilation with a partially opened hatch. That's an acceptable solution except when blue water comes over the bows.

Fifth, some cruisers find it hard to be tidy in center cockpits without conventional sail lockers to place all the usual small stuff. So they make do with various straw baskets holding everything.

On the other hand, there are some solid advantages to center cockpit designs. Usually there's enough room to bring out the navigation desk and install the gear all around the compass pedestal—chart plotters, radar, instruments, VHF, and so forth. And by virtue of the large standup dodger spanning the entire front of the cockpit, there's plenty of room for charts and so forth. In a word, a well-designed center cockpit facilitates bringing the navigation center topside.

If a really good cockpit watertight enclosure is fitted out with a large folding table attached to the forward end of the steering pedestal, one can really live the good life with fine companions and dine outside in style even when it is raining. That's especially handy at anchor or in port or cruising in pleasant weather.

Yet another advantage of a center cockpit design is that it's easier to dock when the helm is positioned in the center of the boat. The helmsman gently eases the boat parallel to the dock and then, having pre-positioned the fenders and lines, merely steps off. However, getting back on a center cockpit boat with high hull sides usually requires a one- or two-step box or mid-ships ladder.

Still another advantage is that the aft deck area is available for stowing fenders along the aft pulpit. Usually there's a large lazarette to store all sorts of gear—lines, electric cords, even some sails. A life raft and deflated rubber boat can usually be stored on top of the aft cabin, or with appropriate gear the aft cabin top itself can be used for sunbathing. Some center-cockpit cruisers even go so far as to use the aft deck to carry dock chairs.

Besides having space to hang fenders and so forth, the aft deck is a great place to troll for fish. There's no boom or winches or steering gear to worry about, and it's easy to clean up the mess.

Like most sailboat compromises, center-cockpit designs have their advocates and detractors. Having logged tens of thousands of miles in center-cockpit designs, I can testify that their greatest advantage is the ability to sustain a truly watertight enclosure usable in all weathers and most climates. Close behind is the ease of engine and equipment installation, followed by superior accommodations below decks at anchor or in port. Against these very real enticing advantages is the very real disadvantage of not being able to fully brace oneself in heavy weather simply because the cockpit is too wide.

On one stormy offshore passage off Cape Hatteras up the East Coast not too many years ago, aboard a well-found 40-ton center-cockpit boat, a rogue wave out of nowhere simply lifted the starboard quarter with sufficient force that the boat's 82-foot mast kissed the ocean before snap-rolling back. I was thrown across the cockpit over the coamings with my nose just inches from blue water. The subsequent snap-roll threw me back into the compass pedestal. Bloodied and bruised, with some fractures, I thought long and hard about how to avoid such episodes. Now when the weather is up we always wear harnesses secured to strong points to prevent being heaved across the cockpit. That was always standard procedure in aft cockpit boats. But center cockpits seemed so inherently secure high above the seas that they give a false sense of security. In a word, center cockpits can be downright dangerous unless you're securely strapped in.

CENTER COCKPIT ENCLOSURES

Fig. 8.2
Aft Center Cockpit Enclosures

Fig 8.3
Forward Center Cockpit Enclosures

Cruisers with center and aft cockpits commonly install a separate dodger forward and a bimini overhead, both with folding metal tube supports. Usually the dodger is made of 3 panels of plastic with zippers allowing the middle or all the panels to be removed. That can be helpful when sailing in hot weather. These easily removed plastic and cloth devices are fairly inexpensive and provide some useful protection from winds forward and from overhead sun.

But protection from rain is quite limited and there is no protection from heavy winds abeam or aft the dodger, nor any protection from the cold. By and large, crew is still exposed to the elements—sailing is an outdoor experience. And the plastic and cloth panels set over light tubing structures require frequent repairs, especially the zippers.

It is possible to build quite robust all-weather center-cockpit enclosures that will readily withstand sustained 40- to 50-knot winds and just about mimic the protection afforded by traditional pilothouse designs of a bygone era. These structures are quite expensive and take repeated visits to the canvas maker to get done correctly, but they offer impressive advantages to the distance cruiser and raise the comfort level to that enjoyed by motorsailers securely ensconced in enclosed pilothouses. One doesn't have to rush below to get foul-weather gear when the heavens open up.

The enclosures greatly expand the sailing season—or more accurately, the range of acceptable comfort. Several years ago we were well off Cape Hatteras on Thanksgiving Day heading for the balmy Bahamas. A good breeze was blowing, it was below freezing outside, and steam was rising from the surface waters courtesy of the warm Gulf Stream. The sun was out, and inside the cockpit it was about 55 degrees. Of course, when the sun went down it was below freezing and out came the Mustang survival suits. Without the sturdy enclosure we would have been rather uncomfortable.

The basic design of these structures is a sturdy frame of 1-inch stainless-steel tubing permanently mounted with bows in front and across the top of the cockpit with several angled support bars at both the front and back ends. Properly done, this reinforced supporting framework is quite sturdy and can take sustained heavy wind loads from any direction, especially the near vertical sides and aft cockpit sections. Installing the correct tubing angles can easily run a thousand dollars or more and takes considerable trial and error to build in sufficient reinforcement. Few canvas makers have experience building such robust structures so there's an all-around learning curve for everyone concerned.

Outfitting the Offshore Cruising Sailboat

The bimini is made of heavy acrylic or Weblon fabric and is attached to the frames independent of either the front dodger type structure or the side or aft panels. This is very important, because the heavy wind loads from any side of the cockpit structure must be transferred to the bimini frame, not to the overhead fabric or side roll-up panels. Similarly, the dodger structure is attached independently to the frames with a roll-up front panel and removable quarter panels that do not roll up. The side panels roll up, as do the aft cockpit panels, but not the removable quarter panels for the aft side of the cockpit. The front and aft quarter panels are more or less permanently mounted to provide adequate security.

For maximum ventilation, all the panels roll up except the two front quarter panels and the two aft quarter panels. The two aft quarter panels are quite sizeable and have suitable openings for handling the various sheets. The usual practice when sailing is to adjust the side roll-up panels to provide for desired ventilation and temperature control. For example, when heading to windward, one or more leeward side panels will be partially or even completely rolled up. With some practice and a handy thermometer, a more or less constant temperature can be maintained.

The fittings for attaching the removal panels to both the bimini above and the cockpit coamings need be quite robust. Conventional snaps will not do the job here. The weak point of any cockpit enclosure is surely the plastic zippers that hold the panels together. We designed a heavy-duty backup system that allows the panels to remain attached without the zippers even in heavy weather. This system is a genuine invention to the best of our knowledge, and so far we have not patented it.

Attached to each edge of the plastic panels and their ubiquitous zippers is a heavy cloth panel that can be fastened to an adjacent edge cloth panel with a heavy-duty marine fastening. Not only do these heavy fabric panel edges completely cover the plastic zippers from the UV rays, but they will also hold the panels together without any help from the zippers. Normally we keep these protective panels cloths in place for the front dodger and for the first side panel. When heavy weather is expected or the enclosure is left closed for extended periods, we also fasten the protective panels over the side panel zippers. The panel edges are strong enough to take green water or a falling crew without collapsing. They are several inches wide.

184

After having green water knock out the front panel zippers, we went one step further and had protective panels made for the top edge of each of the three forward dodger plastic panels. In other words, every zipper in the front dodger now has a secondary attachment system—heavy duty overlapping cloths with heavy-duty fasteners. We've also gone up in thickness for the panels and fabricated a protective white cover for the entire front dodger. That cover completely shields the forward part of the cockpit structure from the sun and dramatically reduces the temperature inside when the panels are lowered.

There are some other wrinkles we've learned along the way. Both plastic and the heavy cloth used for the structures degrade when subject to continued movement against the stainless steel tubing. So some protective cloth was sewn around the frames where they contact the plastic panels. Since the side panels are most frequently raised and lowered, we use beeswax, an excellent lubricant, every couple of days on the zippers.

One of the nicest features of the cockpit enclosure when at the dock or at anchor is how clean the cockpit stays. When leaving the boat, all the panels are rolled down and fastened. Similarly at night. So when stepping out at first light, we find that the cockpit floor and seats are almost always dry. No dew. Keeping the cockpit dry also benefits the various electronic installations and cushions, and zipping the panels keeps out unwanted guests.

It's taken more than a few trips to the canvas makers to get the cockpit structure to the point where it can take some heavy-duty punishment. Zippers have been a perennial problem, but that's been resolved with reinforcement panels. Heavy-duty fastenings are a must, as is heavy-duty fabric that is double or triple stitched. Adjusting the bows so that the bimini fabric is stretched just right and doesn't catch puddles of water took some doing. A particularly nice feature is having plastic panels in the overhead bimini at just the right spot to look up at the mainsail during the day and, with the use of flashlights, during the evening hours. Those overhead panels need covers when not in use.

Despite all our improvement efforts, there are some remaining problems. We have to roll up a leeward panel to get a good fix on the genoa when close hauled. The aft rollup panels have to be partially raised to allow the mainsail traveler to be used. It's taken a few adjustments to get the line openings in the aft cockpit quarter panels just right. If the panels are rolled up for a few days in hot weather, the plastic panels can be damaged. Similarly, in cold weather the panels do not like to be unrolled.

At sea some additional maintenance is required to keep the panels clear of salt water with occasional cleaning with fresh water. Left in place for a while, salt crystals can do a real number on the plastic panels. In port, even in tropic climates where the air is clean, it's surprising how much filmy residue deposits on the panels. On occasion the seams around the plastic windows on top of the bimini need attention with Captain Trolley's Liquid Sealant.

When all is said and done, a complete cockpit enclosure quite dramatically improves sailing comfort, especially for passage-making. Keeping the rain and wind out of the cockpit on a cold night really does lift spirits. One of the unexpected surprises is that off-watch crew like to remain in the cockpit. It's almost always dry and quite comfortable.

The enclosed cockpit is especially helpful late at night when making entrance into unfamiliar harbors. Charts can be readily unfolded in the dry cockpit, providing additional confidence along with the ubiquitous chart plotter and radar. All is not perfect, however, since a side window has to be raised before a spotlight can be used to pick out buoys.

While I was initially drawn to a center-cockpit design by the expected pleasures of a comfortable aft cabin in port and a dedicated engine room, I now put an enclosed all-weather cockpit structure at the head of the list. Not only does it make passage- making much more pleasant in all weathers, but it adds an additional day and night cabin with excellent visibility. In fact, we now spend more time in the cockpit than in any other part of the boat when at anchor or in port. With some portable lights it's a nice place to read or work on the laptop computer. Or just stretch out and dream under the stars.

So far it's taken three years and half a dozen canvas makers to get the enclosure cockpit structure just right. It's been an expensive adventure—about the cost of two mainsails to date. Our enclosed cockpit has held up to an afternoon of 60 knots at anchor and several days of 50 knots at sea from abeam and behind. It's a bear to remove and replace for repairs, so we're always looking for ways to make it more robust. And it will take several hours to remove it ahead of an expected hurricane.

We've learned that the real trick is fixing reinforcing panel attachments so we do not have to depend upon zippers to keep the enclosure intact. The enclosure is as strong as its weakest link, so it's important to have alternative attachments besides the zippers and very robust attachments to secure the panels to the bimini and cockpit coamings. The key is installing very strong stainless-steel tube framing that will handle whatever wind load is placed upon the structure. We've long ago lost count of the dozens and dozens of visitors who've come by to see our enclosure, which has been copied by a few friends.

Our center cockpit enclosure was fabricated by master canvas craftsman Leon Moorer of Royal Canvas in Norwalk, Connecticut. For its 5-year "refit" Leon is putting heavy flaps covering every zipper as well as installing heavy duty "turn snaps" everywhere so that the frail zippers will be a redundant system of attachment. Our goal is to have the enclosure readily withstand 60/70 knot tropical storms.

Fig. 8.4 A Really Large Aft Cockpit
A good cockpit for coastal cruising and big enough to hold a dance. The helmsman has to stand; there's no room to sit behind the wheel or stretch out full length ahead of the wheel. And just a pair of lifelines at the back. Note the double turnbuckle rod: someone cut the backstay too short!

Fig. 8.5 Aft Cockpit Gear
Note the gear conveniently stored on the aft deck of this center cockpit boat —
double radar poles, stern access ladders, crane, outboard motor mounts and a
bevy of safety gear including double life buoys with MOB lights, throw buoys,
life buoy, and MOB pole with light. Also, note the auto release EPIRB on the
starboard radar pole and radar responder on the port radar pole The stern
pulpit is ideal for storing fenders. Celebration carries four 18-inch round buoy
fenders and four 12 x 30 inch conventional fenders each fitted with soft covers
made by Maine Point. In a heavy blow all 8 fenders will keep her safely off the
dock.

9

ACCOMMODATIONS

The interior layout in a cruising sailboat deserves just as much attention as the cockpit, hull, and rig. The basic considerations are whether the designer is more oriented towards the charter/liveaboard market or the traditional requirements of the blue-water cruiser, the difficulty of disassembling parts of the interior when needed to refit, and the perceived quality of the interior woodwork/finish. While the main functional accommodation requirements of the blue-water cruiser have long been well established, modern designers have shown considerable creativity in designing interiors for pleasurable living.

By virtue of longer waterlines, greater width, and greater depth of hull, modern designers have considerably more volume and area to work with than traditional designers for a given length cruiser. Longer waterlines and pushing salon interiors out to the hulls have substantially increased the alternative arrangements that can be fitted into a given boat length. Similarly, the center-cockpit innovation has offered a whole new dimension in liveaboard convenience. Basically the new innovations focus on portions of the interior aft the mast.

Nonetheless, despite the new possibilities, the basic interior accommodation functions have remained unchanged for a century. These include several secure sea berths, a galley usable in heavy weather, a well-positioned head, a dining table, a foul-weather locker, and a navigation command center (chart table). Without secure sea berths and a secure galley, the voyage is apt to be a fairly short one.

Nowadays with most new boats built for the charter/coastal trade, these traditional requirements have been overshadowed by magnificent galleys with Corian counters, large heads with separate showers, double queen-size berths, and highly polished cabin soles. Such interiors, when well done, can be splendid in port, but it's no fun sliding around on a slippery cabin sole at sea.

Over the years the traditional accommodation possibilities became fairly well standardized, in part because the sailboat designer fraternity was a small, close group of folks who typically spent substantial time cruising offshore. Designer commissions were hard to come by and boats were built typically on a one-off custom basis. Bending wood to make fancy interiors was very time consuming, so plain-and-simple interiors dominated. The "Hershoff" time-honored interior finishing style was commonly employed, with painted flat surfaces outlined with modest teak trim.

But with the advent of one-piece interior liners and CAD machine-made interiors, cruising boats now often resemble sculptured works of art rather than straightforward machines for crossing oceans. In contrast to the piece by piece construction of traditional wood interiors, modern designers have taken advantage of highly engineered one-piece prefabricated interiors that are often quite breathtaking, especially when highly finished teak and other natural wood veneers are used.

These modern methods allow finishes and interior cabinetry designs almost unimaginable with traditional methods, but there is a drawback. Some important access areas are difficult or impossible to inspect—chainplates, in particular, come to mind. And refitting equipment, such as running new electric lines and plumbing or even replacing water and fuel tanks, can be quite challenging. Moreover, old-fashioned boat builders usually went to great lengths to make sure that each substantial piece of interior joinery strengthened and supported the hull. Now, inner and outer hull skins are fitted together and pre-fab interiors are just dropped into place.

Storage space has been a major casualty with modern cruising boat interiors. Traditional interiors with their straightforward approach and relatively simple cabinetry encouraged oodles of storage, as did their V-shaped hulls with storage under the cabin soles. Modern hulls are shallow, with precious little storage below the cabin sole. Pushing out the salon interior to the hull sides means lost storage space behind the settees.

Of course, storage space isn't much of a consideration when designing a boat used primarily for charter or coastal use. But blue-water sailing requires a fairly high degree of independence from the local chandlery. Carrying a substantial supply of spare parts requires substantial dry and accessible storage. It's even more important when food stores are considered. Most cruisers routinely carry a month's supply of food, because of the challenge of replenishing where local stores only have modest and often overpriced supplies.

Another casualty has been the venerable foul-weather locker sufficient to house the oilies of the entire crew, along with their boots and southwester hats. In the olden days the first rule when coming below was removing the oilskins and boots and stowing them in an appropriate locker, lest the interior remain forever soaked with salt water. Once the boat is large enough for four, five, or six crew, the sheer volume taken up by foul weather gear is awesome. We currently have an entire large stand-alone shower assembly completely filled up with foul-weather gear, including several Mustang survival suits.

Working in the opposite direction are larger heads and galleys. Modern boats often have heads large enough to do justice to a nice apartment, with a separate shower large enough for several crew. That's nice in port but not so nice offshore. Over the years we've received more bruises both inside the head and getting in and out of the head than anywhere else on the boat. Small heads are preferred offshore, large heads at anchor.

Chart tables are another traditional blue-water cruiser interior feature that has nearly been relegated to obscurity. Alas, the electronic revolution has all but made the chart table obsolete; often it's been simply relocated to the cockpit steering console. However, properly viewed as the vessel's command center, the chart table deserves a prominent place in any serious cruising boat.

An interior made of real solid wood is more likely to remain fresh and intact after many years of hard duty than modern lightweight factory-machined interiors. Some years ago we had a chance to inspect the interior of a high-end modern boat that sank at the dock but was lifted out the next morning. Every interior wood veneer panel had lifted up and separated from its frame. What had been elegant craft with an inspiring sculpture in complex wood veneers was a total loss.

In contrast, many an old-fashioned real wood interior boat that has run up on the beach after separating from a mooring in a storm could be brought back to life without too much effort. Similarly, more than a few boats have a localized interior fire once in a while, especially with a diesel or kerosene recalcitrant heater or with faulty electric wiring. Repairing boats originally built with the old stick-by-stick method is far easier than dealing with highly engineered interiors with exciting compound curves and raised paneling. Stick-by-stick comes apart fairly easily.

In the early days of fiberglass production, builders retained the traditional accommodation arrangements found in wooden boats where the basic func-

Outfitting the Offshore Cruising Sailboat

tion of the boat was providing accommodations for offshore passages. Over many decades the basic accommodation needs were standardized in terms of adequate sea berths, galley, head, eating place (folding table), foul-weather locker, and chart table. That's no longer true. Some cruising boat designs nowadays resemble spaceships.

For smaller cruisers in the 30-foot range, the standard arrangement once was V-berths forward, followed by a head to port with cabinet opposite, in turn followed with port and starboard settees, folding table in between, followed aft by a small galley with chart table opposite. With larger boats, say 35 feet in length, a quarter berth underneath a cockpit locker was added, together with pilot berths above the salon settees. Occasionally a clever designer arranged a second head by the cockpit stairs. With suitable lee cloths, the settee berths (and pilot berths) did double duty as salon seats and secure offshore berths together with the quarter berth. The V-shaped berth forward was used in port or for sail storage.

Over the years, designers have largely shifted accommodation focus towards providing liveaboard amenities rather than outfitting the boat primarily as an offshore cruiser. Most current boats now have dinette tables rather than folding tables. Pilot berths are all but forgotten. In larger boats, swivel chairs often replace one settee in the salon. (Swivel chairs are de rigueur on powerboats.) Galleys and heads have become quite sumptuous. Sometimes the humble chart table is elevated to a stand-alone center of attention as an office away from home, rather than its original function as a navigation command center.

One of the pleasures of viewing the interior accommodation of a traditional wood or early fiberglass boat by a well-known designer is that the interiors work well at sea. Designers actually spent time at sea learning what works and what needs improvement.

To be sure, what makes a comfortable interior is importantly a matter of personal taste. But the basic functional requirements of the interior accommodation for the distance cruiser haven't changed. Well-designed galleys, heads, sea berths, foul-weather gear lockers, and chart table are no less important than a well-designed cockpit, rig, and hull form. Arguably, traditional sailing cruisers had very similar interiors because form did follow function.

192

Accommodations

Fig. 9.1 Accommodation Requirements for Blue-Water Cruising

Secure all weather sea berths with lee cloths adequate for off-watch crew.

Chart table large enough to display conventional navigation paper charts with plenty of stowage space, access to instruments and switchboards.

Galley workable in heavy weather, with deep double sinks, fiddles, rails, gimbaled stove / oven, plenty of storage, bright lights, large freezer, pressure and manual water faucets, pressure sea water faucet.

Locker near cockpit stairs to hold foul weather and safety gear.

Ample stowage for gear under cabin sole and below and behind berths / settees

Accessible head athwartships, preferably near cockpit stairs, with separate shower.

Dorade-type ventilation / fan for each cabin / compartment

BERTHS

Secure sea berths suitable for trouble-free, secure sleeping offshore are a critical interior accommodation issue—perhaps the critical accommodation requirement. Without really good sea berths, crews just become exhausted as one day leads into another. Long-distance cruising with short crews can be physically demanding, and being well-rested in a secure, dry berth is not a luxury but a serious requirement. Sea berths need only be 24 to 30 inches wide, but they should be at least 7 feet long to accommodate tall crews. It's especially important to have sturdily fastened lee cloths that will keep the crews secure even when the boat rolls in a quarterly sea. It's a rare production cruising sailboat that comes fitted out with lee cloths as standard items. In olden days they came standard.

In most small to mid-size aft cockpit boats, the lower salon berths serve as suitable sea berths (together with quarter berths if available), provided the salon is not fitted out with a permanent dinette for comfortable living. That means two crew can rest comfortably below with the watch crew in the cockit. Forward V-berths are usually unsuitable except in mild conditions and sometimes only for small children. Queen-sized aft cabin double berths are usually unsuitable because it's challenging (though not impossible) to fit secure lee cloths. The traditional aft cockpit arrangement allows at least 2 sea berths—the lower settees in the main salon and perhaps one or more quarter berths fitted under the cockpit seats. That old-fashioned design has lasted more than a century.

Outfitting the Offshore Cruising Sailboat

Center-cockpit cruisers usually offer just the lower salon berths and sometimes a berth in a cabin alongside the engine room in larger boats. If there's a dinette table fitted in the salon, there's just one lower settee available as a sea berth—and only if that's properly fitted out with a lee cloth. So quite often one finds a sturdy-looking center-cockpit design splendid for liveaboard but with only one or two really good sea berths despite its imposing size.

Fig. 9.2 A Secure Sea Berth
A secure offshore berth in a "captain's cabin" outside the engine room in a center cockpit design. Note the ready-to-use lee cloth below the bunk. Note the large library of equipment binders and pilots above the berth.

Occasionally in a much larger aft- or even a center-cockpit boat one sees a cabin forward of the salon with upper and lower berths with a head and locker forward followed by the venerable V-berth. This arrangement gives an ample supply of good sea berths sufficient to accommodate large crews and is especially attractive when making delivery trips. Still another arrangement with larger center-cockpit designs is twin cabins forward of the mast with opposite upper and lower berths, together with a cabin alongside the engine room, thereby providing three sea berths plus two pilot berths. Having one's own berth is a major inducement for attracting good crew or charter customers.

Having at least two sea berths on opposite sides of the boat means always having an available leeward berth—far more comfortable than leaning against the lee cloth on a windward berth, which can be tiring when undertaken for long periods. As a practical matter, even the smallest cruiser heading offshore should have, at a minimum, secure sea berths on opposite sides of the salon, typically the most comfortable part of the boat. Having the minimum of two good sea berths also means that three crew can be taken aboard for substantial overnight voyages, where two are resting below with one on duty.

One of the problems with the venerable U-shaped dinettes is that while they are delightful in port, the outboard seat is typically too short to serve as a proper sea berth and it's all too easy to bang one's head getting in and out. However, one can learn to sleep sitting up on the athawrtships portion of the dinette in utter desperation if no other sea berths are available.

Lee cloths need to be sturdily constructed and securely fastened. Typically they're about twelve inches high and a foot shorter than the berth at each end and made of either heavy acrylan or sailcloth, appropriately hemmed with heavy grommets every foot or so. Heavy-duty eye-shaped fasteners are secured to the berth every foot or so along or under the outside of the berth/ seat, together with robust eye fasteners bolted into the cabinets a foot above the berth cushion at each end of the berth. The lee cloth is left securely fastened along its bottom length and a suitable arrangement is made for tying the ends while the crew is in the berth.

All in all, it takes some experimentation to get it just right. Typically the lee cloth is left underneath the seat cushion. In our experience it's worth having a strong lee cloth made for every sea berth. One of the hallmarks of an experienced crew is that they always set up the lee cloth when sacked out—even in mild conditions. Who knows when a rogue wave or line squall lies in wait?

One rarely sees lee cloths fitted out on shiny new cruising boats displayed at boat shows or even sitting on the hard with a For Sale sign. When visiting other boats at anchor, long before the rum, cheese, and crackers come out we cast an eye for the life raft on deck and lee cloths below. Otherwise, the forthcoming stories of derring-do need a huge dose of salt. Lee cloths are the true below-decks hallmark of the serious offshore cruiser.

A few words about seat cushions. Over time, foam cushions lose their resiliency and sometimes (often) become mildewed or moldy. The minimum thickness is four inches for seat cushions, but five or six inches is much better. There's no shortage of cover materials that can be used; even well-made interior fabrics can be quite satisfactory. Usually a pleasant fabric cover design brightens up an otherwise drab interior. After all, careful crews do not as a habit drag salt-encrusted foul-weather gear all over the interior.

Whether fancy or plain fabrics and designs are used for covers, it's a good idea to use a mesh for the bottom to keep the cushions ventilated. If the crews are wont to sit on cushions with their salty foul-weather gear, it's a good idea to fit delivery covers. Keeping cushions dry and free of salt water takes some doing. Some captains require their crew to hang up the oilies in the head or on hooks past the cockpit stairs as a matter of course. When anchored out in sunny weather, drying out cushions helps get rid of the interior aromas.

Clearly there is a sharp conflict between the comfort demands for sleeping at port/anchor and sleeping while voyaging. It's long been noted that most boats spend most of their life either tied up to the dock or at anchor rather than pushing waters aside. So it's understandable why sleeping accommodations at port increasingly take precedence over good sea berths that are used only infrequently or not at all. Moreover, decisions about buying boats are typically made dockside or while the boat is on the hard, so it's easy to ignore the all-important sea berth requirement. But rearranging a cabin interior is challenging.

HEADS

Gone are the old days of a cedar bucket and a trip to the leeward stern rail. Increasingly, the widely denigrated basic mechanical marine toilet requiring hand pumping to retrieve salt water and exhaust effluent has been replaced by electric marvels. Most still use salt water, some use fresh water. Upscale boats often use vacuum pump heads such as Vacu-flush with modest amounts of fresh water to keep everything tidy and fresh.

Whatever the brand, the best advice is to carry spares and mechanically adept crews. Experienced crews know that heads are living creatures with memories always anxious to "pack up" at the wrong time. There is just nothing more irksome when cruising than working on one's knees, in a boat pitching to windward, trying to unplug a recalcitrant head. It can destroy even the best friendship.

Fig. 9.3 Head
A secure fore and aft Vacu-flush head installation usable in all weather with ample side support and grab rails.

Heads have grown in size and function over the decades. Once difficult to access, with just minimal space and a handheld shower, heads have become spacious. Even mid-size boats boast a separate shower. Just about all cruising boats have pressure hot and cold water. Adding a foot-powered water pump is useful in conserving water, both in the head and in the galley. Even better is a pressure salt-water pump at both locations. Many detergents work fairly well with salt water.

Heads are usually located forward the mainmast in both aft- and center-cockpit boats. That's where they're out of the way, in space that's difficult to use anyway. Much better is a head located just off the stairs leading to the cockpit, but this placement isn't often seen nowadays since it interferes with the conventional cabin layout. Nevertheless, such a placement has its advantages, since the head is immediately available when coming below rather than requiring going forward as the boat is moving this way and that. The venerable Ted Hood produced some splendid designs half a century ago with the head just off the cockpit stairs opposite the galley where the head had a separate shower used as a foul-weather locker.

Outfitting the Offshore Cruising Sailboat

Opinions and practice differ on whether the head should face fore and aft or athwartships. Most boats with just one head favor the athwartships arrangement, on the grounds that it's easier to use when the boat is heeling. Actually, that's true if the head is to leeward. In many center-cockpit sailboats the second head in the aft cabin arrangement is often placed fore and aft on the grounds of easier accommodation and that it's likely to be used only in port or during pleasant conditions.

While many sailors consider the head wasted space, the advantages of two heads aboard should not be discounted, especially if they are useable on opposite tacks. Despite claims to the contrary, heads are failure-prone gear. A second head also encourages showers. Modern boats often carry watermakers, so there's sufficient water to encourage daily or frequent showers when offshore. Long gone are the days when the crew showered with fresh water only after the voyage was over or when the heavens opened up. The advantages of daily or frequent fresh-water showers when voyaging in the tropics should not be discounted; they're a good argument for installing a watermaker.

Most boats have opening ports in their heads for ventilation. Even better is an electric ventilation fan leading to a closeable on-deck ventilator. Vetus makes a very low amperage two-speed fan for this purpose, with a computer motor that should last for decades. Having an electric ventilator is a real assist when drying out the head after a shower or hanging up wet foul-weather gear or for crews with occasional intestinal difficulties. With a low amperage exhausting head fan, the immediate cabin vicinity can be readily ventilated in all weathers.

Head floors often get wet. Traditionally, removable teak cabin soles were fitted. These were the hallmark of a real yacht—or at least an owner with deep pockets. We've used removable floors made up of interlocking plastic panels with good results over many decades. They're easy to clean and do not mildew or discolor when rinsed with mild bleach.

A very handy convenience in a head is a drain leading to a sump. This facilitates washing down the entire head. Nowadays the drain in the separate shower compartment leads to the sump rather than requiring a separate failure-prone shower drain pump, or just letting the head floor drain into a smelly bilge.

Some experienced skippers require their crews to wash down the heads after every turn of the watch. Early fiberglass production boats usually used formica on the interior head walls to facilitate cleaning. Later on, separately molded fiberglass interior assemblies were used. These one-piece assemblies are much easier to clean. However, it can be challenging to change plumbing hoses and wiring with one-piece head assemblies.

Besides the ever-present maintenance issues with marine heads, the exhaust hoses require replacement every five or ten years. Otherwise the odors in the effluent as well as gases in the marine environment will seep through the hose wall. Keeping the head smelling fresh requires perpetual vigilance. A daily regimen with Lysol or similar disinfectant brings smiles all around. In our experience, advertisements about "odor proof" hosing for heads is just marketing hokum.

All in all, heads with mechanical/electric toilets and showers are great conveniences. Two are certainly better than one, especially if ladies are aboard, but even with two it's essential to have spares available. Separate floor drains along with separate shower compartments, exhaust fans leading to watertight ventilators, emergency foot pumps for fresh water, and a pressure salt-water spigot round out the usual amenities. The modern-style head is one of the very few interior accommodation improvements worth thinking about when refitting a traditional older craft.

One last comment about heads. In port, the head can't be too large. But large heads at sea can be downright dangerous. With a modest-sized head it's usually easy to brace one's body and avoid being thrown about. Even in rough weather it's usually possible to take a brief shower provided the head or separate stall is small enough so one is not thrown about.

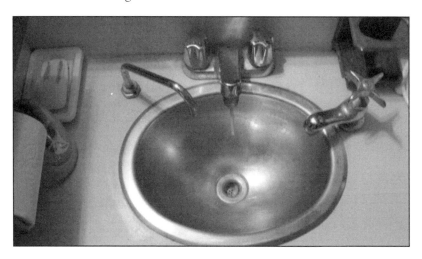

Fig. 9.4 Head Sink and Fixtures
Head sink has manual foot pump spigot for fresh water, pressure fresh water spigot with water saver and pressure salt water spigot.

Outfitting the Offshore Cruising Sailboat

GALLEY

People used to go cruising with ice in the reefer, plenty of cans, preserved foods in Mason jars, and sacks of potatoes and onions. Nowadays it's common to have all the conveniences of home aboard even a smaller cruiser with access to 110-volt power, by means of the ubiquitous inverter/charger. The conveniences of refrigeration, microwaves, and ready availability of frozen foods/dinners have unmistakably altered food preparation. Today virtually anyone can prepare tasty and nutritious meals afloat in settled waters with a minimum of fuss. With deep pockets, frozen gourmet meals can be prepared in just minutes, even in heavy weather.

The venerable and sometimes dangerous (if misused) alcohol stoves and ovens, along with the occasional diesel-powered stoves, have been replaced with propane. More than a few cruisers have installed gimbaled stoves with ovens, and the ovens remain unused: Microwaves are so much faster, especially if using prepared frozen foods. Making bread afloat seems like a lost art nowadays. That's a pity, since the smells of baking bread while at anchor on a chilly, damp day are one of cruising's best pleasures. There was a time when just about everyone sailing in colder climates carried a crew skilled at raising the dough.

Alas, not all galleys are equal. In few places is the designer's experience at sea or lack of it more visible than in the galley. In port almost any arrangement will do. But a really serviceable galley under way at sea requires some serious thought.

Fig. 9.5 A Well-Equipped Galley **Celebration**'s *superbly designed offshore L-shaped galley with 12 feet of counter space is well fitted out for keeping 8 crew well supplied for months at a time. Note the large vertical food storage cabinets, ample-sized separate freezer and refrigerator installations, protective grab rails, outboard storage cabinets, microwave, gimbaled propane stove, and double sinks with manual and pressure water and salt water spigots.*

The primary requirements are to keep the cook secure as the boat rolls, ditto for plates and pots used in food preparation; ease of access to cooking utensils and pots; deep sinks to wash dishes; and plenty of surface area to prepare foods, all the while keeping everything off the floor. A thoughtfully designed galley suitable for sea duty will feature a set of deep sinks, high fiddles, and some grab bars to assist the cook in remaining upright. Good lighting also helps.

Keeping the cook in place while the boat is rolling presents a challenge, especially in boats where the galley is fore and aft. Without grab rails—stainless steel one-inch rails set about three inches above the galley surface—the cook can easily lose balance and fly across the cabin. One traditional means of securing the cook is with a large webbed belt secured to strong points, especially around the stove area. A better arrangement is an athwartships galley, but this is difficult to arrange in a conventional smaller cruiser.

Once a mid-sized cruiser is considered, there's often space enough to construct a U-shaped galley running fore and aft. Here the cook has reasonable protection from being thrown across the cabin. Center-cockpit boats typically have a fore and aft galley set outboard the passageway leading to the aft cabin. Here the engine room wall set below the center cockpit provides good protection, although headroom in the passageway may be limited.

In a larger center-cockpit boat the galley can not only run fore and aft outboard alongside the engine room wall, but also extend in an L shape athwartships into the salon, leaving space for stairs to the cockpit. This arrangement, pioneered in the Gulfstar 50 ketches built for the charter trade, is an especially good setup inasmuch as the cook is protected on virtually all sides. Here the reefer and stove run fore and aft outboard alongside the engine room wall and the sink, with additional counter space form along the L shape running athwartships. One advantage of this arrangement is that the cook is not isolated and it's easy to pass the dishes back and forth from the galley to the dining table just forward of the galley. Also, the cook is right up close to the cockpit for handing up dishes.

Sinks need special attention. All too often the sinks are but six or eight inches deep—far too shallow. Much better are sinks ten or even twelve inches deep. Even better are a set of double deep sinks, one for storing and washing dishes and pots and the other for rinsing. Deep sinks are also helpful for washing clothes and even occasionally for disassembling engine parts or bathing a small child or a dog. Stainless steel is best for sinks, since it can take abuse more readily than fiberglass. However, glass sinks can readily be restored to their former luster with several applications of paint used for coating masts and decks.

Fig. 9.6 Deep Double Galley Sinks
Double deep galley sink with manual fresh-water foot pump, pressure water faucet with water saver, hose extension, and pressure saltwater spigot. Deep sinks not only save water but are handy for doing laundry, cleaning engine parts, and washing small dogs.

Most galleys come with a pressure hot and cold water faucet installed. Better is one with a flexible hose and trigger handle allowing the spigot to reach into the sink. That arrangement uses less water and keeps water from splashing. A good galley foot pump is a handy device. More than one cruiser has learned to their regret that during a passage the pressure water system developed a leak and the water tank emptied. Turning off the pressure water system is good practice running offshore unless one has separate water tanks.

A pressured salt-water faucet at the galley is seldom seen these days, and that's a shame because offshore salt water is ideal for cleaning pots, pans, and dishes. Offshore, salt water can be used to boil pasta and rice. Salt water mixes well with modern detergents and is a great water saver. Having pressurized salt water handy encourages quick clean-up of dirty dishes, a good sanitary practice. Pressurized salt water also helps in the head and elsewhere: We've pointed out its utility in the engine room where a salt-water pump can substitute in an emergency for a distressed engine or genset. Prior to inexpensive watermakers, salt water was widely viewed as the poor man's water tank extender.

Salt-water manual pumps at the galley and head(s) were fairly common. But with substantial battery installations commonly aboard cruisers today and the low-cost wash-down saltwater pumps, it makes sense to install an electric saltwater utility pump. Some care is needed to find a robust faucet that will resist salt water. Salt water at the galley is also helpful in cleaning out the sink drains periodically. Rather than use several gallons of precious fresh water, letting the saltwater pump run for ten or fifteen minutes does the job nicely.

Let's turn to storage in the galley. A cruising boat can never have too much storage for food and utensilss. Any proper cruising boat should be able to store food enough to feed crew for several months without replenishment. Eating well at sea is even more important than when on land, since the corner grocery store is a long way off. Since the major market for cruising sailboats is the charter and local offshore market, it's not surprising that food storage gets short shrift on conventional cruising boats. Typically there are a just a few cabinets sufficient to store a week or two of groceries. That's a shame, because then one has to find alternative places and it takes a notebook to keep track of where food stores are located.

Here a center-cockpit design has some advantages, since food cabinets can be located outboard the galley—sometimes, in a large enough boat, above the galley along the outside hull above the countertops. In any event, besides looking to see if there are suitably placed sea berths, one of the first things to look for when inspecting a boat down below is food storage capabilities. Cans (properly protected with Vaseline and whatnot) used to be stored below the cabin sole. But modern designs, with their shallow hulls, usually have scant, if any, storage below the cabin soles. Moreover, bilge water tends to slosh around in flattish hulls, so the cans tend to rust if not protected in plastic sealed bags. A really well-thought-out galley will not only have adequate food storage for several months supply but will also have sturdy cabinet hinges and fiddleboards to protect the contents from sliding out. Storing food in shallow plastic containers is good practice, since it's easier to remove a plastic container with a dozen cans than to sort through the entire cabinet to find that last can of beans.

Most cruisers nowadays have refrigerators; larger boats have both refrigerators and freezers. Typically the freezer is much smaller than the refrigerator, demonstrating that the designer has limited offshore sailing experience.

For voyaging it's the freezer, not the refrigerator, that's critically important. Perishables in a refrigerator can last a few weeks, but food kept frozen can last months and months. We keep our freezer running for months at time, even occasionally as long as a year, save for brief monthly intervals to defrost, and with few exceptions have had no difficulty with foods stored for months. Freezers are ideal for storing frozen meats, juices, milk, bread, prepared meals—especially high-carb pastas and pizzas handy for quick meals—and frozen vegetables almost indefinitely. If we're lucky enough to catch a good-eating fish, the freezer is always ready.

Since most of the really interesting places to cruise are distant from a convenient grocery, it makes good sense to have the largest freezer possible. Not often seen on cruising sailboats are the external freezer units commonly seen on offshore sport fisherman. Typically 4 to 5 feet long and somewhere between 18 and 24 inches in height, these units are designed to run continuously from either 12 or 110 volts. With a medium-sized mid-ship cruiser, these units can be stowed aft attached to the stern pulpit. After their contents have been used up they make ideal deck storage boxes.

A few words about stoves. Making a gimbaled stove is not complicated, but it's rare to see a stove that has sufficiently high protective fiddles around the perimeter or a good system of holding a variety of different-sized pots and pans in a seaway. Building a protective barrier using 2" or 3" wide by ⅛" thick aluminum flat stock can help here. Stove builders used to build heavy stoves with added weight down below so their oscillating motion when swinging was dampened. Nowadays the mode is lightness, using highly polished stainless steel. In any event, a pot filled with a gallon of boiling pasta can do considerable damage to both the boat and cook when it becomes airborne. Sometimes a few bricks stowed in the oven can dampen the motion.

Propane stove installations are required to have cut-offs where the tanks are stored below-decks in watertight containers, together with remote on/off switches within sight of the stove. Over the years we've found that the propane tank electric switches last just 3 or 4 years, so replacements are often recommended. Similarly, rubber or copper tubing runs between propane tank and stove. We much prefer the neoprene rubber runs. Money is well spent for aluminum or fiberglass propane tanks (over conventional steel ones) and spare tank fittings.

Most galleys have some sort of modest molding that serves as a fiddle. But really good fiddles should be at least 3 inches high. Easier than redoing the existing moldings is placing stainless steel tubing several inches above the outside of the galley in critical grab areas. These are usually installed in front of the stove but are handy elsewhere, especially in front of the sinks since that's where the cook spends a great deal of time. Steel grab rails are also handy for the refrigerator/freezer, since they usually open from the top and once the food is removed, the rails keep the contents from flying on the floor.

Wide-open galleys are nice for houses, but for serious blue-water cruising boats of any pretension the galley needs careful attention to protect the cook in serious weather. When the going gets rough, eating well becomes important. If the galley isn't serviceable during such times the crew doesn't eat well. Here is where the microwave saves our souls. Even with the least inspired galley, a microwave can within the space of 4 or 10 minutes turn out a hot meal, tasty or otherwise, from a frozen prepared package. If the budget is large, gourmet prepared frozen food dinners can really lift spirits, even with an indifferent galley.

Some thoughts about an ideal galley. Placement matters. The galley is adjacent to the stairs leading from the cockpit, either a U-shaped galley running fore and aft in an aft cockpit arrangement, or an L-shaped galley for a center-cockpit design. Either way, there's a narrow entrance for the cook with protection all around.

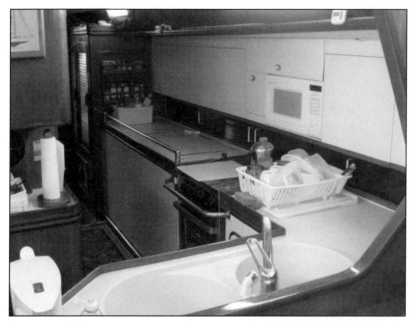

Fig. 9.7 L-Shaped Galley
Another view of **Celebration***'s L-shaped galley. Note the sturdy protective*
safety rail in front of gimbaled propane stove, substantial fiddles all around
the counters and safety rail on top of the freezer and refrigerator. Note the
spare propeller shaft stored at the bottom of the freezer / refrigerator structure
—a handy spare when venturing to faraway places.

Having bright light from large windows helps, along with dimmable bright lights above. Large fiddles and plenty of stainless steel grab rails, where appropriate, are essential. Your galley should have an oversized freezer, to be sure, and separate from the refrigerator. You want big, deep, double sinks and lots of counter space, together with storage space outboard and hopefully above and below. One can never have too much food storage space on a cruising boat. You also need not only pressure hot and cold water but also a foot pump and a pressured salt-water pump. For the brave of heart, a pressure cooker can work wonders. The real question is how the galley functions offshore. A well-fed crew will endure heavy weather with far better spirits.

CHART TABLE

Chart tables were regular fixtures in sailing cruisers before the electronic age relegated navigation instruments mostly to the cockpit. Traditional cruisers had chart tables large enough to fully open up charts, with chart storage drawers below, cabinets for signal flags, various Pilots, a sextant, various cruising guides, and a dimmable light above with a red lens. Up above was room for the radar, instruments, and various radios. Smaller cruisers made do with opening charts over the icebox. With a 5- or 6-foot-wide chart table that's 2.5 to 3 feet deep, there's ample space to use paper charts in their entirety.

Fig. 9.8 Chart Table
A large table is a highly desirable feature in any offshore cruiser.

While current fashion places the major navigation instruments and screens in the cockpit securely mounted in a large steering pedestal, the traditional chart table still has its virtues as the vessel's command center. It's a good place for computers and peripherals, guidebooks, pilots, and other reference books. In addition it offers drawers to store all sorts of small items and navigation tools.

Outfitting the Offshore Cruising Sailboat

Big or small chart tables are found either athwartships with a bench seat or fore and aft with the navigator seated outboard in a swivel chair. Most designers favor an athwartships table, since it fits in better with the overall accommodation. After all, airplane pilots face forward. Alas, sailboats rock and roll and it's challenging to brace oneself in the bench seat. Much preferred is the athwartships chart table set against the outboard hull with the navigator firmly seated in an outboard swivel seat. Suitably arranged, the navigator is secure in any weather.

Arguably a proper chart table runs athwartships with the navigator secure in a sturdy adjustable swivel chair bolted to the floor. With the feet braced on the hull side and the navigator secure in the swivel chair, the occupant is well positioned to remain at the table for extended periods. The only argument against such an arrangement is that it takes up too much space. Then again, many long hours will be spent at the chart table at sea and even longer hours at port working at the computer to communicate with the rest of the world, to manage one's portfolio, or even to write books.

Fig. 9.9 Library
A large library of equipment manuals belongs on every offshore cruiser.

TABLE

As with berths, the dining table is a compromise between utilities of offshore cruising and in-port activities. The U-shaped dining table has all but become ubiquitous in cruising boats, reflecting both the importance of eating comfortably and of spending time in quiet waters. Offshore with the boat rolling and pitching, save in the gentlest of conditions a dining table is useful only for looking at large paper charts. Eating typically takes place sitting in a salon settee or cockpit seat. Traditional builders understood the importance of dual utility and typically built fold-down tables in small to mid-size cruising boats. Such tables often folded down from the wall partition just ahead of the mast or even attached to the mast itself.

For larger boats, traditional builders built dining tables with substantial fiddles all around the edges to keep the plates from sliding off. Sometimes the fiddles had interlocking pieces so plates on the table would be kept in place. More than a few tables in larger offshore traditional boats were actually gimbaled fore and aft to keep the plates in place. Some builders even arranged cabinet openings in the center of the tables to hold spirits, silverware, and so forth. Alas, utilities such as serious-size fiddles are rarely seen anymore. After all, fiddles would interfere with elegant eating around the table in port. Nor are tables often built so they collapse around the U-shaped settees and form into a double berth to serve extra duty in port. In early fiberglass production boat building days such arrangements were often used to boost the berth numbers of a particular design.

Our old wooden ketch had this arrangement. It was the only double berth on the boat, and the favored berth at that. It came with a supply of serious removable fiddles not only around the table edges but actually crossing fore and aft and athwartships. Even in a minor blow it was possible to keep the china and silver off the sole. But keeping track of all those fiddles was a chore, as was setting up the berth.

Nonetheless, tables have great utility in port, and with the advent of the venerable chart table moving electronically to the cockpit, the dining table remains the only space where a large paper chart can be unfolded. That's especially handy when entering an unfamiliar inlet or set of low-lying islands. Any table worth having should be sturdily built and firmly bolted to the cabin sole. Having a table that can also be used a double berth is a handy arrangement.

Outfitting the Offshore Cruising Sailboat

Tables are often works of art in higher-end boats, with splendid wooden inlays and high-gloss varnish. Some high-end builders delight in creating inlays with their firm's initials built into the tabletop. Over the years we've improved our table finish and now have 20 coats of varnish, so it's a veritable mirror.

One of the great advantages of the U-shaped table is that the surrounding settees allow substantial storage space. Given the shallow hulls commonly built, the traditional storage areas under the cabin soles are long gone, so storage spaces in modern yachts are always at a premium. Unfortunately, the settees around the U-shaped table are fair game for installing the refrigerator compressor and/or an air conditioning unit. We've long used these valued spaces, when available, for storing tools, paints, and especially for spare parts and motors.

In many ways a cockpit table hinge mounted off the steering pedestal is ideal for sharing a meal, provided it has large fiddles. The table itself need not be large for an aft cockpit. But for a center cockpit, a substantial table can be fitted. With a sturdy cockpit enclosure there will be ample opportunities to dine in style.

Sometimes in the marine supply store one can find plates and soup bowls with rubber feet. That's nice and they do look yachty. But nothing beats real, big china bowls useful for salads and soups. They tend to stay in place by sheer weight, especially in the cockpit, and encourage both the cook and crew to accept the importance of one-pot meals. Even better are the large bowls made of high-grade plastic, called Corian china, that can survive an occasional flight to the cabin sole. In any event, eating out of one's lap is the time-honored tradition of real salts. A salon dining table is primarily useful when in port entertaining guests.

LOCKERS

Since sailboat production focuses on the charter industry's residing in warm, sunny climates, it's not surprising that the venerable foul-weather locker has faded into obscurity along with clothing lockers. Even our own vessel, designed to take eight souls to the ends of the earth, lacks a suitable foul-weather locker. So the shower of one of the three heads is now devoted to storing foul-weather gear plus safety gear and several Mustang Survival Suits. Absence of a suitable foul-weather locker is by itself a decent argument for having a second head with separate shower.

In traditional boats, foul-weather lockers were serious business and always situated adjacent to the stairs leading to the cockpit. Remember that these were the days before dodgers and biminis became commonplace. Sailors got wet and their oilies needed a place to dry. A nice touch in the olden days was venting the foul-weather locker into the engine compartment and fitting a drain into the bilge.

Along with foul-weather lockers, vertical clothing lockers have also become scarce items. Good clothing lockers are even more important for liveaboards. Sailors who venture from tropical climes are especially disadvantaged by absence of storage space for coats and suitable cold-weather gear. All too frequently, once the tropics are reached the winter gear is stuffed into duffel bags and stowed away. Sometimes the stuffed duffel bags are used as pillows for unsuspecting crews. Typically the clothing locker is relegated to the owner's cabin, while the rest of the crew makes do with duffle bags.

VENTILATION

Just about all cruisers have various opening hatches and an assortment of opening ports. Builders of wooden craft made do with just one deck hatch for stowing the sails in the forepeak, together with the sliding hatch at the forward end of the cockpit. Nowadays the number of installed deck hatches can be awesome as builders take advantage of the possibilities with fiberglass. Hatches are certainly handy to bring in light and fresh air.

But once in the tropics, deck hatches can be a double-edged sword under the blazing sun. Most cruisers eventually learn to install external cloth covers to keep out the rays. Some even install insulated flexible aluminized materials. Covering hatches also delays the UV degradation of the plastic hatch lens. Hatches left open are also wonderful devices for flooding of the interior during unexpected thundershowers when exploring ashore.

While deck hatches are nice in port, what happens when sailing in rough or wet weather or when the boat is closed up for extended periods for trips home? If there is no provision for serious ventilation, the interior becomes ripe with mildew and mold. So some serious thought needs to be given to ventilating the boat when it's all bottled up, either when at sea or at the dock/anchor for extended periods. Experienced tropic cruisers are ever vigilant against mold.

Outfitting the Offshore Cruising Sailboat

Most cruisers have one or more deck ventilators. Typically there's one for the head, one or more for the engine intake/exhausts, and sometimes one over the galley. With ventilators what you see is largely what you get. The large Dorade-type ventilators originated by Olin Stephans in the 1930s work just fine. These have rectangular boxes with an interior opening forward and an opening for a large scoop ventilator aft with a divider in between to keep the water out. In really rough weather the scoop can be removed and replaced with a screw cap to make the whole proposition watertight. An improvement over the wood box is one made of heavy fiberglass for use on the foredeck. Whether made of wood or glass, the Dorade boxes need to be securely fastened (bolted) to the deck so they can take abuse from an errant crew snagging a line or from heavy boarding seas.

Fig. 9.10 Dorade Ventilator on the Foredeck
A secure fiberglass Dorade ventilator mounted to the deck at the foredeck.

The basic problem with Dorade ventilators, besides their expense, is that they tend to snag lines, so often they are protected by a contraption of stainless steel tubing, which means more fastening holes in the cabin top. A varnished Dorade box with a gleaming chrome-plated bronze or cast stainless air scoop

212

with a red interior is one of the best ways to dress up a yacht. On occasion one sees nearly a dozen shiny Dorades on a goldplater just 40 or 50 feet long shouting, "Look at me!" The cost of a dozen such magnificent embellishments can easily exceed that of an ocean-certified life raft. Maybe two of them.

While Dorade boxes can be purchased from many marine supply houses, they often make good projects. Typically the boxes need be carefully adjusted to account for the camber of the deck. Teak is often the wood of choice, but many cruisers have made do with plywood. While it's the surface that captures attention, what really matters is how well the Dorades are put together and bolted to the deck.

A step down from the standard venerable Dorades are ones made of plastic. These are smaller and less obtrusive but our experience has not been satisfactory. Plastic is not wood or glass and is susceptible to breakage and degradation under ultraviolet rays. It makes no sense to cut holes in the deck unless the holes can be securely made watertight under all reasonably expected conditions.

Another venerable design is the low-profile deck ventilator, usually made of metal. Mariner Hardware makes beautiful, robust, stainless steel versions with diameters of about 4 inches. The tops can be screwed down tight or left open in ventilation position rising to just 3 or 4 inches above deck. These heavily built ventilators can take lots of abuse. They can also be used on vertical or near-vertical cabin sides to ventilate heads or the galley.

Fig. 9.11 Mushroom Ventilator on Cabin Top
A robust Mushroom ventilator on the cabin top is unlikely to be snared by lines. Note the heavy dinghy support cradles forward of the mast and hatch covers to keep out the hot tropical sun.

While there are many other ventilators on the market, they are generally difficult or impossible to make completely watertight and therefore are not suitable for serious voyagers. Any ventilator worth its name should resist several feet of water on top of it. Otherwise the interior cabin sole becomes wet, and a wet cabin sole is dangerous. Quality ventilators should also be able to be opened or closed from below decks.

With ventilators it often seems that more is better. But once offshore with a good breeze it's surprising how much air can be extracted with just several ventilators. Ideally each sleeping area should have its own dedicated ventilator that can be closed from below. Ventilators are useful when installed on a lazarette, and when made especially robust, on the foredeck as well. Ventilators equipped with fans are especially useful in heads.

All serious ventilators should have robust metal screens. Otherwise our little rodent and roach friends will find their way into the food lockers. Finding and removing rodents and roaches and cleaning up the mess is truly nasty work. A good working assumption is that every dock and boatyard has rodents and roaches. So leaving the cabin open while walking down the docks to have lunch ashore or discussing the weather with a neighbor is taking a risk. An elegant solution is a ventilated hatch door with suitable screening.

Ventilators are also important for the engine room, both for intake and exhaust. These, too, must be able to made watertight and have rodent-resistant screens. A nice feature of a center-cockpit boat is that it's easy to install ventilators in the cockpit right above the engine room in an aft seat. The usual arrangements are one ventilator for engine room intake, another for the powered exhaust fan. Our experience is that the best arrangement for engine room ventilators is to also use Dorade boxes mounted well away from oncoming seas.

While cruising boats continue to have opening side ports, our experience is that all makes and models eventually leak—usually under the most dire conditions. So we screw them tight and leave them undisturbed save for an annual inspection and cleaning. For ventilation we depend on opening hatches and our trusty ventilators. Often in the tropics aluminized insulation panels are used to keep out the sun's rays on the larger salon windows when in port or anchored.

While there is no shortage of hatch manufacturers, our favorite is the extruded Bomar hatch with a reinforcing bar (or two) down the middle. These hatches can take the weight of a large crew member without any problem, since the metal reinforcing bar or bars absorb the weight, not the plexiglass or lexan lens. Moreover, even if an adventurous soul does remove the plexiglass, the bars prevent injury. We have the chisel marks to show that the bars really do work to keep out intruders! After some time the neoprene rubber gaskets must be replaced, so some spares are handy items to have aboard. Unless protected with covers, the lenses themselves will craze and also need replacement.

HATCHES

Hatches transmit sunlight that in the tropics heats up the interior. Tinted plexiglass (or lexan) helps. Even better are custom-made covers of Acrylan that fit more or less permanently over the hatches. While the covers reduce the light entering the cabin from above, usually the side ports have ample light-admitting properties. Properly made, the covers will last for years and even survive tropical storms.

Traditional cruisers had small ports on the sensible grounds that wood was stronger than glass or plastic. Modern cruisers have much larger ports and frequently have large fixed windows both on the cabin sides and even on the cabin tops. No doubt these create bright, pleasant interiors. But sooner or later an ambitious cruiser will experience heavy seas running over the boat, or a crew banging into a large window, or someone dropping a heavy winch handle, or an errant spinnaker pole. While the window may or may not be strong enough to resist damage, the seals will invariably leak when subject to abuse. Once upon a time, storm windows were fixed, typically ½" plexiglass (Lexan). They're still a good idea for large salon windows and add a nautical blue-water look.

At the very least, some premade plywood panels should be made up with suitable fasteners so that if a large window or port pops open, the damage can be contained. Our own preference is to carry several panels of ¼" aluminum that can be used for emergency hatch and window repairs. They are easily stored under a forward berth. A tube or two of rubber goop or sealant is also handy.

For some mysterious reason hatch manufacturers use either ³⁄₁₆" or ¼" Lexan or Plexiglass in their hatches. Neither material is as strong as the fiberglass deck itself. Boats built for heavy weather are best built with ½" Lexan or

Plexiglass. Even better, with a larger budget, are hatches and ports built with heavy tempered glass. That's thick enough to merit the appellation of bullet-proof. Any hatch worth its mettle should take the full weight of the heaviest crew. After all, a cubic foot of sea water weighs 64 pounds. In a word, when it comes to hatches, less is often more. In particular it's worth investing in the very best forward cabin hatch available.

10

BUYING THE BOAT

THE MARKET

As a practical matter, the domestic cruising boat market is mostly a market for used sailboats. Three well-established volume producers target the coastal cruising and tropic charter markets: Beneteau, Hunter, and Catalina. There are small volumes from several domestic builders such as Island Packet, some custom builders, and imports from Europe and Asia. Finally, there is a significant supply of imports from Asia built during the early days of fiberglass production. Quality issues often preclude these boats built 30 to 40 years ago from active consideration as blue-water cruisers.

Even in the best of times, the used cruising sailboat market is a small one dominated by production builders from the early 1970s and on. Most domestic builders over the past several decades closed shop during the economic downturns in the 1980s, when the demand for leisure goods fell away. These include Gulfstar and Morgan in Florida, Pearson and Bristol in New England, and Columbia on the West Coast. Since fiberglass hulls have proved unusually durable, most production fiberglass cruising sailboats remain available and will likely be so for the foreseeable future.

Current estimates midway into 2010 suggest total broker-assisted sales of used boats in the United States at about 35,000 for the year. Using the 1 to 2 percent market share generally attributed to broker-assisted sailboat sales suggests somewhere between 350 and 700 sailboat sales for the year, with most of those oriented toward smaller boats, with perhaps 100 to 200 cruising sailboats changing hands. Figures for the privately held volume producers and small producers are typically held close to the vest. Even so, the market for cruising sailboats in the United States, new or used, is likely no more than 300 to 500 boats annually, depending upon economic circumstances.

Powerboats, long the dominant recreational craft, define the boating industry in terms of production, design, product innovation, accessory sales, engine innovation, architectural and engineering talent, marinas, boatyards, and brokers. Even

Outfitting the Offshore Cruising Sailboat

in the best high-end sailboats, engine and even electric installations are well behind the standards of most production powerboat builders. So it makes good sense, as part of the learning curve, for cruisers to visit and explore powerboat equipment installations to keep abreast of best practices and innovation.

Florida has long been the major boating market, with about 20 to 25 percent market share for broker-assisted sales, followed by West Coast. Transport costs fairly effectively isolate the East and West Coast markets for mid-size and larger cruising sailboats. However, shipping costs can be reduced significantly by overland transport between Texas and California.

Unlike the West Coast, where only the open Pacific beckons the adventurous, the East Coast is a north-south market. It's relatively easy to ship or move boats throughout this market on their own bottoms courtesy of the intercoastal waterway (ICW). Florida has the special advantage of offering easy access to the prime cruising grounds of the nearby Bahamas and the more distant Caribbean, so most East Coast cruisers eventually find their way to Florida.

Not surprisingly, with its unparalleled supply, shoreside refit, and repair facilities and dockage, Florida is the premier boat market in the United States. Florida also has a large number of individual contractors working out of do-it-yourself yards and boats stored in the many canals behind private homes. Florida is the one East Coast boating market open year-round. It's a good place to begin one's explorations for a new boat, power or sail.

The sheer number of world-class marine facilities centered in and around Fort Lauderdale and nearby Miami is breathtaking. Even if one lives some distance away, it's good advice to visit the offerings in and around Fort Lauderdale just to see the sheer breadth of the cruising sailboat market. Odds are pretty good that one's affordable dream cruiser awaits there. And it's not a long drive to Miami, where boats are seemingly everywhere.

Because they are used only seasonally and often stored on the hard during the winter, Chesapeake Bay and New England cruising boats often command a market premium compared to those stored afloat in Florida. However, since coastal cruising conditions are fairly mild during the sailing season, mid-coast and northern boats tend to be outfitted only for coastal cruising. With only seasonal use, it's fairly common for northern boats to continue with their original rigs and engines for several decades. After all, there's almost always a boatyard nearby. So while older sailboats—the kind most cruisers can afford—are apt to be in better condition in the middle and northern East Coast markets, because of only seasonal use, they're likely to be more expensive to acquire.

Another disadvantage of purchasing cruising boats in the Chesapeake or New England is that it does take some time to get to Florida and then hop off for the Islands. An ICW trip mostly by motor can easily take 3 to 4 weeks, but can done almost any time year-round from the Chesapeake. Running offshore from New England down to Florida even in favorable weather almost always takes at least 7 to 10 days and requires a well-fitted vessel and experienced crew. Cape Hatteras, where the Gulf Stream frequently meets a norther, has a well-earned reputation for white-knuckle sailing.

There's also an offshore passage weather constraint. October is the preferred month for heading south after the hurricane season ebbs, while April to June offers the southerlies for boats heading north. As a practical matter, relatively few sailboats transit the East Coast directly offshore. Even in October and especially in November it can be bitterly cold. That's when the Mustang Survival Work Suits are needed. On the East Coast, blue-water cruising almost always begins in Florida no matter where the boat has been purchased.

SOME PEARLS OF ADVICE FOR BUYING A CRUISER

In a perfect world, a broker or a fellow cruiser would call with the magic words that there's a blue-water cruiser about to come on the market of just the size and price that you're looking for. Moreover, she has a recent rig and engine and is outfitted for serious cruising, having been built by a reputable builder. You're told that the current owner has a "change in plans" and is just selling her because of health, finances, etc., and the boat is in simply wonderful condition. Clean as a whistle.

PEARL NUMBER ONE

Nothing matters so much in the longer term enjoyment of the cruising sailboat as size—providing, of course, reasonable limits. The corollary is that a cruiser large enough for comfortable blue-water cruising with extended time living aboard may well be larger than needed for subsequent coastal or more modest cruising endeavors later on. Costs and maintenance are disproportionately related to size of boat, so size is a two-edged sword in some respects.

As size increases, volume increases by the cube. A 40-foot cruiser will have twice the interior volume of a 30-foot one. When discussing size, it's the waterline length rather than the overall length that counts, since the former creates the possibilities for the interior accommodation. Within reasonable limits, everything about the boat can be changed save its original structure. Absent considerations of pocketbook or of health, relatively few cruisers who spend substantial time aboard and make serious passages look forward to smaller boats.

Size matters because size yields benefits of more storage space; also because, other things being equal, longer boats typically sail faster, with a more pleasant motion. Size also provides occasional privacy in the accommodations when taking on additional crew.

Size is also related to where one cruises. There is no shortage of 20- to 25-foot sailboats cruising comfortably about the Bahamas, while most cruisers aiming for the Caribbean Islands are 35 feet and upwards. Yet it's worth remembering that in the early days of fiberglass production when cruising boats first became affordable, a 22- to 25-foot boat was certainly considered adequate for serious blue-water cruising. Times change.

PEARL NUMBER TWO

Almost every boat one sees when out blue cruising is different. So far, no builder has created the "ultimate" boat. Practically speaking, that means that for a given size budget and requirements, there's a wide assortment of boats that, properly outfitted, will do quite nicely. Readers of the celebrated Monthly Bulletin of the Seven Seas Cruising Association (SSCA) will quickly become aware of the broad variety of makes and models of successful cruising boats. Few cruisers voyage in shiny new ones.

More than a few intrepid cruisers have made remarkable voyages and cruising adventures in what most of us would consider problematic boats not suited for offshore cruising. All in all, it's the crew capabilities and attitudes, having essential cruising gear on board, and owning a reasonably fit boat that makes for successful voyaging.

PEARL NUMBER THREE

Remember the 30-70 rule: the builder makes 30 percent of the boat and buys the remaining 70 percent from other suppliers, some good, some not so good. As a corollary, almost all of that 70 percent has to be periodically re-placed from time to time. Consequently, a 40-year-old boat that's had a recent near-complete refit might well be more suitable (and less costly over the long haul) than a 20-year-old boat whose entire equipment and gear inventory is also 20 years old.

Well-built fiberglass sailboat hulls seem to last forever if well maintained, so age alone should not be a criterion in selecting or rejecting cruising sail-boats. It's how they are equipped and their condition that really matters. In-stalling a new or recent engine and rig on an older hull in good shape is often the quickest way to secure a suitable cruising boat. An important corollary is that with a fixed budget, an older, proven fiberglass boat that's been recently refit and fully outfitted with the essential cruising gear is a much better bet than a newer boat where's there's no budget left over for essential cruising gear. It's also less costly to maintain and insure.

The 30-70 rule helps explain why sail (and power) boats have such fero-cious rates of depreciation. Most of the materials (gear) involved in their original building need periodic replacement. Quite often after a decade or so a new boat will have lost 50 percent or more of its original value. Moreover, model runs seldom last for as long as a decade. And after two decades or so the depreciation can be as large as 75 percent. The upshot is that for those with limited budgets (most of us), cruisers a decade or two decades or even three decades old can be relative bargains compared to the acquisition costs of brand new, shiny boats. The fact that boats are depreciating assets with high maintenance and upkeep makes blue water cruising possible for the vast majority of cruisers. Very few of us can afford to purchase brand new boats and those who can afford to buy new boats typically haven't the time to take off and enjoy blue-water cruising.

To be sure, there are some builders whose products depreciate more slowly than others, but in hard economic times even those craft with the stron-gest reputations depreciate noticeably. Reputations are often a reflection of the boat's original cost. Over the years we've observed that the more expensive or high-end boats seem to come on the market more frequently than their less elegant counterparts, which are more likely to be out cruising.

Moreover, reputations change, as once well-remembered but long-gone builders are forgotten by newer generations. Many senior citizen cruisers can easily reel off a dozen once-high-quality wooden boat builders and designers whose names are mostly unknown to the younger generation.

Outfitting the Offshore Cruising Sailboat

PEARL NUMBER FOUR

Focus on the total cost of the acquisition and expected refit, not just the acquisition cost. Every used boat requires serious refit outlays before it can be taken cruising. No boat is ever turnkey ready—not even a new one, or one "professionally maintained" or maintained with "an open checkbook." That's just broker-talk. All too often, cruisers go for broke to buy the best, latest, largest, most prestigious boat from the best builder and designer they can find. Then they're hard pressed to undertake the refit, purchase the requisite cruising gear, or even afford to go blue-water cruising, so their plans are delayed. There's no shortage of blue water-cruisers on today's depressed market.

PEARL NUMBER FIVE

Avoid being beguiled by a long list of seemingly impressive gear and equipment. Most probably requires replacement. Cruisers rarely remove old, outdated gear, but that doesn't mean it's worth keeping aboard. It's important to remember that one is buying a sailboat focusing on its two critical components, the rig and the engine. Most likely the boat will be outfitted with new equipment prior to serious cruising. To be sure, a long list of gear and equipment indicates some serious spending by the current or former owners, but in and of itself that doesn't automatically mean there's much value in such an inheritance.

For example, a non-certified 10-year-old life raft doesn't have any real value. Its inclusion in the equipment list is often a good indication that the seller/broker has overvalued the offering. Similarly, there's not much value in outdated electronics—and they get outdated pretty fast these days. In fact, it's often a bloody chore to remove outdated electronics and their associated wiring.

Surveyors usually report what gear is aboard and whether it's operable, but rarely do they go to the trouble of identifying its age or whether it's operating correctly.

PEARL NUMBER SIX

Be skeptical about claimed seller outlays for new gear or major maintenance. Question whether such claimed outlays really add value to the boat. Brokers and sellers alike know that cosmetics help sell boats. Avoid being beguiled by cosmetic claims of "new paint," "varnish stripped and recoated with 10 coats," and "new soft goods." Whether the hull has a new or recent Awlgrip paint job may reflect pride of ownership but has no bearing on cruising capabilities.

Similarly, claims of recent money spent on maintenance and refits should be looked at with skepticism. Brokers are only obligated to report what owners tell them, not to investigate the real facts of the matter. Generally we've found that most sellers are short on documentation of their claimed outlays. For example, does "new anchor chain" add significant value to the boat? Not if anchor chain is an expected part of the boat's normal inventory and it's already outfitted with a chain windlass and anchors.

As a general rule, replacement of inventory is part and parcel of boat ownership and doesn't usually add significant value to the boat. Of course, if an owner of an older boat has taken particular pains to refit the rig, replace the engine, and replace all the other major gear of the boat, then it's a different matter. On occasion one finds an owner who has gone the whole nine yards to get an older boat ready for serious voyaging and then has to bail because of health, financial, or other reasons. That can be a real opportunity. In the days of wooden boats more than a few individuals building their own boats simply waited too long to do the deed.

Matters are more complicated when it comes to claims of "new sails." Well, new sails do add some value, but only if they were made by a reputable sailmaker. But certainly the entire cost of the new sails should be substantially discounted. After all, sailboats are expected to come with sails. Few cruisers sport new sails and new sails become used sails pretty fast.

Matters get dicey when the seller claims a recent engine rebuild. Here's it's important to know if it was done by an authorized dealer, if it was a "top end" or complete overhaul, if it was done in frame or removed from the boat, if there any transferrable warranties, and so on. Authorized dealers invariably charge more for rebuilds than a local firm or "Jack the mechanic." But failures in the rebuild are likely to occur miles and miles distant from the place of original repair. So the more expensive authorized dealer may be cheaper in the long run. The long and the short of it is, be skeptical about engine rebuilds unless they were done by a well-established authorized dealer, and always ask why the seller didn't simply replace the entire engine with a new one.

PEARL NUMBER SEVEN

When looking at a boat for the first time, focus on the really important stuff. For example, how recently were the critical elements of the rig replaced, *e.g.* wire stays, furlers, halyards, sheets, sails, and so forth. When was the engine rebuilt or replaced, where was it done, and are there any warranties? Focus on the big ticket refit items, not the teak cabinetry or the recently revarnished glossy cabin sole.

When it comes to claims of serious money spent on engines, matters become much more complicated. How long should engines be expected to last? That's a matter of age, the engine builder's reputation, maintenance, and current condition. More than a few 4-107 Perkins diesels have clocked more than 5,000 hours with careful maintenance, and double that for the venerable 6-436 Perkins. But that doesn't automatically mean that a 30-year-old boat with only 600 hours on its original Perkins is a good prospect. Usually insurance companies do not consider that rebuilding or replacing existing engines adds significant value to the boat. Boats are expected to have operable engines.

Clearly, in an older boat, say one twenty or thirty years old, a new engine does add value but only a relatively modest proportion of its total installation cost. After all, if the boat required a new engine, any prospective owner would have to figure the new engine installation cost beforehand. In many ways newly replaced engines are like recent Awlgrip hull paint jobs. They help sell the boat, and while the seller may have evidence of large bills incurred to properly position the boat for selling, that doesn't mean that all of those outlays create value for the buyer.

PEARL NUMBER EIGHT

Beware of fancy interior joinery and the liberal use of external teak. High-end boats are high-end mostly because of their interior and exterior joinery, not because the guys who laid up the fiberglass hull were chemistry wizards or because the guys doing the plumbing or electric work were actually following an engineering diagram. Fancy joinery is expensive (lots of man hours) and nice to look at, but it doesn't make the boat a better cruiser any more than a recent hull Awlgrip painting. Moreover, boats with fancy joinery interiors cost more to buy, and that money is better spent on gear and equipment and perhaps a larger boat.

Maintaining fancy teak mounted externally, *e.g.* toerails, is hard work in the tropics. When cruising offshore, the sun literally burns through the salt left by the spray on the once-glistening varnish. Exterior teak looks nice on a seasonally used boat, but really is something of a maintenance nuisance in the tropics. Take a tip from the boats built for tropical charter work: no external teak visible anywhere.

PEARL NUMBER NINE

Whenever possible buy a boat designed by a reputable naval architect rather than an inspired builder. The dynamics of moving solid objects through the ocean have been pretty well identified and require some serious higher math. To be sure, there are some rare builders who have the intuitive feel of solid design and do it the old-fashioned way. But they are very rare, indeed. Naval architects with established reputations seek out builders with good reputations and vice versa. That's why so called "pedigreed' boats are usually (but not always) identified by their designers rather than their builders, because it's presumed that a designer with a strong reputation wants a well-built product.

PEARL NUMBER TEN

Not all builders are equally competent. Some are quite competent at building adequately for the coastal cruising and chartering trade. Others know how to build a boat that can survive serious storms with minimal damage and that has all the space that long-distance cruisers consider necessary. The money in boat-building oft lies with the racing crowd. In a word, boat builders specialize. So if distance cruising is your dream, look for builders who build cruising boats with good reputations, boats that get sold fairly quickly when they come on the market. In just about all cases, builders that remained in business for several decades or more producing well-regarded cruising boats earned their reputations the hard way: word really did get around. Often to find the real skinny about particular cruising boats, just ask veteran cruisers and surveyors.

Outfitting the Offshore Cruising Sailboat

PEARL NUMBER ELEVEN

By their very nature, cruising boats are always works in progress, just as are their crews. Over time, by virtue of age and experience, our ideas and demands change. Sometimes by the time we swallow the anchor we really do understand what a near-perfect cruising boat would look like. But by then we've had our adventure and it's time to move on. It's far more important to correctly equip and maintain a proper cruising boat than spend time and effort looking for the next cruiser. It's an open question whether anyone ever found the perfect cruiser. At day's end most every cruiser wishes they had left the dock earlier in life and spent less time and money finding and outfitting the really "perfect" boat. Time is the real enemy, not finding the perfect boat.

PEARL NUMBER TWELVE

Know thy limitations. It is possible to have a boat that's too big to maintain, equip, and operate. Most folks comfortable with a 30-footer can readily adjust to a 40-footer. But to move up to a 50-footer requires some mechanical assists. And a 60-footer will require a whole bevy of very expensive mechanical and electric assists for a small crew to handle in rough weather.

The costs of maintaining and equipping a modern, well-outfitted 50- or 60-footer can easily run into the 6 figures yearly. Professional crews can be required simply to assist in the maintenance and repair. Boat yards love large sailboats—that's where the money's made. One can easily spend upwards of $100,000 and more removing and refitting the rig of a 60-footer, enough to buy a quite nice cruising boat in the 35- to 40-foot range.

Size of boat is often a function of age of owner and whether substantial liveaboard arrangements for extended periods are envisaged. When living aboard, either at anchor or even at the dock for extended periods in out-of-the-way places, interior accommodations and amenities grow in importance. The flip side is that medium and larger cruisers can be a handful offshore in rough conditions and can require some expensive sail assists for small crews. It's an interesting tradeoff. Smaller boats are invariably more fun to sail, easier to maintain, and easier to purchase, while larger boats offer more space and amenities at higher acquisition, outfitting, and maintenance costs. Even with a large budget, one must be careful not to acquire the largest boat possible. If

226

the boat isn't really manageable at sea by the owner/crew, then the cruising adventure is invariably handicapped and the boat becomes a liveaboard.

PEARL NUMBER THIRTEEN

Think long and hard about the boat's accommodations in heavy weather. If the boat doesn't have really good sea berths that can be used offshore when the weather turns nasty, the crews will become fixated with weather forecasts and counting miles to the next port or harbor of refuge. Queen-sized berths in the V-section of the bow and aft cabin are lovely in port, useless in heavy weather. A good, solid berth in the salon, or captain's cabin or quarter berth for the off-watch crew, is a must-have. Make sure the berths are long enough for full size humans—7 feet—and that they are equipped with strong lee-cloths.

PEARL NUMBER FOURTEEN

Crews, like Napoleon's armies, travel on their stomachs. Galleys can be large or small, plain or fancy, but the question is whether the galley can be readily used in heavy weather to whip up tasty meals. Proper galleys need adequate shelf space, high-edge lips to keep stuff off the floor, a decent stove, and a large freezer to store prepared foods. No cook wants to slide around for an hour making everything from scratch. Without a serious-sized freezer, i.e. 6 cubic feet or more, best to bring along crew with heightened fishing skills.

The galley of a capable blue-water cruiser is not a kitchen but a secure place where good meals can be prepared in any weather by any member of the crew. Appetites typically blossom during voyages, and eating well takes on increasing importance as the passage lengthens. A good galley at sea requires some serious thought. It's a matter not of size but of real functionality.

PEARL NUMBER FIFTEEN

Marine toilets can fail—usually at the most awkward time. Having spares is nice, but a second head and spares is much nicer. Even better is a head near the cockpit stairs. Slipping and sliding to get to the head forward of the mast in a heavy quartering sea is no mean feat. Happy is the crew that has a head reserved for the ladies, one for the boys. Whenever possible, look for a boat with two heads. One can always be used exclusively for showers and stowing foul-weather gear. No one ever complains about too many heads on a board. But there often are too many useless so-called berths.

PEARL NUMBER SIXTEEN

Make good friends with your engine. Be sure that you have ready access to all its parts without disassembling the boat. Hands down, the engine is the most important part of any cruising sailboat. If it's difficult to access the engine, the odds are it hasn't been well maintained by previous owners and will be difficult to repair. Some builders understood the importance of easy engine access. Most focused on the interior joinery.

Arguably it's much better to set off with an older boat with a new engine than a 20-year-old boat with its original engine or one that has been just rebuilt without warranty by "Jack the mechanic." Engines are the real Achilles Heel of cruising sailboats and oft have their sweet revenge. Make sure there's a good list of engine spares aboard. Carry extra engine and transmission oil. Always remember that vigilance is the password with engines. They never fix themselves.

Conscientious blue-water sailors understand the importance of a reliable engine. So a well-painted, clean, rust-free engine in a sweet-smelling engine compartment speaks volumes. So does an engineering log, engine workshop/parts manuals, and an ample supply of essential spare parts. Be cautious about "yard maintained" engines. That all too often means the engine was looked at perhaps once a year to change the oil.

PEARL NUMBER SEVENTEEN

Stuff doesn't always happen to the other guy. Deep or skinny pocket, take safety seriously. That means a good, solid life raft for ocean duty, annually certified; several EPIRBS; some good alternative radio devices; and all the usual required safety gear. Remember, one can never have too many anchors, bilge pumps, lifejackets, or good sailing comrades. Always remember that the primary mandate for any captain/master is to bring the crew and vessel to port/harbor safe and sound under all conditions, without excuses. Safety gear is just an important as a sound rig and reliable engine. So from the outset, plan on putting aside sufficient funds when purchasing a new boat to fully take care of the serious safety gear needs.

PEARL NUMBER EIGHTEEN

When buying another or first boat, ask the opinions of well-qualified friends and fellow cruisers. Odds are, others will be less impressed with cosmetics and interior joinery. Moreover, they may well have known other cruisers who have been aboard similar boats. And don't hesitate to spend serious money on a pre-purchase survey by a well-qualified surveyor. Learning the real skinny about the cruising life takes time and experience and can't be completely learned either from books or from leafing through magazines. When it comes to boats, there are no dumb questions.

PEARL NUMBER NINETEEN

Learn about the boat's history. Where did she sail, where was she stored, and how many owners did she have? Was she babied by a loving owner or kept as an unwelcome relative? Where did she cruise, or did she spend her life sleeping at the dock? Did she spend part of her life sitting on the hard for years and years? Boats, like horses, like to be used. What kind of work did the yard do, or did they take care of the boat? Why did the owner put her on the market? Well-maintained, fairly valued boats often sell just by word of mouth among friends.

If the boat is documented, then spend $25 or so to obtain an Abstract of Title from the U.S.C.G. Vessel Documentation Center and learn the boat's history of owners and if there are current liens on the boat. Often the Abstract of Title can provide useful information on where the boat has traveled. For example, if the boat was always documented in Boston but is now berthed in Florida, the odds are fairly good she spent her life up north. But if she was documented in Miami then the odds are fairly good she's been to the Islands.

If you know the boat's current name and/or documentation number, simply by searching the Web you can learn from the USCG Documentation Center the current and former owners, past names, where the boat was built and when. Most well-established brokers have no difficulty in learning about the boat's history from their colleagues if they are asked.

PEARL NUMBER TWENTY

Look for records. Some owners kept an engineering log of the boat's maintenance and repairs, with lists of spares, lists of up-to-date paper charts, and so forth. A caring and knowledgeable owner who kept good maintenance and refit records and made them available to the next owner along with a good set of charts, is a real find and a good bet even if that owner's boat costs more. A caring and knowledgeable seller wants the object of his affection and good times to continue on with a new owner. Providing records is a good sign the boat was well cared for. If substantial recent work was done at a yard, one can often find out some useful information about how the boat was used, taken care of, and where she traveled.

PEARL NUMBER TWENTY-ONE

Try a serious sail with the boat—not just up and down the harbor—before signing on the dotted line. Some boats are heart-throbs just sitting at the dock, especially with gleaming teak and a new paint job. A short test sail with the surveyor isn't likely to give much serious input about how she sails. If possible, dig down and charter a similar boat for a week or so, where there's a real opportunity to see how she sails. With boats, what you see isn't what you always get. It's hard to fix mistakes after taking ownership. The transaction costs of buying and selling boats are very high, so tread carefully. Even experienced cruisers buying their third or even fourth boat are almost always surprised at what they overlooked.

PEARL NUMBER TWENTY-TWO

There is a good reason most hulls in the tropics are painted white. It's hot. Navy blue hulls are fine up north in the Chesapeake or in New England. We've spent serious money painting our hulls navy blue over the years—it's a nice color. But the interior temperature difference between dark and white hull colors in the tropics is really awesome. Besides, white finish lasts longer and is easier to see at a distance.

A corollary is to avoid teak decks. To be sure, they denote high-end or pedigree boats. But a good tropic sun will make the teak decks hot enough to

230

burn one's feet. Moreover, every teak deck fastened with screws and bungs leaks. It's only a matter of time.

PEARL NUMBER TWENTY-THREE

When in doubt, walk away. Unless the boat inspires real passion it's the wrong boat. When I first laid eyes on a two-year-old wooden 36-foot Dickerson ketch named Robin sitting on the hard at Consolidated Boatyard at City Island more than four decades ago, it was love at first sight. It has been the same for every boat I've owned since.

If it's not real love, then why bother? Cruising boats are dream machines merely awaiting life's best shipmates and prospects of meeting new ones. It also helps to visit the boat in good weather, bring along a trusted friend or crew, some sandwiches and drinks, and spend some real time aboard. If the broker/seller has "appointments" elsewhere, then it's time to move on. Despite our best efforts at objectivity, there's a good deal of emotion involved in buying cruising boats.

THE PROFESSIONAL BROKER

Most cruising sailboat purchases involve a broker. Typically there is some serious money involved: the seller usually has an outstanding loan balance, the buyer needs financing, there's state taxes to be paid, registration forms to fill out, usually USCG documentation forms, and so forth. It's helpful to have a fiduciary to handle manners. Moreover, brokers usually work for firms and have standardized contracts available. In most states the broker is the seller's agent, so the buyer is pretty much on his own.

But in Florida all brokers must be licensed and bonded, and brokers are obligated to fairly represent the interests of both the seller and buyer. They may only act for both the seller and the buyer with the knowledge and written consent of both parties. All Florida brokers are required to have State registered escrow trust accounts for deposits and all other monies pertaining to the sale/purchase of a boat. The yacht sales business is a major multi-billion dollar business in Florida, so the state has gone to greater lengths than elsewhere to protect the best interests of the boat buying public. Moreover, Florida yacht brokers have worked hard to raise their professional standards.

Outfitting the Offshore Cruising Sailboat

Fig. 10.1
Bob Zarchen of Sparkman & Stephens, Ft. Lauderdale office, is past president and currently treasurer of the Florida Yacht Brokers Association. Bob is one of the country's most knowledgeable offshore sailing yacht brokers, with a formidable background as a Yale-trained engineer, engine specialist, experienced blue-water cruiser, and professional captain.

Most everyone has unflattering broker stories, and to be fair, brokers are like the rest of the human race—some good, some not so good. Over the long haul, measured in terms of decades, the really good brokers build strong reputations. That's how they get plum central listing assignments and repeat business. If the broker does his job correctly then it's a good bet he'll have the listing when the boat is once again up for sale. Any broker worth his salt with a well-established reputation has a list of well-qualified clients looking for good boats fairly priced. The real skinny is that from the brokers' perspective there's always a shortage of listings of good, well-maintained boats and owners with reasonable expectations.

From the seller's part, the broker is expected to produce well-qualified prospects either by previous contacts or by marketing with other brokers and/or the public. The seller also expects the broker to exclude "dreamers" or those without adequate financial resources. There's no benefit to either the seller or broker with a client who ties up the boat with a deposit while looking for funding beyond his means. A really good broker can size up the potential of a prospect in fairly short order, especially the prospect's ability to follow up with the financial wherewithal and complete a sale.

For example, a prospect new to sailing coming out to look at a high-end 50-footer has either come into a new inheritance or is just fantasy shopping. Serious prospects usually have pretty good ideas about what they are looking for. To be sure, some brokers really work hard to "sell" the boat, but they are in the minority. Good brokers know the real task is to find the right boat for the client rather than find a client for the boat their office is listing.

A really good broker with long experience and a solid reputation is fun to work with. They may not always tell everything they know about the boat, but they usually take some pains not to misrepresent. After all, if the broker does a good job executing the sale it's likely he'll be used when the boat comes up for sale again, and that broker will be recommended to friends. Boat brokerage often seems like a pleasant way to make a living so it attracts a sizeable number of new entrants who then leave. The real skinny, I'm told, is that well-established brokers in Florida who work year-round do very nicely in normal economic times and usually don't have the time to spend on their own boats.

Well-established brokers typically go to great lengths to maintain lasting relationships with their clients. Every boat that gets purchased eventually gets sold, and many clients purchase several boats over their boating careers. Clients often use brokers as good sources of information as to where to get repairs done, how to hire captains/crew, and so on. Well-established brokers work hard not only selling boats, but also maintaining lasting relationships with clients.

Of course, owners can have unrealistic expectations. Sometimes when the owner of a high-end boat is in financial difficulties, the owner may want the broker to move heaven and earth to find a buyer simply to stop the monthly outlays. Occasionally there really are great buys when a good boat can be purchased well below its fair market price. But it doesn't happen very often, even in distressed economic times. Beware the phrase "estate sale" or "recently donated." That doesn't translate into a giveaway. Well-established brokers almost always have lists of potential clients looking for a particular type and price of boat. So if a true bargain really does become available, the odds favor that the broker already has a list of qualified folks to call. That's all the more reason to establish relations with one or more well-qualified brokers when beginning a serious search for a new boat.

Sometimes buyers go to great lengths to whittle down the price by a few thousand dollars once armed with a not-completely-perfect survey. On occasion the broker will dip into the expected commission and "contribute" in order to complete the sale. But that often leaves a bad taste. Few owners take calls from new purchasers for information after the sale, after having being nickeled and dimed. Ditto the broker. Of course, there are always some new owners who call up the previous owner years afterwards for "critical information."

For would-be cruisers new to the game, a reputable and knowledgeable broker can be a real lifesaver and source of vital information. Long-term brokers often have encyclopedic knowledge of the sailing industry and long-gone builders with good reputations. Frequently they have reference libraries of marketing brochures with plans of boats built decades ago. Despite an occasionally published "book of plans," there really is no comprehensive source about sailboat builders over the past several decades. The market is just too small.

Reliable pricing information for older cruising sailboats is often sketchy or inaccurate or just reflects the particular circumstances of a forced sale or an over-eager buyer. Brokers often look back for past sales information for clues about current pricing. But even for two identical-sized boats from the same builder in the same location, their conditions can be quite different. So it's often apples and oranges. A newly painted boat recently repowered with new sails and serious cruising gear can often command $25,000 or even $50,000 more than a tired sister hull and be a better buy. Pricing history for used boats is difficult to come by outside the brokerage industry. Most, but not all, brokers share pricing history with other brokers.

After listing the boat with a broker, most sellers can't wait to see their former love advertised in the boating publications. After all, the boat is being advertised with some of the proceeds from the broker's expected commission. But in this modern age the important place to list the boat is on the Web. Moreover, there is a strong incentive for the broker to call his list prospects before the boat is officially advertised and thereby obtain the full commission rather than split with other firms. Well-established brokers often like to deal with clients who have boats from well-known builders and designers that have been well maintained, with good equipment lists.

Brokers can be especially helpful when it's time to sell the boat during difficult circumstances, especially for an estate sale. Here is where trust, reputation, and long-established relationships come into play. It is nice knowing that the boat will find a proper new owner and that one's companions or relations dealing with the sale or donation for a deceased owner will be well and fairly treated. No one wants to envision their pride and joy being sold to a true innocent and then slowly decaying on the hard in some remote boatyard.

Maintaining contacts with one or more favored brokers or spreading the word among fellow cruisers can often be more fruitful that scanning the ads

234

and websites when looking for another dreamboat. Occasionally when looking for another boat, a broker with whom we've had a good relationship calls with the magic words and our lives are forever changed: "I think you should take a look at a boat that's just about to come on the market."

AN OLD PRICING RULE OF THUMB

One of the more useful rules of thumb in establishing used boat values is the centuries-old method of quoting new builds and used boats/ships in dollars per pound. For example, modern production builders can often build new sailboats for between $15 and $20 per pound. (Customer builders charge $50/60 and up.) So a 30,000-pound boat (medium-sized cruiser) before major options may have a new build cost of between $450,000 and $600,000, for example. After 5 years the market value might be $10 per pound and perhaps after 10 years as low as only $5 per pound. Over time, cruising boats from known builders in reasonable condition seem to bottom out at between $4 to $5 per pound. Of course, for high-end or custom specialty boats the figure may drop to just $10 a pound. But as a rough rule of thumb, between $4 and $5 a pound is quite useful, especially when deciding how big a boat one can buy for a given budget.

To see how this rule works out, consider a 20- to 25-year-old 40-foot cruising boat weighing in at about 30,000 pounds. Against an acquisition cost of about $120,000 ($4 a pound), there's a substantial refit ahead. For example, redoing the engine could easily cost $15,000 and the rig half as much. Similarly with new paint, tender, genset, refrigeration, life raft, safety gear, new soft goods below, and canvas. Let's assume the refit will equal the acquisition cost. Of course, if the new owners fully realized at the outset that they might eventually spend upwards of $180,000 to $200,000 on their dream boat over the next decade, they might have second thoughts. But owning a boat has strong appeal for cruisers and at 40 feet the accommodations become quite pleasant. Most boats one sees out cruising are in the 40- to 45-foot range.

Going forward it seems fairly reasonable that cruising sailboats will decline in value but require ever-more-expensive refits, so they will remain expensive commodities. There will always be a market, limited as it may be, for new cruising boats from offshore builders. At, say $20 to $30 per pound fully loaded with options, the semi-custom low-production sailboat offshore builders will need to charge roughly a million dollars for a new 50-footer before major options. The final price could easily top $1.5 million. At those figures there should be no shortage of cruisers willing to refit used boats. The key point is that used cruising boats are inexpensive relative to new ones, but still fairly expensive when the inevitable refit is completed. But even with the refit they often cost just one half or less compared to a new build, and the market for new-build cruisers is pretty thin even in the best of times.

THE SURVEY

Fig. 10.2 Valuation and Purchase Survey Components

1. *Integrity of the hull, deck, and interior assembly*
   - *bulkhead attachments to interior hull, floor structures*
   - *chainplates*
   - *rudder, running gear, seacocks and thru-hulls, steering gear*
   - *hull/deck excessive moisture, delamination, stress cracks*
   - *port and hatch seals*

2. *Installation of major equipment to industry standards*
   - *engine, genset, electric systems, stoves, heaters, plumbing, tanks, batteries, water system, bilge pumps*

3. *Visual inspection of rig and sailing gear components*

4. *Listing of installed equipment and age if known*

5. *Brief sea trial*
   - *raising sails*
   - *noting engine RPM, temperature, and boat speed*

6. *Report with notice of deficiencies*
   - *required and recommended and estimate of approximate market value*

A standard provision of yacht sales contracts calls for the buyer to obtain a valuation and condition survey for his intended insurance company and that the survey results be satisfactory to the insurance company and the buyer. Insurance companies usually require the surveyor affiliated with one of the two nationwide groups, NAMS and SAMS. The surveyor's valuation of the boat usually approximates the agreed purchase price of the boat unless there is a noticeable defect or omission. Surveys are also required if the boat is being purchased with a mortgage. Of course, if the boats are being purchased for cash and no insurance is involved, more than a few buyers do their own surveys.

As with being a yacht broker, being a yacht surveyor on the surface looks like an interesting lifestyle. Yet most well-established surveyors rely on commercial vessel surveys, and those inspections are typically hard work in unpleasant conditions. Some surveyors have extensive engineering backgrounds and decades of experience examining sizeable, complex ocean-going vessels. All in all, surveying sailing yachts ranks pretty far down the list in the skill sets of most well-established surveyors. Moreover, spending a full day examining the boat and then perhaps another half to full day writing up the report for less than a thousand dollars is fairly modest compensation.

In contrast to the one-day sailboat surveys, upwards of a week is often involved in surveying mid-sized or larger powerboats, especially ones with metal hulls where a hull thickness assessment is undertaken. In a typical mid-size and larger powerboat survey, in addition to the surveyor, an engine surveyor is called upon together with surveyors for specialized systems, e.g. stabilizers, A/C, refrigeration, and electric and electronic systems. It's not uncommon to spend between ten and twenty thousand dollars for a well-fitted-out mid-sized and larger powerboat, especially one with a metal hull. For larger boats, surveys can involve some very serious figures.

Typically the conventional condition and valuation survey involves just a day. It begins with an interior inspection of accommodations and hull structure and noting of installed equipment. The surveyor will often ride the bosun's chair to briefly inspect the rig. Then the boat is hauled and the hull is inspected, and finally a brief sea trial is undertaken noting readings on engine gauges. At day's end the surveyor offers some general comments to the buyer, and within a few days a formal, written survey is forwarded to the buyer.

Survey expenses, including hauling, are borne by the buyer and are usually charged by the foot. For a medium-sized boat the survey and hauling charges typically range between $1,500 and $2,000 and vary considerably by geography—higher in the north, lower in Florida. For a medium and larger boat, surveyors will sometimes be hard pressed to complete the survey in one day. Since the survey is purchased by the buyer, it may or may not be shown to the broker and/or seller.

The standard condition and valuation surveys are often a source of considerable confusion. Their primary focus is whether the boat is a suitable "insurable risk" and meets industry standards as regards installation of basic equipment such as engines, stoves, seacocks, plumbing, and so forth. Also, the survey notes the installed equipment. The survey does not typically evaluate the condition of the installed equipment, its age, or whether it is working as designed. Nor does the survey typically identify equipment that needs be replaced or is outdated, outside of requirements, *e.g.* flares.

The standard condition and valuation survey does not answer the important question of how much will it cost to refit and equip the boat for extended blue-water cruising. In other words, the standard survey is part of the acquisition process but provides little guidance on the next step—refit and outfit. Here another survey is often used— a valuation or pre-inspection survey, although the terms are somewhat misleading.

For example, when boats are donated to a nonprofit, a valuation survey is normally required to establish the value of the donation for tax purposes by the donor. Such valuation surveys may just include a brief inspection of the boat in the water and after a brief haul, note the surveyor's estimated market value and involve no sea trials or even a listing of the installed equipment. Other valuation surveys may just note the installed equipment, overall observed condition and not require either a dry-docking to inspect the hull or a sea trial. Obviously the donor is typically interested in a valuation survey that reports a high estimated market value. When the boats are eventually sold by the nonprofit, their selling prices are typically just a fraction of the original donated market value. The original valuation survey will typically have little value for the subsequent buyer.

Newcomers and even experienced cruisers will sometimes order what is loosely called a pre-purchase and valuation survey, in which the seller agrees for a surveyor paid by the buyer to fairly and completely evaluate the operating condition of the boat, noting whether the installed equipment is operating satisfactorily, its current suitability, and any need for replacement. Often a haul out and extensive sea trial will be conducted. Here the emphasis is upon making a truly informed judgment about the boat's current market value and estimated costs of refit and outfitting for cruising. Such surveys are commonly undertaken

238

where some serious money is involved in a purchase. After all, how else is a buyer able to make an informed judgment on what a boat is really worth.

Having paid for several dozen surveys and read upwards of a hundred of them, I offer here some suggestions. First, as within any profession, surveyors with well-established reputations and broad experience are actively sought after, even though they may not charge appreciably more than others. Typically, experienced surveyors have a treasure store of information about boats or types of boats that they regularly survey. Some are willing to share information informally. Unless there are overriding considerations, it's worth waiting for a surveyor with a well-established reputation to become available.

Second, for the buyer the key elements of the typical valuation and condition survey are the surveyor's assessment of the hull, rig, and engine—the most costly elements of the cruising sailboat. The surveyor will bang away with a phenolic hammer, read the moisture meter on the hull and deck, carefully inspect the hull (especially the rudder) and decks for damage, and carefully examine the boat's interior structure (bulkheads and floors).

It may look easy to a casual observer, but considerable skill and experience are required before the sounds of the phenolic-tipped hammer can be interpreted. Most recent hulls are cored with either balsa or plastic foam and are subject to both voids and delamination. Similarly with using the moisture meter on both the hull and the decks, especially around the high stress areas such as chain plates. Careful surveyors spend considerable time around the boat's running gear and through hull areas. Rudders receive particular attention. Over time, water often migrates into the rudder's core, corroding the internal metal structure and threatening eventual failure. Also, they look for evidence of previous hull damage, assess the quality of the remaining bottom paint, and inspect for incidence and seriousness of blisters and evidence of epoxy barriers.

On the decks and cabin tops the surveyor looks for evidence of structural weakness and soft cores. Seals of ports and hatches receive attention, as do the various stress cracks that are part of the hard life of fiberglass decks. A good surveyor will work the moisture meter over the deck and cabin surfaces with special attention to high stress areas such as the external chainplate fittings. Unlike on the hull, where moist bottom paint interferes with moisture readings, the moisture instrument is particularly effective on the deck and cabin tops, providing the weather is clear and the decks dry.

Inside the boat the surveyor focuses on the structural connections between the hull and bulkheads. These are often problem areas resulting from stress on the hull from vigorous sailing or improperly installed bulkheads. On larger boats the surveyor will usually examine at least one of the chainplates. Examining the full set of chainplates typically requires the removal of substantial interior joinery and may require the yard's assistance. Some surveyors and some knowledgeable buyers will insist that all the chainplates be inspected, especially on older boats. In a larger boat, the cost of removing the interior woodwork and joinery to gain access to the chainplates can equal the cost of the survey itself. Also, the surveyor tries to examine the supports in the bilge, support structures for the cabin sole, and the operation of seacocks.

A thorough engine survey—beyond noting gauge readings, boat speed, and whether the engine reaches its designed maximum revolutions—requires a separate engine survey. In turn that requires a more extended sea trial and could well cost upwards of $1,000. From the insurance company's perspective, it's only important to note whether the boat has a satisfactorily operating engine. Of course, the buyer has a different perspective.

Having spent several thousand dollars on a survey, buyers will often use that survey to negotiate a reduction in the agreed-upon selling price. Sometimes a hard-nosed buyer will demand that the broker "kick in" something to remedy the deficiencies. That's bound to sour future relations with the broker, and most well-established brokers will demur such requests. Typically the insurance company provides several weeks to remedy "mandatory" and "suggested remedy" deficiencies. Just about every boat will have deficiencies. Even buyers of expensive new boats typically hire surveyors to oversee the construction process itself.

Sometimes a broker will recommend that the seller of a high-valued craft hire a surveyor to establish the realistic value of the boat and note deficiencies that can be corrected in anticipation of a sale. Such valuation and inspection surveys are sometimes made available to serious buyers.

Another wrinkle when purchasing a boat is asking to see past surveys, including the one made when the seller originally purchased the boat. They often contain useful information about past deficiencies. On fairly rare occasions one finds a seller who has a complete file of all past surveys on the boat and her major repairs.

Since the surveys themselves are inherently nondestructive and subject to obvious time limitations, the surveys are always conditional. In older high-end boats it's not unusual for the surveyor to take core samples of the underwater hull. Of course, the buyer pays the considerable expense of repair and refinish. Tanks are one of the most difficult areas to properly inspect without obtaining access. But few surveyors require the tanks be filled to look for leakage or undertake a hydrostatic pressure testing. Most boats do not permit inspection of the tank's interior.

Surveyors can make errors and omissions. Once the boat's been purchased there's an opportunity to bring down an experienced rigger and ask him to spend a day looking over the rig. Similarly with hiring a knowledgeable diesel engine mechanic and, if the budget allows, a skilled electronics technician to make recommendations about what should be junked and what new installations should be considered. Trying to obtain these assessments within the short confines of the one-day conventional condition and valuation survey is a mission impossible. However, if the boat is 25 or so years old and still has the original rig and gear, the prudent mariner will just refit the rig, replace/rebuild the engine, and install some modern electronics.

Over the years we've found that reputable brokers have a pretty good idea of the boat's condition prior to survey. It's their business to know the real skinny. After all, there's no merit in taking the time and effort to have a client survey a boat and then find major deficiencies that cancel the sale. Odds are that when that happens, the broker loses both the sale and, more importantly, the client. Just about all the professional yacht brokers we've dealt with over the years have visited and inspected the boat prior to our visit, even when it's not their central listing.

Fig. 10.2 Code of Ethics of Florida Yacht Brokers Association, Inc.

Section 1. It is the duty of the member to protect the public against fraud, misrepresentation, or unethical practices in the yacht brokerage profession. Member should endeavor to eliminate any practices which could be damaging to the public or to the dignity and integrity of the yacht brokerage profession.

Section 2. In accepting employment as an agent, member pledges himself to protect the interests of his client. This obligation of absolute fidelity to the client's interest is paramount, but it does not relieve the member from the obligation of dealing fairly with all parties to the transaction.

Section 3. Since the member may be representing one or more parties to the

transaction, he should not accept compensation from more than one party under any circumstances without the full knowledge of all parties to the transaction.

Section 4. Member, for the protection of all parties with whom he deals, should
see that financial obligations and commitments regarding brokerage transac-
tions are in writing and express the exact agreement of the parties. Copies of
such agreements must be placed in the hands of all parties involved at the time
the agreements are executed, or as soon as possible thereafter.

Section 5. Member must segregate from his own funds all monies being held
for other persons. Separate special bank trust accounts should be used for this
purpose.

Section 6. Any offer submitted to either an owner or to a cooperating broker
must be related in its entirety and must specify the exact nature of the earnest
money deposit, i.e. cleared funds, personal check, telex advice that the deposit
will follow by wire transfer, etc.

Section 7. In the event that more than one formal written offer on a specific vessel is made before the owner has accepted any offer, any other formal
written offer presented to the member, whether by a prospective purchaser or
another Broker, should be transmitted to the owner for his decision.

Section 8. Member should neither acquire nor sell an interest in, or buy for
himself, any member of his family, firm, or any entity in which he has substantial interest, vessels listed with him, or his firm, without making the true situa-
tion known to the listing owner or prospective purchaser.

Section 9. Member should use his best efforts to ascertain all pertinent facts
concerning every vessel, including the correct model year of manufacture as it
appears on the ship's document, for which he accepts the agency so that he may
fulfill his professional obligation to avoid error, exaggeration, misrepresentation, or concealment of pertinent facts.

Section 10. It is the duty of the member to be well informed on current market
conditions in order to be in position to advise clients as to the fair market value
of vessels.

Section 11. Member should not undertake to make an appraisal or render an
opinion of value on any vessel where he has a present or contemplated interest
unless such interest is specifically disclosed to all parties of the transaction.
Member should not undertake to make an appraisal that is outside the field

of his experience unless he obtains the assistance of an authority on such type of vessels, or unless the facts are fully disclosed to the client. In such circumstances, the authority so engaged should be identified and his contribution to the appraisal should be clearly set forth.

Section 12. Member should always recommend the timely employment of an independent qualified marine surveyor as a condition precedent to the completion of a brokerage transaction.

Section 13. Signs giving notice of any vessels for sale, rent, lease, or exchange should not be placed on any vessel by more than one member, and then only if specifically authorized by the owner.

Section 14. Member should not submit or advertise vessels without written authority and in any offering the price quoted should not be other than that agreed upon with the owner as the offering price. Central listings must be in written form for a minimum period of 30 days, signed by the owner or his legal agent, and must provide cooperating brokers adequate protection in the case of a transaction between the owner and the cooperating broker's client.

Section 15. Members should not advertise other members' listings without their permission. Prices advertised on other members' listings should not be other than the listed offering price.

Section 16. Member should not engage in activities that constitute the practice of law and should recommend that legal counsel be obtained when the tax liability or legal interest of either party requires it.

Section 17. Members should cooperate with other members on vessels listed with him whenever it is in the interest of the client. Negotiations concerning a vessel listed exclusively with one member should be carried on with the listing broker, not the owner, except with the express consent of the listing member. All shared commission agreements should be negotiated prior to the submission of any Offer to Purchase.

Section 18. The agency of a member who holds an exclusive or central listing should be respected. A member cooperating with the listing member should not invite the participation of a third party without the express consent of the listing Broker.

Section 19. A member should not voluntarily disparage the business practice of a competitor, nor volunteer an opinion of a competitor's transaction. If his opinion is sought, it should be rendered with strict professional integrity and courtesy.

Section 20. A member should seek no unfair advantage over his fellow members and should willingly share with them the lessons of his experience and study.

Section 21. In justice to those who place their interests in his care, the member should endeavor always to be informed regarding laws, proposed legislation, governmental orders, and other essential information and public policies which affect those interests.

Section 22. Member should keep himself informed as to movements affecting recreation and yachting in his community, state and the nation so that he will be better able to contribute to public thinking on matters of taxation, legislation, marine use, waterfront planning, and other issues affecting boating interests.

Section 23. A member should so conduct his business as to avoid controversies with his fellow members. In the event of a controversy between members of the Florida Yacht Brokers Association, Inc., such controversy shall be arbitrated in accordance with the regulations of the Association rather than litigated.

Section 24. When a member is charged with unethical practice, he should place all pertinent facts before the proper tribunal of the Association for investigation and judgment.

Section 25. Controversies between members who are not members of the same local chapter should be submitted to the Florida Yacht Brokers Association, Inc., Board of Directors for arbitration. The decision of this Board is final and binding upon all members.

Section 26. When a dispute involves both members and non-member parties, the Florida Yacht Brokers Association, Inc. may conduct an independent investigation at the request of any interested party.

Section 27. It is in the best interests of society, of his associates, and of his own business that the member be loyal to the Florida Yacht Brokers Association, Inc. and be active in its work.

11

END NOTE

Other than initially buying a cruising boat that's too large, too expensive for one's budget, structurally uncertain, or poorly designed, the main impediments towards undertaking blue-water cruising usually focus around spending time, energies, and funds in outfitting the boat beyond the essential cruising necessities. This phenomenon, known as "endless outfitting," is a real impediment not only to getting started, but also to enjoying the cruising life. In part it reflects that one's own cruising sailboat affords a unique environment to tailor one's environment in a way not usually available elsewhere. The boat becomes a reflection of one's personality, technical sophistication, and installation skills. All too often at the planned date of departure the boat is literally filled with boxes and gear that must be stowed or installed, so the departure date keeps getting postponed. Or the gear is shoehorned somewhere for installation at a later date when safely anchored somewhere.

Just about every cruiser we've met has been or remains afflicted by the "endless outfitting" phenomenon. If anything, it's getting worse as the possibilities for sophisticated gear accelerate. Closely associated with the endless outfitting phenomenon is the "next boat will be better" search. We, too, have been afflicted with this disease. It's fairly uncommon to find cruisers who start out and end up with the same boat after a decade or so of blue-water cruising. It's easy to understand the "next boat will be better" search. After all, every cruising boat is a compromise and spending time aboard illustrates the compromises and the deficiencies—real or imagined.

Looking backward, we would have done much better with fewer boats and would have had much more time to go cruising had we remained less focused on the search for a better boat. In part, the search for the next boat is encouraged by reading boating magazines illustrating the latest go-fast designs and the latest technological wizardry. After several decades of cruising with conventional designs, we opted for a complete change of pace and purchased a high-tech offshore racer that had been outfitted for the Kenwood Cup. It came

Outfitting the Offshore Cruising Sailboat

with 22 mostly Kevlar sails and we were utterly mesmerized with the fancy hydraulics, unfamiliar go-fast doodads, electric winches, tall mast, a maze of sheets, and teak decks. Initially we were excited at how well she sailed close-hauled in really light airs and how she racked up the miles offshore with her sharp bows. But then in heavy weather we learned that the boat required far larger crews than we had available, that she was really wet going to weather, and that she had a most uncomfortable, squirrely motion when the wind was aft abeam. Offshore she'd run at double digits in following and quartering seas. She was gorgeous at the dock with black spars, teak decks, and royal blue hull and always attracted admiration. We couldn't wait to find her a new owner.

Where we have benefited over the years from purchasing more than our proper share of boats is redoing basic interior systems. Unlike production powerboat builders, where the system installations are generally done to a reasonably high engineering standard, sailboat builders focus on other matters. So we've undertaken fairly major systems restoration projects in most of our boats. The guiding mantra has been to make every component readily accessible, based on the premise that what gets installed in a boat, eventually has to be replaced.

Focusing on systems accessibility over the years has led us to realize the advantages of center-cockpit designs with separate engine rooms, together with their opportunities for installing really secure all-weather cockpit enclosures. But if truth be told, our happiest sailing memories were in traditional designed, aft cockpit boats with simple systems. Aft cockpit boats are just more fun to sail, and being close to the water it's easier to connect to the rhythm of the seas. There's a lot to be said for leaning over the cockpit sides and dipping ones hand into the water into soft seas with the moon overhead and stars hanging like candles ghosting along.

All cruisers are afflicted by the dilemma of choosing among the comforts and conveniences from ever-more-complex systems aboard, but dreams of a larger boat with the opportunities that increased size brings must be weighed against the realities of time, energies, and expense of outfitting another boat. It is part and parcel of the cruising challenge.

When starting out on my cruising career, I heard the following advice: "Just go—the boat will never be perfect." It's still good advice. Hopefully this modest volume will encourage would be cruisers to just go sooner rather than later and focus on the really essential refits—the rig and the engine—rather than getting ensnared by the endless refit possibilities and prospects of a better boat. Like their owners, boats are never perfect no matter how hard we try. Cruising is always about the voyage.

Outfitting the Offshore Cruising Sailboat

INDEX

ABOUT THE AUTHOR

Peter I. Berman has cruised more than 100,000 miles in the Atlantic, Pacific, and Caribbean Oceans over the past 45 years in nearly a dozen different designs ranging from traditional CCA designs to modern high-performance craft. He's owned and extensively refit a wide variety of craft: medium to large wooden and fiberglass ketches, centerboard ketches, sloops, cutters, aft cockpit, and center cockpit designs.

An engineer by training, he managed a large wire and cable factory devoted to building mil-spec cables for the United States Navy, including submarines, and has extensive knowledge of electric installations aboard U.S. Navy and Coast Guard craft. He's been on-site in virtually every significant commercial marine and ship repair facility in the United States. He was also the manager of a firm that manufactured proprietary stuffing tubes to the commercial marine industry and proprietary marine electric equipment.

His first ocean-going craft—a 36-foot wood Dickerson ketch built in Trappe, Maryland in 1965—is still going strong in Anchorage, Alaska. Much of his early cruising was done aboard one of Ted Irwin's first large fiberglass cruisers built in the early 1970s, a 45-foot CCA designed aft cockpit centerboard ketch. Over the past decade he's owned and actively cruised 50- and 60-foot Gulfstar center cockpit ketches between the Caribbean and New England.

Looking back, Peter says the well-built Dickerson, primitively equipped by today's standards, was his favorite cruiser and at a cost of $16,000 the most affordable. When ashore, Peter lives in Norwalk, Connecticut next to a forest preserve but alongside a pond. His first sailing adventure was as a 12-year old crewing aboard the celebrated black-hulled *Black Witch*, a 72-foot wooden schooner moored in Oyster Bay, New York. He says he would like to own and cruise aboard a traditional gaff-rigged wooden schooner just to complete the circle.